P9-BIW-134

The First Canadians

A Profile of Canada's
Native People Today

Second Edition

Pauline Comeau and Aldo Santin

James Lorimer & Company, Publishers
Toronto, 1995

© 1995 by Pauline Comeau and Aldo Santin

All rights reserved. No part of this book may be reproduced or transmitted in any form or by any means, electronic or mechanical, including photocopying, or by any information storage or retrieval system, without permission in writing from the publisher.

James Lorimer & Company Ltd. acknowledges with thanks the support of the Canada Council, the Ontario Arts Council and the Ontario Publishing Centre in the development of writing and publishing in Canada.

Canadian Cataloguing in Publication Data

Comeau, Pauline, 1956-
   The First Canadians
   2nd Ed.
   Includes bibliographical references and index.

ISBN 1-55028-479-7 (bound) ISBN 1-55028-478-9 (pbk.)

1. Indians of North America — Canada — Government relations — 1951. 2. Indians of North America — Canada — Politics and government. 3. Indians of North America — Canada — Social conditions.
I. Santin, Aldo, 1954- . II. Title.

E92.C56 1995   323.1'197071   C95932094-6

James Lorimer & Company Ltd., Publishers
35 Britain Street
Toronto, Ontario M5A 1R7

Printed and bound in Canada

Contents

AUGUSTANA UNIVERSITY COLLEGE
LIBRARY

Acknowledgments

When we first sat down with the editors at the *Winnipeg Free Press* in June 1988 to discuss our next assignment, we had no idea it would soon take on a life of its own. Five months later, the *Free Press* published "Indians, Strangers in Their Own Land," a twenty-four-page supplement that explored twenty years of native issues in Canada using the plight of Manitoba's aboriginal people to highlight the problems. During the five months we spent on the project, we both interviewed dozens of people — native leaders, bureaucrats from all levels of government, social scientists, doctors, nurses, and native people from all walks of life. In the political field, we personally interviewed federal Indian Affairs Minister Bill McKnight; Liberal MP Keith Penner, who headed a committee investigating native self-government; Manitoba's Premier Gary Filmon and Northern Affairs Minister James Downey. We also reviewed twenty years of documents, everything from government annual reports to academic journals; and compiled data based on the information found there. We were also able to obtain hundreds of pages of information, particularly on the events surrounding the 1969 White Paper, through the federal Freedom of Information Act.

But at the end of the project, we found ourselves with many loose ends. Time restraints and space restrictions had forced us to leave much of the original material on the cutting-room floor or completely untouched. And so, the idea for the book was born. In these pages, we take the original twenty-year focus beyond Manitoba's borders and examine many of the same issues on a national scale. To prepare for the book, we read more scholarly accounts, government reviews, conducted dozens of additional interviews with national spokespeople and government and native representatives from a variety of regions. We also applied for more information through the Freedom of Information Act. Included in this second round were personal interviews with some of the original players who were front and centre in 1969.

We are deeply grateful to all of those who gave so freely of their time and energy to pass on their personal experiences and knowledge of native issues during the two years it took to put this project together, and again for the revision.

A special note of thanks must also be extended to our employer the *Winnipeg Free Press* for first introducing us to the subject of the plight of native Canadians and then for allowing us ready access to research material first obtained for the newspaper. We would like to specifically thank Wayne Hanna and Harold Cardinal for their time.

Aldo wishes to thank his wife, Pamela Pyke, for her patience and support. Both Pauline and Aldo would also like to thank all their friends and colleagues for the much-needed support.

Pauline Comeau
Aldo Santin
July 1995

Introduction

In 1989, a senior Indian Affairs bureaucrat with more than a decade of experience in the field stared out the eleventh-storey window of his Winnipeg office tower at the vast prairie. "What are you going to do with this information?" he asked a reporter who had arrived to cart away several boxes of data. The bureaucrat waved his arm in a gesture at the unnamed public below. "They don't give a damn about native people you know. They couldn't care less."

That same year, Nona Pariseau, a curious and opinionated Grade 11 student who had recently moved to the Prairies from Halifax, approached us for help in doing research for a history class. She was researching contemporary native history and had come armed with a question: "What is it that these Indian people want, anyway?" Speaking in tones edged with frustration, she decried what she saw as native demands to return to the time of the buffalo hunt and the teepee while the rest of the world moved on. "I never saw an Indian until I came to Winnipeg," she admitted later with a tinge of amazement. "I never knew they were here, in this country, first."

Five years ago, when the first edition of this book was released, these anecdotes highlighted the extremes of apathy and ignorance that existed across this country when it came to Canada's aboriginal residents. How quickly some things have changed. In the early 1990s, the *Globe and Mail* reported on a poll that indicated that 65 per cent of Canadians supported native self-government. Just a few years earlier, it would have been difficult to find a Canadian who had even heard of the term.

Despite this, the problems plaguing native communities in this country continue to abound. While there have been some major gains, simple or easy solutions to the ongoing suffering of Canada's native people are not evident. As well, as readers will discover, there is no single enemy or event that explains the current situation. Undoubtedly, racism has played a key role and continues to do so. In

January 1995, a federal court judgement was released that called the Indian Act a "racist" document. The judge charged that the document "favours" aboriginal people over the rest of society. "It makes financial dependents of those who pay no taxes as an eternal charge on those who are taxed to meet the expense of such dependency," wrote Mr. Justice Francis Muldoon. If the Indian Act was subject to the Canadian Human Rights Act (the human rights legislation exempts the act), "human rights tribunals would be obliged to tear apart the Indian Act," wrote the judge.

During the past twenty-five years, international human rights bodies, including the United Nations (UN), have also criticized Canada for its often discriminatory native policies. In 1989, and again in the 1990s, the Canadian Human Rights Commission declared the treatment of the country's aboriginal people a national tragedy.

Serious students of native issues in Canada are well aware of the mountains of information available on almost every aspect of native life that can be found at any library or book store, or in government archives. In this book, we attempt to provide an overview of that information both for those who are just beginning their studies and for those who seek a basic understanding of how the relationship between the Canadian federation and its native people has evolved.

The First Canadians uses as its starting point the 1969 "White Paper," a document introduced by Jean Chrétien who was the Indian Affairs minister at the time. The goal of the policy was to remove from native Canadians their "special status" and to hand over primary responsibility for the country's first residents to the provinces. Achieving this goal, reasoned the government philosophers of the day, would help native Canadians to assimilate and, eventually, to take their place as equal citizens in Canada. Once this had occurred, the Department of Indian Affairs and Northern Development (DIAND) would no longer have a purpose and would be disbanded.

In 1994, Indian Affairs minister Ron Irwin stood in the Canadian Parliament to make a surprise announcement. Manitoba had been chosen as the testing ground for another major native affairs initiative, and, once again, the result would be the dismantling of the Indian Affairs department. This time, however, assimilation was not part of the plan.

The Canadian government's evolution from its 1969 position to its current viewpoint is explored in this book. In this second edition, we present updated statistics and new policy initiatives. It becomes apparent that, while significant change may be on the horizon, an abundance of data indicates that little has happened to change the day-to-day lives of a suffering people.

The federal government has spent billions of dollars over the past twenty-five years to provide services and programs for native people across Canada. What has been the result of all this spending?

The majority of the country's 500,000 registered Indians still live in conditions that other Canadians imagine exist only in the Third World. (In large part, this book deals with the experiences of the country's status Indians, i.e., those who come under the auspices of the Indian Affairs department. Others, such as the Métis and Inuit, are also mentioned when their debates cross the registered Indian debate.)

According to 1995 statistics, the average life expectancy of native Canadians is almost ten years less than that of the Canadian population as a whole, and this discrepancy has not improved significantly in twenty-five years. Furthermore, native Canadians are only marginally better educated today than they were twenty-five years ago; they continue to be jailed at rates that far exceed what their population would indicate is possible. In fact, some experts suggest that a native Canadian is about three times as likely to land in a jail cell as in a high school graduating class. Aboriginal people destroy themselves at a phenomenal rate through violence, accidents, and suicide — a fact that was brought home to many Canadians in 1994 when the attempted suicides of a number of children on the Davis Inlet reserve made headlines across the country. As one western newspaper columnist noted in the late 1980s, in a story about a young native boy's suicide: "We used to hang them. Now they hang themselves."

However, it was not always this way. Long before the new settlers arrived on Canada's shores, the country's aboriginal residents lived in largely co-operative social structures, complete with a governing power and a system of justice. However, the functioning of these societies came to a sudden halt when the settlers arrived and set about taming the "savages" they found here. Despite the insistence by a few officials that only the best of intentions motivated the newcomers, the reality was that the non-native settlers, with their overwhelming arrogance, rejected everything indigenous. In the early days, these settlers passed laws to stop Indian ceremonies. Later, when travel to remote areas became more accessible for missionaries and government officials, native children were taken from their parents and placed in schools where non-native teachers made attempts to erase their languages and cultures.

More than 200 years after the arrival of the Europeans and with a disturbingly familiar arrogance, non-native officials in Ottawa announced a solution to this national tragedy. In 1969, the newly elected Liberal government of Prime Minister Pierre Trudeau attempted to rework the national native agenda to solve the problems afflicting native Canadians once and for all. In the glow of Trudeau's "Just Society" came the now infamous White Paper. The new policy was driven by a goal of equality among all Canadians. Both the special status conferred on Canada's registered Indians by the Indian Act and the separate federal department overseeing the administration of their welfare would be eliminated. The provinces would assume the burden of financial responsibility for native services, reserves would disappear, and Indians would eventually become a welcomed part of the Canadian mosaic, no longer the victims of discrimination.

Native leaders were furious. Besides making the naive assumption that something as deeply rooted as racism could be wiped out by decree, the document also served as proof that Ottawa had failed to understand the message that native leaders had been trying to communicate for centuries: native people sought the right to live their lives without the hand of Ottawa meddling in their affairs. In response to the White Paper, native leaders united as never before and spent a year fighting the proposal. This fight comprised their first successful lobbying effort against a federal government initiative, and the leaders would draw from this experience again and again through the 1980s and 1990s.

With the official withdrawal of the White Paper, Ottawa was left without an overriding national agenda on native issues. In its place have been a thousand small skirmishes waged almost daily — from local disputes over areas of independence, to the clash of visions with cynical civil servants or idealistic politicians, to battles in the national courts and various international arenas. *The First Canadians* takes a closer look at some of those skirmishes and finds, among the complexity and frustrations, evidence that the issues are, in fact, moving forward.

Perhaps the most telling indicator of change has been the introduction of the term "native self-government" into the Canadian political domain. When the White Paper was introduced, such an idea would have been inconceivable. Today, following two major political confrontations (the Meech Lake and Charlottetown Accords), native self-government has become the stated goal of another federal

Liberal government initiative, this time with former Indian Affairs minister, Jean Chrétien, as prime minister. From the start of his mandate, Chrétien has sought a significant rewriting of the native agenda. Unlike the goal of Chrétien's 1969 initiative, however, the current objective appears to be in keeping with the stated intentions of many of Canada's native leaders.

This is not to suggest that all outstanding native issues will be solved when the new millennium dawns. The struggle for Indian self-government has encountered many problems, not the least of which have been the lack of experience on the part of many native leaders and the difficulty of uniting a small, often fractured, aboriginal population. The ultimate native vision proposes a country dotted with hundreds of First Nations (today's reserves), which will have the status of a third level of government, equal to that of the provinces. For much of the past twenty-five years, Ottawa has offered Indian people bits and pieces of control; some offers have been made in response to native demands, but most provided a way for the government to satisfy an agenda of reducing its own financial and constitutional responsibilities.

In 1994, the agenda appeared to change again; this time, the stated intent was to give Indian leaders what they had been asking for. But even this new direction is not without its potential pitfalls and its critics. Even some band members are unsure whether their leaders can be trusted to take control, especially in light of the drug smuggling and gambling schemes that have served as the main economy for some reserves. As a *Globe and Mail* editorial noted, serious questions continue to surround the issue, including the century-old problem of defining the term "Indian" and determining who is responsible for providing the definition. "The acceptance of Canadians of the general notion of self-government attests to the best of liberal impulses: namely self-determination and a desire to make amends for past wrongs. The policies flowing from those impulses, however, clash with other deeply held principles: non-discrimination, democracy and the idea that rights accrue to individuals as a function of their humanity, not their racial heritage. Then again, self-government becomes meaningless if natives are stripped of the ability to define themselves."

In *The First Canadians,* Indian leaders describe their own gains and losses in the fields of economic development, health care, education, child welfare, and justice. These policy areas have served as the working laboratories for self-government, offering evidence that many native leaders are more than capable of handling their own affairs and improving the lives of their people. Leading the way are the men and women and their political structures, which have evolved over the past years from small, single-issue lobby groups to complex, multifaceted organizations led by individuals able to hold their own in any battle.

In 1969, few Canadians could name a native leader. Today, it is difficult to find someone who has not heard of Liberal member of Parliament (MP) Elijah Harper, a central player in the 1990s, or Assembly of First Nations (AFN) head Ovide Mercredi. However, while there is no doubt that much has changed, there is also much to suggest that native leaders believe their work is not done. As the federal Liberal government's pre-election "Red Book" notes: "The aboriginal population is an overwhelmingly young population. If we do not focus on the potential of these young people, we will face increasing costs to our social security, health and justice systems, and we will have lost a generation able and willing to make a contribution."

These same ideas were presented at the end of the first edition of *The First Canadians* by a native leader, and they are worth repeating here: "We can't sit back for a minute....If we quit, what will happen to our children?"

1

The White Paper and Other Policy Initiatives

On June 25, 1969, Indian Affairs minister Jean Chrétien stood before the first session of the Twenty-Eighth Parliament to read from a thirteen-page document titled "The Statement of the Government of Canada on Indian Policy."

Watching from the visitors' gallery were dozens of Indian leaders from across the country. They had been called to Ottawa to be on hand for what, from all appearances, was to be a historic occasion. For months leading up to this June day, native people had been taking part in a series of consultations with federal government officials that, they had every reason to believe, would soon lead to a new Indian policy. This policy would, ultimately, give them greater control over their lives. That afternoon, the invited native leaders had gathered briefly with the young, enthusiastic minister of Indian Affairs. Then, they were directed to their seats in the parliamentary gallery. Following a short debate, Chrétien stood to read the document known in native circles today as the White Paper. What the aboriginal guests heard that day stunned them.

The six main points in the new policy were all based on the same idea: the different legal status conferred on Indians by the federal government had kept them from attaining the same privileged position as their non-native counterparts in Canadian society. The solution? The Indian Act, drawn up in 1876 to formalize the relationship between the British Crown and native people, would be repealed, leaving the country's 265,000 registered Indians with a status no different than that of any other Canadian. As a result of this devolution of authority, DIAND would be dismantled within five years. Other federal departments and levels of government, particularly the provincial ones, would provide services for Indians in the same way they provided services for other Canadian residents. Indians would be given control of Indian lands. Canadians would be educated so that they would recognize the "unique contribution" that native people had made to the country. Those native communities and individuals furthest behind would be helped the most. And finally, "lawful obligations" would be met by the federal government. The Indian Policy Group, later called the Implementation Group, and, still later, the Consultation and Negotiations Group, was named to carry out the government's plan.

In an interview twenty years later, David Courchene, Sr., leader of the Manitoba Indian Brotherhood at the time of the White Paper's release, still remembered the anticipation of that day. "We didn't know anything about the 1969 White Paper until we were called to Ottawa by the minister," says Courchene, sitting in his log home on the Fort Alexander Indian reserve in 1989. "All the national native organizations, the General Assembly Group it was called then, were there. There must have been hundreds of us in Ottawa that day." Throughout the rest of the interview, Courchene's voice rose with the same anger that he and the other native leaders felt that day in 1969.

In the fall of 1994, another Indian Affairs minister stood in the Parliament of Canada to make a historic announcement about Canada's aboriginal residents. This time, no specially invited native visitors were watching from the gallery, no national or public consultations had taken place. In fact, the information did not even come as the result of any special announcement. Instead, Indian Affairs minister Ron Irwin, appointed just months before by Liberal leader, and current prime minister, Jean Chrétien, stood to respond to an inconsequential question posed to Irwin by native leader and fellow Liberal MP Elijah Harper.

Irwin, who upon his appointment had been called a "nobody" by AFN leader Ovide Mercredi, revealed that a historic agreement was about to be signed. The goal of the agreement, being worked out with the sixty-one bands in Manitoba, was to create a model for issuing true authority over native affairs to native bands. Over a three-year period, Ottawa would relinquish jurisdiction in several areas, including education, health, and social services. At the end of the experiment, bands would administer about one-fifth of the department's $5 billion budget. And, once again, Ottawa proposed a full-scale dismantling of the multibillion dollar department of Indian Affairs. In 1969, it was estimated that this work would take five years. How long would the Indian Affairs department continue to exist this time?

"The ministry," said Irwin, "will probably be there long after I am gone."

The philosophy behind the new proposal was as different from that of the 1969 White Paper as the way in which the initiatives were announced. In 1969, Indians were seen as wards of the federal state, barely able to fend for themselves. In 1994, the Jean Chrétien government assumed that native people in Canada had an inherent right to self-government and that they were more than capable of handling the complexities of their own affairs.

A Change in Native Policy

When the Canadian government is preparing to take a new public stand on an issue, it announces its "intended" policy direction in a document called a "white paper." After debate and final shaping, these documents are filed in the national archives and then, more often than not in the case of native policy papers, forgotten.

For Canada's aboriginal people, one particular document, among the volumes of other policy papers gathering dust in Ottawa, remains in their collective conscience. Its official title rarely recalled, the 1969 document lives on as simply the "White Paper"; these two words can trigger heated discussion, debate, and anger more than a generation after the paper's creation. Why? For native people, the document came to symbolize just how ignorant of native history and of native hopes and dreams the Ottawa-based overseers could be. For Ottawa politicians and bureaucrats, the White Paper became an example of how *not* to change policy directions.

A few years before the release of the White Paper, Indian Affairs decision makers had begun digesting data from a document prepared for the department by anthropologist Harry B. Hawthorn. *A Survey of the Contemporary Indians of Canada* was three years in the making, and it included 151 recommendations, such as the continued use of a modified Indian Act. The 1966 document was described by Indian Affairs bureaucrats at the time as a "thorough and scholarly" paper offering "sound research and...practical recommendations." The report concluded that notions of integration and assimilation were not reasonable avenues to pursue for Canada's aboriginal people; it called instead for an all-out effort that focussed on education, programs that would increase Indians' income potential, and improved health care. As well, Indians should be regarded as "citizens-plus," a group with rights beyond other Canadians, because they were the country's original residents.

As has been said, in the months before the new policy appeared, native leaders had also taken part in a series of nineteen meetings between Indian leaders and government officials. The meetings had been sold as a consultation process that was to have led to a new native policy. Discussions in these meetings had largely revolved around the Indian Act and ways that it could be amended to give native people more autonomy and control over their lives. At least, that was what Indian leaders *thought* they had been discussing.

A speech by Chrétien early in the consultation talks adds weight to charges by Indians that they had been led astray. "As a result of the consultations we have had with them until now," Chrétien told the House in late 1968, "it is obvious that under the terms of the new Indian Act, we will give them more authority on both the reserve and band levels in order to enable them to control their own destiny...."

With the White Paper's release, however, the consultation process suddenly seemed a farce. None of the concerns raised by native leaders, particularly regarding improvements to the Indian Act, were addressed in the policy by government officials. "They spoke with a forked tongue," says Harold Cardinal, the young and assertive leader of the Indian Association of Alberta in 1969. According to Cardinal, since the meetings had concentrated on improving the Indian Act, Indian leaders naturally believed that there would still *be* an Indian Act when the new policy was announced. "And all the while, the internal process was that, if the government was going to pursue their policy of equality, then there was no need for special legislation."

Cardinal suggests another reason why native leaders were so unprepared to react to the affront. Since the passing of the Indian Act in 1876, Indians in Canada have been waging a battle to gain recognition of what they see as their right to exist as a separate political entity. Their vision of self-determination, which would not be given the currently popular term "self-government" until the 1980s, was understood by Indian elders and their students, but by virtually no one else in the country. Ultimately, the goal in the 1960s was to gain the right to make decisions on those issues which affected their lives. Discussion about the actual mechanisms needed to carry out those decisions was left for the future.

Cardinal points to several key events that led to the slow emergence of a clearer, more publicly defined vision. First came changes in the Indian Act during the 1950s that gave Indians the legal right to organize. Then, the right to vote in federal elections was granted in 1960. With those two events behind them, Indians turned their focus away from the federal government scene. For all intents and purposes, they were working in the late 1960s under the assumption that the question of their legal status had been resolved, if not in any concrete, legal sense, then at least as an understood and accepted long-term goal of government. Thus, native leaders had turned their attention elsewhere, says Cardinal. When the White Paper was released, they were busy with other projects — including building their own political organizations, which they saw as the next stage in gaining recognition as an integral part of the political equation in Canada. "There was this notion that since this first step [voting rights] was achieved in the native political agenda in terms of having the Indian person recognized, that the next step would be to have the Canadian nation state recognize the collective entities that made it possible for Canada to be what it is today. That's our Indian nations," says Cardinal.

The most contentious point of the White Paper policy was the main assumption. According to the authors of the paper, the Indian Act was the key reason for discrimination against Indian people. The special status conferred on them by the act, along with the separate government department established to care for their needs, was deemed to be the major stumbling block to progress in native issues. "Special treatment has made of the Indians a community disadvantaged and apart," announced the paper's prologue. Chrétien would add later: "The policy of separation has become a burden. This 'differentness' must not be enshrined in legislation." Remove that distinction, the bureaucrats reasoned, and the rest would almost take care of itself.

"We couldn't believe it," says Courchene, his voice rising in memory of the shock he felt. "We were being pushed like the Métis people into the hands of the provinces who didn't look after the Métis. He was transferring everything to the provinces and washing his hands of the Indians. And he said he had consulted with us. That was bullshit." If the plan succeeded, Indian people would have no more right to self-determination than other Canadians. "They didn't want to recognize us as Indians, and I think that was why our reaction was so strong," Cardinal says. "We thought at least that basic step had been passed in 1960."

The Indian Reaction

Within hours of the announcement, it became clear that something was seriously wrong. Indian leaders met and the next day released a letter denouncing the government's intentions. "One hundred years from now our grandchildren will reap the consequences of the actions we take in the next few days — just as we are the inheritors of a legacy brought about by the actions of our forefathers," stated the six-page response signed by eight chiefs and co-chairs of the National Indian Brotherhood (NIB). "The Minister has made a mistake. We appreciate the Minister's concern and do not question his good will." According to Courchene, the leaders, who had long been criticized in the past for internal bickering and their failure to reach consensus, had no trouble speaking as one that day.

Indian leaders insisted that, despite Chrétien's assurances, the result of implementing the new policy would be assimilation, or "cultural genocide," as the NIB called it. In turn, assimilation would lead to the eventual loss of control over lands. For Indians in 1969, as now, any perceived threat to their control over land was cause for grave concern. Dreams of Indian sovereignty and power over their lives are rooted in their rights to the land.

Included in the deluge of mail that arrived in Chrétien's office following the White Paper's release were dozens of letters written by Indians. "We got to keep our special rights," wrote one. "Take them away and you leave us nothing, you, and your 'just society'. One last thing. We are Canadians by birth. We don't need a law passed to change us into Canadians. So I suppose the law is to tell the white man what we are. And if it takes a law to do that, God help us."

Whether or not the new policy was a *fait accompli* was another point of contention. The federal New Democratic Party and others joined the native protest. As the critics pointed out, Indians were apparently being asked to "consult" only on *how* to implement the policy, not on whether the policy should exist at all. The government, fearing derailment of the plan due to the impression that there was no room for Indian input, changed the title of the main co-ordinating body, the Indian Policy Group, to the "Implementation Group." "The proposals contained in the policy paper are subject to consultation with Indian people," Chrétien wrote in September 1969 in a letter to the NIB. "Indians will be offered every opportunity to participate in further development of the proposed policy and in bringing it into effect."

But Indian leaders were in no mood to be persuaded. They were sure that the bureaucrats would not change direction, even if every native person in the country spoke out against the policy. Internal memos indicate that the leaders' suspicions were well grounded. While the approach might have been open to debate, the philosophy upon which the document had been built was not.

In August 1969, an Indian Affairs department deputy minister, John A. McDonald, sent a letter to his staff. He stated that the White Paper "sets forth not only certain principles, which are incontrovertible, but also a number of proposals or actions which are subject to modification in substance in the light of alternatives that may be suggested by the Indian people...."

Meanwhile, Chrétien was facing an increasingly hostile and emotional Indian population. In Alberta, bands refused to meet with him, saying they could not guarantee his safety. A memo to the government written by an Indian Affairs superintendent on a Six Nations Indian reserve described a meeting this way: "Councillor Mrs. Rena Hill almost broke down in the middle of her talk. She asked the Indians to unite and avoid violence, reminding them that the Six Nations were dignified, and proud Indians." A petition was sent to the Queen, asking for intervention on the grounds that Canada planned to unilaterally remove rights that had been bestowed on Indians by the British Crown. In Winnipeg, Indians burned the government document in front of Chrétien. And Chrétien's reaction to the chorus of protest? "He couldn't believe us," recalls Courchene. "Just as we couldn't believe him."

In his autobiography, written years later during a hiatus from politics, Chrétien wrote about the White Paper controversy, recalling with discomfort meetings at which Indians accused him of speaking with a "forked tongue."

"I was always looking bad; it became an image problem," says Chrétien in *Straight from the Heart*. "To correct it, I asked to speak first at these meetings and then I invited the Indians to give me hell...."

Despite such discord, Chrétien found something positive in the experience. In his autobiography, he recounts that some chiefs told him that it was the first time a minister had ever sat and talked with them. "That was a necessary start to an evolution that may take a couple of generations to complete...." As well, Chrétien was criticized by those unprepared for a government engaged in any dialogue with Indians. "Some people accused me of creating my own problems by deliberately consulting with the Indians, helping organize Indian associations across the country as instruments for negotiation and discussion, and, in effect, financing my own opposition. That may be true, but I felt it was essential that the native people be given opportunities to express their views even if they put me in an awkward position."

The Provincial Response

Despite all the efforts to diffuse the situation, the list of critics continued to grow. The provinces, which were being asked to accept primary responsibility for native people and the programs supporting them, joined Indian leaders in denouncing the plan.

In February 1970, Chrétien wrote to Manitoba premier Edward Schreyer, outlining the federal government's view on how the provincial takeover of Indian responsibility would unfold. According to the basic scheme, Ottawa would sign an agreement with the provinces guaranteeing funding at current levels for Indian services. In the decade following the signing of the agreement, the funds would increase as the native population grew. In the next decade, the financial pay out would be constant, and in the third and final decade, the payments would be phased out. "Over the entire period of the agreement, we see the Indian people improving their economic position and their earning ability and, as a consequence, producing a substantially greater proportion of provincial tax revenues," wrote Chrétien. Chrétien also said that Ottawa believed Indians would continue to migrate to urban centres in large numbers, resulting in the eventual demise of remote reserves. The more they heard, the less provincial leaders were interested. "We do not want the problem thrown on our hands," said Saskatchewan premier Ross Thatcher, several months after the paper's release. Other provincial leaders insisted that they had no wish to ignore their responsibilities to Indians as residents of their provinces; however, they felt that they could do nothing until the Indians and the federal government had settled their differences and until Ottawa was ready to reimburse the provinces for the extra financial burden.

Is it any wonder the provinces backed off? Not only have reserves failed to disappear in the past twenty-five years despite the growth of the urban Indian population, but a massive infusion of money has failed to improve the economic status of Indians regardless of where they live. Today, Indians are not even close to the point where the provinces could consider them a tax bonus instead of a burden.

The public response, as measured in the media by the government, was also largely negative. Editorial writers and columnists delivered an especially pointed series of attacks. In a July edition of the Vancouver *Province*, Eric Nicol wrote: "The Indian Affairs minister has offered the Indians equality with the white man. Naturally, the Indians rejected what they saw as a retrograde step — like offering the snow goose equality with Donald Duck." Another article stated: "As all species reproduce only their own kind and no other, thus the new policy...is a baby white elephant of the same breed as its parent, the Department of Indian Affairs."

Within weeks of the first volley of criticism, Chrétien and his staff began insisting that the problem was confusion about what the policy actually meant. "I believe you have misunderstood the intent of my policy proposals," repeated the thousands of form letters that poured out of Ottawa. Chrétien began touring the country and eventually developed a speech that focussed on "what this policy does *not* say," in an attempt to clear up the confusion and deflate the growing protest. "This statement is *not* a final policy," he said, in a speech in Regina in October 1969. "This statement does *not* propose or suggest that Indian reserves be abolished. The statement does *not* propose that provincial governments should take over responsibility for Indian land." On and on he went, responding to the growing fears of native people and others across Canada.

The Department's Defence

A behind-the-scenes examination points to several elements that contributed to the official withdrawal of the federal government's Indian policy. First, there was a profound naiveté not only about the roots of the Indian problem, but also about the consequences of the policy. The bureaucrats predicted that not only would the massive Indian Affairs department fade away within five years (an estimate many laughed at), but the deep-rooted socioeconomic problems facing Canada's aboriginal people would be solved within a mere thirty years.

Chrétien's own attitude was another factor that contributed to the policy's demise. In his autobiography, Chrétien writes: "Trudeau and I had been bothered by the charges that the Indians were the victims of discrimination because they lived on reserves and came under the authority of the Indian Act. They described themselves as second-class citizens, and the reserves looked like ghettos to outsiders. But when we offered them in all sincerity to abolish the department, to give the Indians their land to do with as they pleased, and to make them fully equal with other Canadians, they were shocked by the challenge."

Chrétien reveals a similar attitude towards the prediction by Cardinal and others that the new policy would lead to assimilation and the loss of any rights to control their destiny. "They talked about the threat of 'cultural genocide,' " writes Chrétien, "and admitted they needed affirmative action in their favour. After that, no one could use the old rhetorical exaggerations about the reserves or the special laws because the Indians themselves had chosen to keep them."

In the midst of this chaos, Prime Minister Trudeau made the now-famous statement that aboriginal rights could not be recognized "because no society can be built on historical 'might have beens,' " as well as other less-than-sympathetic words of wisdom. In a television interview in March 1970, Trudeau left little doubt as to how he felt history would unfold if Indians rejected the White Paper. "We are not forcing anyone to do anything," he said. "We'll keep them in the ghetto as long as they want." The words reflected Trudeau's belief at the time that Indians had no claim to aboriginal rights. He expanded on these points and offered several rather prophetic warnings in that November letter to Chrétien.

Although Trudeau suggested a flexible approach with Indians, he felt a more forceful one was needed with the provinces. The prime minister wanted to move quickly before provincial leaders united behind Alberta and British Columbia, the two early dissenters. "A common front of the provincial governments and the Indian communities would make negotiations very difficult," wrote Trudeau. "In the same manner, the participation of the Indians in the negotiating meetings of the two levels of government concerning the transfer of services, seems to me to pose serious difficulties. If the Indians are present in a capacity other than as technical advisors of their respective governments, they would, by that fact, acquire a status at par with the status of the government." (This is, of course, the very status native leaders were seeking.)

Trudeau also suggested in the letter that the government's discussions should include not only registered Indians but all of Canada's aboriginal people, including the Métis. Since the White Paper's release, status Indian leaders have accused governments of purposefully undermining the growing strength and visibility of Indian groups by drawing all aboriginal people into the debate. However, there is no hint in this letter that Trudeau's thoughts about including the Métis had any duplicitous intent. He simply gave no credibility to the notion of a separate native level of authority; thus, he was left with plenty of room to ponder the larger philosophical questions of exactly who was and who was not an Indian and what the term actually meant from a practical perspective. "Those not registered are as numerous as those registered; they are living, to a large extent, in the same localities, share the same set of values and are suffering from the same discrimination on the part of white society," wrote Trudeau.

Upon the White Paper's release, the government sent bureaucrats to sell this ideal of assimilation. Negative reaction was usually met with typical bureaucratic self-confidence. According to internal memos, government officials believed that Indians were simply over-reacting because of their historic distrust of anything related to the government. They expected that things would calm down once everyone had had time to digest and accept the policy's proposals. This misguided response proved to have serious repercussions for the survival of the White Paper.

Added to this misjudgement was a major flaw in the process — the lack of a solid strategy for carrying out the plan. Internal documents show that the general policy outline gave few specifics (beyond the announcement that a land claims commissioner would be appointed). The policy provided absolutely no mechanism or blueprint for restructuring government departments in order to guarantee service delivery across the country. In the months following the policy's release, bureaucrats complained to head office about problems such as an insufficient number of copies of the policy, the lack of copies written in aboriginal languages, and the timing of the document's release (during fishing season when many Indians were in the bush).

In addition, Indian Affairs employees had been informed that their department would disappear in five years, but then were given no guidelines on how to proceed. With no direction, those in the field could not answer the simplest questions and often gave conflicting responses. As well, there was some evidence that even basic research had not been done, which in turn led to more questions about the policy's origins. Academics wrote to newspapers criticizing the government for pilfering a well-known American policy, which had failed during the 1950s. But documents show that the bureaucrats were unaware of that policy and had researched the issue for only six months after its introduction. "We do not now have the precise information we need respecting the position of Indians in each province vis-à-vis the extent to which they require services and the degree to which they contribute to the provincial economy and treasury," wrote one bureaucrat in October 1969, adding that the cost/benefit information would have major bearings on discussions with provincial leaders.

The Demise of the White Paper

Finally, after more than a year of fighting, Chrétien had no choice but to admit that the objections ran deeper than simple misunderstanding and overreaction. In the spring of 1970, the White Paper was officially withdrawn, and Ottawa coined a new phrase: "A Search for Common Ground." More than a year after the release of the White Paper, native leaders submitted their official written responses. They delivered two major reports, consisting of hundreds of pages detailing the direction Indians wanted to take. Cardinal's *Citizens Plus,* with a name borrowed from the Hawthorn study, is often referred to as the "Red Paper." The document dealt with land claims and economic policies and was presented to Prime Minister Pierre Trudeau on July 4, 1970. David Courchene's report from Manitoba, *Wahbung, Our Tomorrow*, was released in October 1971. The document covered a wide spectrum of native issues in detail, everything from land claims and culture, to housing, education, and on-reserve government. The government conceded that an entirely new approach was needed, one that would include Indian leaders right from the outset. These were conciliatory words, but what became of them?

Indian leaders and some scholars have insisted for decades that the White Paper simply went underground and continued throughout the 1980s to be one of the driving forces behind various native policy initiatives. There is some evidence to support that charge.

In a document dated April 1, 1970, Indian Affairs deputy minister David Munro pieced together for a newly appointed bureaucrat the history of the White Paper. Munro advanced several notions about how the government should proceed since the paper's withdrawal. Not once in the document did he suggest that the government's basic premise had been flawed. Despite the debates and protests, Munro still believed that Indian leaders had simply "failed or declined to understand the policy proposals." He went on to outline "obstacles to further progress" and suggested "tactical" changes: "We can still believe with just as much strength and sincerity that the policies we propose are the right ones, and we should inform and persuade the Indian people to that end with the greatest effort we can muster. If our concepts and proposals are indeed correct, they will be accepted by all but a few once they are understood."

Munro was convinced that the policy, would be realized. "But the pace of acceptance will vary in accordance with the degree of acculturation and sophistication of the groups of people concerned." On the issue of the removal of special status, he wrote: it "must be relegated far into the future....If pressed on the question, we should respond to the effect that the government considers the elimination of special status to be ultimately desirable but it is not about to force the issue now." He suggested that the government make two "concessions": First, it should issue statements about the need to discuss aboriginal rights. Second, "for an interim period," the government should return to Hawthorn's recommendations, especially the allocation of considerable funds to education, health, and economic development. Considering Munro's other views in the memo, it is likely that he thought these expenditures would only be required for a short period of time. Once Indian leaders had accepted the White Paper policy or, as Hawthorn predicted, most Indians had moved from reserves into urban settings and become, by default, the responsibility of others, this funding would not be necessary.

Indian leaders take some pride in the fact that their early protests, while unsophisticated when compared with later efforts, were nevertheless effective. "We stopped [the White Paper] anyway," says David Courchene, with more than a hint of resignation. "It was not made into national policy." However, Cardinal and Courchene have often lamented that, overall, their battle had little effect on the endless attempts by government to ignore their long- and short-term aims.

As evidence, they point to the fact that, with no official agreement on the table, the provinces have acquired a greater degree of responsibility over the administration of Indian Affairs dollars. Between 1982 and 1987, a study showed that Indians and provincial governments shared almost equally the spoils of what the federal government had relinquished. In that five-year period, the provincial share of control almost tripled: in 1988, the provinces controlled 13 per cent of the federal government's $1.7 billion Indian Affairs budget, for a total of $219 million.

"If we had been successful, we would have been involved in negotiations through the Prime Minister's Office on the question of disbanding Indian Affairs...," said Cardinal in 1989. "If we had been successful, we would have independently funded political organizations....We would have Indian control over a university and technical training programs to tackle the development program. On most fronts we lost bad. I think we failed. And in some ways, it is really tragic.

"I think the White Paper was one of the most destructive documents to ever come out," Cardinal adds. "I think there was a political revival taking place right across the country among various Indian people. It was fuelled by the kinds of rights movements that were occurring in the U.S....There was a basic yearning for democracy, and the government of the day had an opportunity to join forces with that. I think the White Paper sidetracked the kind of developments that had to go on."

Still, the aftermath was not completely negative, say others. The political vacuum that followed the White Paper's withdrawal created opportunities. Over the years, historians, bureaucrats, and some Indian leaders have identified the White Paper as a major catalyst for the growth of a renewed vigour among the Indian leadership. Some have called it a major contributor to the advances Canada's aboriginal people have realized since 1969. "For the first time, the real problems of Indian people, and the basic issues at stake were clearly revealed, considered and argued over," stated one Indian Affairs civil servant, one year after the paper's release. "The old paternalism and tolerance of legislative discrimination has gone forever," maintained another. "And so has the apathy of the Indian people so evident three or four years ago. There is, indeed, a new spirit abroad."

Even Cardinal gives some credit to the new policy: it forced Indian leaders to regroup and work on their counter-attack. Cardinal says that the conflict and point-counterpoint pattern established then still continues, only the tide has turned: now it is the native people who have a very clear sense of what they want and who have remained consistent in their demands, and it is the federal government that is struggling for some sense of direction.

On the native front, things have gone in a different direction, with the financial help of the federal government. Of the billions spent on native issues since 1969, a significant amount can be linked to the White Paper initiative to fund Indian organizations. Initially, the idea was to strengthen those organizations so that their leaders could become the chief negotiators with Ottawa in carrying out the White Paper's proposals. Instead, the money has helped these native groups take their battle for rights into other forums.

Still, the withdrawal of the White Paper from the political arena left the issue of aboriginal rights without an overriding political scheme or direction. As a result, the battle to define aboriginal rights within the federal government has been waged almost on a policy-by-policy and department-by-department basis. The process that emerged became known as "devolution," a concept that took root during the 1970s as the government's response to native calls for self-determination. Devolution involves the government relinquishing control over chosen administrative services to Indians in various stages. Ottawa, however, maintained the role of overseer and overall policy director and still, for all intents and purposes, held the purse strings. In large part, native leaders accepted what they were given, but rejected devolution as only a half-measure; they began to make the big push for native self-government.

Native people made important gains on a number of other fronts, including in the country's courtrooms. In 1973, Trudeau found himself rethinking his statement about historical "might-have-beens" after the Nishga band of British Columbia succeeded in taking the first comprehensive land claims case before the Supreme Court of Canada. Six of the seven judges ruled that native people had a right to the land they occupied. Three judges ruled that the band's claim to land in northern British Columbia still existed, three said it did not, and the seventh gave no opinion, dismissing the case on a technicality. Although the case was not an out-and-out victory, Indian land claims could not be so easily dismissed again. Harold Cardinal says the ruling forced Trudeau, an expert in constitutional law, to rethink his government's approach: "Trudeau took a step back and said, 'Well, I guess we were wrong, there's something in there.' At least there was a willingness to deal with that. On that basis, I think the federal government initiated discussions, some of which are still going on today."

In comparison, Cardinal mentions another court victory. The issue of the federal government's historic responsibility as trustee of Indian rights and claims on behalf of the Crown was the essential ingredient in the 1985 Musquiam case in British Columbia. In a decision that Indian leaders believed could have far-reaching implications, the Supreme Court of Canada awarded the Musquiam band

$10 million to cover its estimated losses in the development of a golf course that the federal government, in its role as trustee, had overseen since striking a deal in the 1950s. The court rejected the government's position that its role as trustee fell within the political arena and could not be subjected to court action. "In a number of very fundamental policy points of view, the Supreme Court sustained, adopted, accepted, or ratified the fundamental positions that our people have been taking," states Cardinal. "But the federal government has adopted what I call a trench warfare mentality, or a containment policy," he says about the response of the Conservative government under Prime Minister Mulroney. "They have, I think somewhat successfully, succeeded in burying that court decision." Cardinal believes the government's aim is to wait for more court tests on the trust question. "They have been found guilty in not fulfilling their trust responsibility in the way land disposal was handled. So they said, 'Maybe in the context. But we will wait and see more tests.' "

Repatriation

In the late 1970s, Canada's native leaders would again find reason to unite in fighting the federal government. This time the cause was Prime Minister Trudeau's plans to create a made-in-Canada constitution. With their historic connection to the British Crown, Canada's native people viewed the repatriation plan as both a threat and an opportunity. If the fundamental tenet under which the treaties had been signed was to undergo a change, then native people must be part of the negotiations to protect their interests, they argued. And so began the first serious struggle to win recognition of native rights in Canada's Constitution.

Native leaders had learned much from their White Paper battle, and they applied everything they knew to this new challenge. Originally left out of the discussions, they eventually pressured Prime Minister Trudeau, who was seeking allies as the Quebec referendum neared, into giving them limited opportunities to present their case. They worked every angle and lobbied government officials for recognition of their rights in the constitution. They conducted new research in an attempt to find any evidence, legal or otherwise, to support the argument that their fundamental place as Canada's aboriginal people and their rights as envisioned by the treaty process must be written in the new document. During this period, research into the native political movement in the United States yielded the term "self-government."

The native leaders did not stop there. In October 1980, in the midst of the constitutional debate, the NIB opened an office in London with the hopes of lobbying British MPs to block the resolution until it included a provision for aboriginal rights. That same month, an international tribunal on human rights, held in Amsterdam and sponsored by the Bertrand Russell Peace Foundation, issued a ruling against the Canadian government based on native claims, declaring it guilty of "ethnocide" in its treatment of native people. While neither event caused an about-face within the Canadian context, the initiatives did force the debate onto a broader stage.

Many Canadians know from their reading of contemporary history that Quebec was left out of the final negotiations and horse-trading that led to the constitutional deal. Many will not recall, however, that on the same night that Quebec would declare it had been delivered the most insulting humiliation, clauses dealing with native people and women were also eliminated from the package. After intense last-minute scrambling and with the support of others, native Canadians succeeded in persuading the government to include the following provision in the new Charter of Rights and Freedoms: "That existing aboriginal and treaty rights would be recognized."

In his book, Chrétien describes the frustration of the 1982 constitutional battles. As justice minister and the man assigned by Prime Minister Trudeau to oversee the constitutional debate, Chrétien outlines some of the changes that were proposed in an attempt to persuade Quebec to sign on, despite a conviction that Parti Québécois (PQ) leader René Lévesque would never sign anything. Chrétien says that dropping women and natives from the package was the only way he could persuade the majority of the other provinces to sign on. "Allan Blakeney opposed the women's rights clause," writes Chrétien, and Alberta and British Columbia objected to the native provision. The three joined forces to block the initiative.

"So the three of them forced the rest of us to abandon women and natives," says Chrétien. "Our only consolation was that we could come back to those clauses later, and I sensed that we would be back sooner rather than later."

Within hours of discovering the cuts, women's groups and native leaders were up in arms. Somehow, the press found out that Saskatchewan premier Allan Blakeney was the sole opponent to the women's clause. Chrétien then suggested to Alberta premier Peter

Lougheed that he too might find it uncomfortable as the lone hold-out on the native issue. "Alberta was worried about recognizing aboriginal rights when it didn't know what that meant or implied," says Chrétien in *Straight from the Heart.* "We debated the meaning again and again until finally I said to Alberta's Attorney General, 'Look, why don't we just talk about the rights that exist, the "existing right"?'

"The inclusion of the word 'existing' puzzled some of the constitutional experts and didn't please many of the native leaders, who thought it would put the onus on them to prove that the right did exist. But I was confident that it wouldn't affect anything. In the view of federal lawyers, a right either existed or it didn't exist. Yet the change was enough to satisfy Alberta, and that was important for me. I have never believed in seeking perfection at the risk of losing everything."

It had been a long, exhausting, and ultimately expensive fight for the country's relatively new native organizations. By the end, divisions among them, in part stemming from a difference in opinions about wording and meaning, had become apparent. This discord has often been cited by constitutional scholars as another reason for the weakened wording in the final document.

But once again, for every loss there were gains; at least recognition of existing native rights had made it into the country's fundamental document. And, as part of the constitutional deal-making, Prime Minister Trudeau had offered native people a series of First Ministers Conferences (FMCs), the first to be held in 1983, to discuss "additional" native rights that might be introduced into the constitution since "existing rights" had now been recognized.

As the first FMC approached, yet another study of Canada's relationship with its aboriginal residents was in the works. It provided reason to hope that positive changes would occur. Prepared by a parliamentary committee and chaired by Liberal MP Keith Penner after months of study and travel across the country, the 1983 "Penner Report" recommended that Indian First Nations should be recognized and treated as equal to the provinces in all respects, including in their financial dealings with the federal government. The report called on the government to allow native people to set their own priorities, which would be supported by direct, unconditional grants. The report also accepted band councils as both governments and the bodies that would foster self-government. Penner's report also called, once again, for the dismantling of Indian Affairs, but suggested that it be replaced by a smaller ministry that would guarantee the preservation of Canada's obligations to native people. The report was supported by all three federal parties and, in principle, by the AFN. Said one expert, "Its foremost contribution is that it provided the first holistic picture of what Indian government might look like."

Different Expectations

As might have been expected, however, the two sides entered the FMC discussions with different goals. Governments arrived to discuss the possibility of "new" rights; native leaders, to restore and clarify the rights they say have "existed" for centuries. However, the word "existing" was defined differently by aboriginal leaders and the government, notes a 1987 Indian Affairs booklet titled *A Record of Aboriginal Constitutional Reform.* "In the view of governments, the existing aboriginal rights that were given protection by section 35 related to traditional use and occupancy of land such as hunting, fishing, gathering and trapping, or rights that now exist or may be acquired through land claims agreements," states the document. The government also insisted that the section did not restore aboriginal and treaty rights lost through agreements that had been reached prior to the proclamation date of the new constitutional document. "By contrast, the aboriginal leaders held the view that the protection offered extended to a full range of rights that they argue aboriginal peoples had exercised in the past and which continue to exist."

At the first FMC, held in March 1983, the provinces (except for Quebec) and aboriginal representatives and leaders of the territorial governments signed an accord. This agreement established an agenda for future FMCs and included a resolution to amend the constitution (proclaimed in 1984). The amendment confirmed that the constitutional recognition of treaty rights subsumed those rights of the aboriginal peoples that exist as a result of current land claim agreements or those that may be signed in the future. As well, the accord indicated that the guarantee of existing aboriginal and treaty rights applied equally to men and women. It further made a commitment that, before the government amended any other sections of the constitution that related directly to aboriginal peoples, aboriginal leaders would be invited to participate in an FMC to discuss the proposed changes. Finally, the accord set the dates for additional FMCs on native issues, the last conference to be held in March 1987.

The most significant development at that first meeting was that the term self-government was officially entered into the Canadian political psyche. In fact, as the 1987 Indian Affairs overview attests: self-government emerged as the "pivotal issue."

Various participants proposed a range of options to deal with the self-government issue, from constitutional recognition of an inherent and unqualified right to aboriginal self-government, to recognition of the right only after its full definition. The challenge of the next FMC was to find a workable consensus.

Setting the tone for the 1984 meeting was what appeared to be a new attitude of the federal government of Prime Minister Mulroney. During that year, the Nielsen task force report on government spending was released. It suggested as the White Paper had in 1969, that responsibility for Indians be shifted to the provinces as a cost-saving measure. Once again, native leaders had ammunition to support their assertion that the White Paper and the government's hopes for assimilation were alive and well in Ottawa: the possibility of a successful FMC began to fade.

While a clarification of positions did occur during the March 1984 FMC, the parties did not reach an agreement. Federal officials proposed a constitutional amendment that would commit governments to establish "institutions of aboriginal self-government" in accordance with federal and provincial legislation. Aboriginal representatives, on the other hand, sought immediate entrenchment of self-government as a right. This idea was unacceptable to most of the provinces and to federal government officials, who felt that such a right could have unknown consequences and should not be left to be defined by the courts.

By the 1985 meeting, the federal government was proposing that any local self-government agreements reached between federal or provincial governments could be given constitutional protection. This approach, the argument went, would allow the development of various self-government models, which would be suited to the individual needs of the diverse native population.

At that meeting, Prime Minister Brian Mulroney stated: "Constitutional protection for the principle of self-government is an overriding objective because it is the constitutional manifestation of a relationship, an unbreakable social contract between aboriginal peoples and their governments."

An "unprecedented level of consensus was reached," notes the Indian Affairs overview. Seven provinces appeared ready to accept a modified version of the proposed federal draft, if the aboriginal associations at the table agreed. Two did not. The AFN refused to accept anything less than entrenchment of an inherent and unqualified right to self-government in the constitution. The Inuit Committee on National Issues rejected the proposal because it would give provinces a mandatory role in the negotiation and constitutional protection of self-government agreements. In June 1985, a ministerial meeting on these issues also failed to produce an acceptable solution.

Emotions were running high at the fourth and final aboriginal FMC, held in March 1987. The meeting ended with no agreement on the constitutional recognition of native self-government. Key provincial leaders joined with their Ottawa counterparts to argue that the concepts of "self-government were too vague to be approved." At the closing ceremonies, native leaders spoke gravely and with bitterness about the future.

Still, some observers note, the process had given native groups yet another opportunity to educate others about their concerns and to emerge with a clearly defined message — that their rights to self-government had never been extinguished. However, says Mary Ellen Turpel, a native legal expert who was part of the AFN negotiation team, the conferences were "abysmal failures in terms of affecting actual change."

The Meech Lake Accord

Just weeks after the final FMC, Prime Minister Mulroney and the provincial premiers emerged from Meech Lake, Quebec, to announce with great fanfare that they had struck an agreement to bring the province of Quebec back into the federation. One of the key pillars of the deal was an agreement to recognize within the Constitution that Quebec was a "distinct society." The irony of both the government's inability to define that phrase, and the responses to critics that its meaning could be determined at a later date between the two "founding nations of Canada, the English and the French," was not lost on Canada's native people. Here was further evidence that Canada's aboriginal residents were not an integral part of the collective Canadian psyche.

The Meech Lake Accord was given three years to be ratified by all provincial legislatures. As the 1990 deadline approached, it appeared that Prime Minister Mulroney's contribution to Canada's young constitutional history would be realized. However, native leaders had other ideas. Once again they united and, using their collective experience, they launched a strategy to kill the accord with a single-mindedness not seen before.

In June 1990, Elijah Harper, the lone aboriginal member of the Manitoba legislature, aided by procedural errors on the part of the provincial Conservative government, blocked the passage of the accord and became a hero to both Canada's aboriginal people and a growing number of other Canadians who opposed the accord for a variety of reasons. Harper, with the extensive assistance of some of the top native leaders in the country, including the head of the Assembly of Manitoba Chiefs, Phil Fontaine, and the AFN vice-chief, Ovide Mercredi, raised the profile of native issues as never before. Suddenly, Canadians who had never seriously considered the plight of the country's aboriginal residents were asking important questions, and politicians were being called upon to give answers.

Those questions became even more pointed in the weeks after the demise of the Meech Lake Accord. A violent stand-off erupted in Oka, Quebec, between natives and local authorities over the ownership of land being prepared for the expansion of a golf course. Afterwards, AFN grand chief Georges Erasmus suggested that the negotiation of modern-day treaties could prevent similar crises in the future; the treaties, in turn, would be protected by "existing constitutional provisions." But if Erasmus was hoping for support for the idea across the country, he would be disappointed. Polls after the seventy-seven-day stand-off indicated that the violent confrontation, which left one police officer dead and saw the Canadian army called in to quell the dispute, had caused many Canadians to question their support of native causes. According to a *Toronto Star* poll, 31 per cent of Canadians had become less sympathetic towards natives by the end of the conflict. In Quebec, that number stood at 43 per cent.

Still, the fallout from both the Meech Lake Accord and the Oka stand-off pushed native issues to a new level within the Canadian political framework. One of the first major announcements to arise during this period was that Prime Minister Mulroney would establish a Royal Commission on Aboriginal Peoples. He had presented this option in the dying days of Meech Lake in the hopes that native people would allow the accord to pass in exchange for future opportunities.

The Royal Commission

The royal commission was launched in August 1991. It began with sixteen full-time staff and four hundred part-time researchers. It was co-chaired by the former AFN leader and Dene, Georges Erasmus, and Mr. Justice Rene Dussault of the Quebec Court of Appeal. Other members of the commission included former Supreme Court judge Bertha Wilson; Viola Robinson, a Micmac and former president of the Native Council of Canada; Mary Sillet, a Labrador Inuit and former vice-president of the Inuit Tapirisat of Canada; and Paul Chartrand, a Métis and professor of native studies at the University of Manitoba. Former Saskatchewan premier Allan Blakeney was also appointed, but resigned in April 1993, complaining the commission was dealing only with generalities. He was replaced by Peter Meckison, a political science professor and constitutional expert from the University of Alberta.

The goals of the royal commission were broad: to investigate the evolution of the relationship between natives and the rest of Canada and to examine all the issues relevant to natives. By January 1994, the *Globe and Mail* reported that the body had heard testimonies from more than 2,200 people in 112 communities, spent half of its $48 million budget, and produced more than 60,000 pages of transcripts. Blakeney would not be the royal commission's last critic. In 1993, AFN chief Ovide Mercredi said that he too was disappointed with the lack of concrete answers from the commission; he expressed frustration over what he saw as just another study into native issues. Mercredi stated that native self-government initiatives would move ahead without the commission's input. "My people won't wait for no study," he commented.

Ron Irwin, who had taken over the post of Indian Affairs after the Liberals won the 1993 election, was also critical. In a 1994 interview with *Ottawa Citizen* native affairs reporter Jack Aubry, Irwin said that the commission's budget, which was then being listed at $58 million, could have been put to better use on the "poorest of Canada's poor." He added that the report of the commission, the release of which was delayed several times and is now expected in 1996, could be too late to benefit native people because the report would be released past the mid-point of the Liberal mandate, making action difficult. "If I had my druthers, I would build a thousand houses with the $58 million...," Irwin told the House of Commons.

Still, the work of the commission will be impossible to ignore. To date, it has written reports suggesting shared land use, development, and jurisdiction as a way to resolve outstanding comprehensive land claims. Each of its reports is covered extensively in the media.

The Charlottetown Accord

Another outcome of the summer of 1990 was that Grand Chief Ovide Mercredi and the AFN became an integral part of the negotiations in an attempt to recoup something from the failure of the Meech Lake Accord. Aboriginal concerns were a key issue to be addressed in the Charlottetown Accord, and after some negotiations, native leaders were treated as equals in the process. Finally, after centuries of neglect and frustration, native people were no longer simply the "technical advisors" during a major Canadian political debate on the country's future.

As one of the AFN constitutional advisors explains, participation in the Charlottetown Accord went a long way to correct the historic imbalance in the relationship between native people and the Canadian government. "Instead of viewing aboriginal peoples as distinct political entities with the capacity to have a relationship with the Crown and as pre-existing governments in Canada, the Constitution has fundamentally only envisioned the inferiority or wardship of aboriginal peoples and the superior wisdom and guardianship of the Crown," writes Mary Ellen Turpel in an article titled "Charlottetown Discord and Aboriginal Peoples' Struggle for Fundamental Change." "This imbalance is the very premise of the Indian Act — this scheme of administration of 'Indians' in Canada sees the all-powerful minister of Indian Affairs as having final authority over all aspects of the life of 'Indians' — from birth to the disposition of an estate."

Correcting this imbalance, says Turpel, could not have been a unilateral exercise. "The Charlottetown Accord round of discussions was the first opportunity, outside of the early treaties, in the history of Canada where change was discussed with aboriginal peoples, based on aboriginal ideas for a new relationship." The imbalance still existed in the amending formula under which the changes would be made to the Constitution — with native people having no input; however, "the act of meeting as equals around a multilateral negotiation table was no small breakthrough when seen against the uniform history of exclusion," says Turpel. The appointment of Neil Sterritt, a Gitskan hereditary chief, as co-chair of the working group responsible for proposing amendments on aboriginal issues, was another breakthrough. Turpel states that "his participation at this level was an important symbolic statement of inclusion."

The aboriginal input into the accord was also apparent in the final document, which offered, says Turpel, the "largest package of proposals for reform on Aboriginal issues in the history of Canada." Some of the native proposals that made it into the final document "were the subject of outright ridicule when they were introduced." The fact that they survived to emerge in the accord, albeit in an altered form, was a testament to the success of aboriginal leaders, according to Turpel.

Among other things, the accord recognized aboriginal governments as one of the three orders of government in Canada, and there would be seats for aboriginal senators and a provision for the conclusion of an accord for the Métis to deal with their historical grievances. Furthermore, in what Turpel terms a "truly critical breakthrough," the government would redistribute power between the federal and provincial levels: this restructuring would be done in such a way as to maintain aboriginal or treaty rights, the federal fiduciary responsibility for aboriginal peoples, and the jurisdictions or rights of aboriginal governments. Constitutional conferences every two years beginning in 1996 on native issues were also promised.

Perhaps the primary gain was the recognition of the inherent right of self-government (pre-existing and not granted by the Constitution). However, the accord set three limitations in this regard: the inherent right would apply "within Canada"; it would be subject to federal and provincial laws in the interest of peace, order, and good government; and it would include a provision that no new land rights would be created by implication. The provinces insisting on these limitations were Alberta, Newfoundland, and Quebec.

In Turpel's view, "These concessions were painful during the negotiation process and were often motivated by what I could only describe as mean-spirited objections to self-government, based on stereotypes about aboriginal peoples as peoples without the sophistication to govern themselves." Native leaders knew such restrictions would make the package hard to sell to their own people. "The question the leadership faced, like that faced by all social reformers, was whether significant although incomplete change was better than none." The four aboriginal organizations that had been involved in the negotiations — the AFN, the Native Council of Canada, the Inuit

Tapirisat of Canada, and the Métis National Council — endorsed the document and called on their people to vote for it.

But it was not to be. On October 26, 1992, the country defeated the Charlottetown Accord in a referendum vote. The estimated aboriginal vote was 8 per cent of the 1.5 million people who turned out. The majority of native people who voted (more than 60 per cent) cast a negative ballot. (Precise figures are impossible to obtain because the Charter deems identification of a voter by race illegal.)

Among the aboriginal detractors was one of the four native women's groups — the Native Women's Association of Canada. The association argued that it had a right to be at the negotiating table to protect aboriginal women's interests. Other detractors argued that the implications of the "within Canada" restriction could not be determined. Leaders such as Elijah Harper and Phil Fontaine maintained that the central problem was the lack of time for digesting the ramifications of the concessions that had been made.

In the aftermath of the rejection of Prime Minister Mulroney's second constitutional initiative, native leaders faced an exhausted Canadian public. Native issues were no longer front-page news, and no politician would dare suggest the reopening of the constitutional quagmire. Native battles once more moved into the background. During the 1993 federal election campaign, which saw a change in government, politicians barely mentioned native issues. This lack of attention was lamented by AFN head Ovide Mercredi. He told Geoffrey York of the *Globe and Mail* that the Oka and Meech Lake episodes had raised the Canadian conscience. "I would think that should be sufficient to keep the issue as a high priority, but it doesn't appear to be the case in this election," said Mercredi.

A constitutional solution to native problems in the near future seemed remote. "I find it highly doubtful that there could be constitutional reform on specific issues, like aboriginal peoples, given the nature of the amending formula and the kind of constitutional politics in which first ministers have engaged since repatriation," says Turpel. "My impression is...that there will be no further constitutional-reform discussions in Canada unless we are on the brink of Quebec secession."

Native Rights in Quebec

The election of Jacques Parizeau and his separatist PQ in September 1994 once again brought the question of native rights to the forefront.

Within weeks of the election, Quebec native leaders sent a message to the new government: "Indians hold a veto over Quebec separation." In October 1994, the *Ottawa Citizen* reported that forty-one Quebec chiefs had unanimously approved a political declaration stating, among other things, that Quebec's 60,000 natives have the right to redraw the borders of a separate Quebec. "The chiefs said aboriginal consent is required for any change to the 'political constitutional framework,' " reported Jack Aubry. Premier Jacques Parizeau has repeatedly scoffed at the notion that Quebec's borders can be altered and noted that he has international legal opinions to prove it. But Quebec natives argue that their historic agreements were with the British Crown and the federal government, and that the right of Quebec's native people to remain part of Canada must be protected by Ottawa, which maintains a fiduciary responsibility for native people.

Exactly where the federal government stands on the issue remains largely a mystery as the referendum vote, expected some time in 1995, nears. Prime Minister Chrétien commented that "there is no mechanism in the Constitution to permit separation of some part of the Canadian territory." However, fearing that any comment could inflame the situation, Ottawa has said little else about Quebec's referendum plans and even less about the plight of Quebec's native people in the event of a "yes" vote.

However, in May 1994, less than six months before the PQ election victory, Indian Affairs minister Ron Irwin offered a hint of the federal position when newspapers, including the *Globe and Mail,* reported him as saying that Quebec's native people had the right to remain in Canada with their territory if Quebec separates. "The point is, [native people] have been here for 10,000 years and they want to remain a part of Canada and I think they have that right," Irwin told reporters during a two-day, self-government meeting with native leaders and provincial and federal officials. "The separatists say that they have a right to decide, then why don't the aboriginal people who have been here twenty times as long have the same right? It seems logical to me." Irwin also said he had assured native leaders that the federal government would not abandon its responsibility under the treaties to protect native interests. But Premier Parizeau argued that the federal government had already abandoned its fiduciary responsibility for Quebec Crees when it signed the only modern-day treaty, the 1975 James Bay and Northern Quebec Agreement. The PQ also insisted that pressure from governments of the United States, Mexico, and other countries terrified of a precedent would force Canada to reject native sovereignty.

Since then, Irwin and other federal officials have remained silent, leaving native leaders to respond to the PQ. Quebec Cree leader Mathew Coon-Come's response is that the Quebec government and the province's aboriginal people will fight for international recognition if separation is approved. He notes that, without aboriginal consent, other countries will not recognize an independent Quebec.

As in the past, one of the principal challenges may be for native people to stay united on the issue. Before winning the election, the PQ spoke of reaching an agreement with Quebec's native people on a constitution for an independent Quebec prior to the referendum. However, soon after the election, this idea was dismissed as impossible, and the goal became to sign agreements with individual nations. Quebec has ten native nations. The PQ announced that it would deal first with the Montagnais, Attikamek and the Inuit. In December 1994, the PQ offered a $400 million deal to the Montagnais and Attikamek groups, which included a promise to double their territories. The deal also offered royalties over resource development and exploitation. Native leaders said they were willing to consider the deal if it benefited both themselves and Quebec. The two groups have few links to English Canada, stated the *Globe and Mail* when the deal was announced, and, historically, relations with Quebec have not been as strained as those with other First Nations in the province.

In March 1995, Mathew Coon-Come indicated that he was unwilling to let the issues wither away and again called on federal government officials to break their silence. "What we dispute is Quebec's right to hold a referendum on the future of Eenou Astchee (the Cree territory) and Eeyouch, the Cree People," said Coon-Come, referring to the 240,000 square kilometres of land in northern Quebec. "I want to be clear. We are not Canada's Indians. We are not Quebec's Indians. We are our people — Eeyouch, The Crees."

Quebec's native leaders know they will need outside help if Quebec separates. Historically, polls have shown far less sympathy for the native situation from Quebec residents than from the rest of Canada. After the Oka affair, polls indicated that the majority of Quebecers (56 per cent) believed that few native land claims were valid, and 14 per cent believed that none were valid. The majority also believed that native people should assimilate. In October 1991, AFN leader Ovide Mercredi faced a hostile audience during a visit to the province when he tried to persuade Quebecers that First Nations shared their aspirations for self-determination and were natural allies in constitutional reform talks. *La Presse* carried the following headline during the visit: "Natives Don't Have the Means to be Sovereign." Comments about AFN plans to seek federal government protection for native rights in the event of separation, and Mercredi's reminder of outstanding land claims in the province, did not help the mood.

Mercredi has suggested that the Quebec government will be forced to the constitutional table once again as Ottawa faces Quebec's threat of separation, and he believes that native self-government will be on that agenda. Perhaps; but other developments, domestic and international, may make that unnecessary.

The Future

In 1989, David Courchene, Sr., said in an interview that the final battles for native rights may well be waged on the international stage. As has been mentioned, Indian leaders first tried their hand in the international arena in 1969. In response to the White Paper, a delegation travelled to London to ask the Queen to intervene on behalf of native people. Since then, several of Canada's First Nations, in particular the James Bay Cree and the Inuit Tapirisat of Canada, have gained extensive knowledge and international experience. In the 1980s, the James Bay Cree were given official status at the UN, allowing them to take part in the official business of various bodies, including the Working Group on Indigenous Populations. "I believe that the Canadian Indian and the American Indian can develop a court case against the governments of Canada and the United States to go before an international court or tribunal," Courchene said before his death in August 1992, adding that the exact forum would be decided at some future date. His words may well prove prophetic. In the 1990s, crusades at the international level are gaining momentum among aboriginal peoples around the world.

In 1994, the UN Year of Indigenous Peoples, a Draft Declaration of Indigenous Peoples Rights began its journey through the final stages of approval at the UN. The five-member Working Group on Indigenous Populations began discussions on the declaration of indigenous rights in 1985, three years after the expert body had been established. While the document still must find its way through the political quagmire known as the UN General Assembly, the exercise has shown that unity is growing among the world's indigenous peoples and among others who want to make serious improvements in their lives that may require control over their own destinies. Considering the competing political pressures within the UN, the draft declaration is especially striking for its unequivocal statement that "Indigenous peoples have the right to self-determination." This assertion is qualified by certain restrictions under international law that aim to protect the integrity of existing states. Some governments argued that few will accept such wording once the document reaches the UN General Assembly, the UN's ultimate authority.

Canada has long opposed any such statement at the international level, arguing that it may suggest that native communities have the right to secede. So concerned was the Canadian government about this issue, in fact, that it led an initiative at the 1994 UN World Conference on Human Rights in Vienna and succeeded in having the "s" removed from the word "peoples" in the final declaration of the conference. Native leaders sought the inclusion of the word "peoples" as recognition at the international level that they are peoples as defined under international covenants and declarations, which include the right to self-determination. This recognition would allow them to assert all rights conferred on collectives in such international codes as the International Bill of Human Rights and the Covenant on Civil and Political Rights. While native leaders lost the fight at the Vienna conference, they remain hopeful that they will have time to persuade the government before 2005, the final year of the UN Decade of the World's Indigenous Peoples.

Some of Canada's native leaders have also become more optimistic due to a change on the domestic front. Twenty-four years after he introduced the White Paper in the House of Commons, Jean Chrétien is back — as prime minister.

Signs of yet another shift in Canadian government policy towards the country's aboriginal peoples emerged during the 1993 election campaign. First, Chrétien called for the negotiation and implementation of the inherent right of self-government outside a constitutional reform process. Second, as he had more than two decades before, he advocated the dismantling of the Department of Indian and Northern Affairs (previously, the Department of Indian Affairs and Northern Development). As part of their election strategy, the Liberal Party released the "Red Book." The document outlined the promises the Liberals vowed to keep after their election. If they failed to live up to those promises, Chrétien often repeated, the Canadian public would be able to hold up the book and demand answers.

Plans for the Indian Affairs portfolio, which the Liberals referred to as "Renewing the Partnership," were extensive. Students of government policy regarding aboriginal people heard echoes of the White Paper. Chapter Seven, titled "Aboriginal Peoples," begins: "The priority of a Liberal government will be to assist aboriginal communities in their efforts to address the obstacles to their development and to help them marshal the human and physical resources necessary to build and sustain vibrant communities."

It continues: "The place of Aboriginal peoples in the growth and development of Canada is a litmus test of our beliefs in fairness, justice and equality of opportunity. For generations, Canadian society has failed this test....Past and current ways of dealing with these conditions are not working. It is time for a change."

The book then set out five goals of a Liberal government:

1. Aboriginal people will enjoy a standard of living and quality of life and opportunity equal to those of other Canadians;
2. Aboriginal people will live "self-reliantly, secure in the knowledge of who they are as unique peoples";
3. All Canadians will understand that they have been "enriched by aboriginal cultures" and be committed to the fair sharing of the potential of our nation;
4. Aboriginal people will have the positive option "to live and work wherever they choose"; and
5. "Perhaps most importantly, aboriginal children will grow up in secure families and healthy communities, with the opportunity to take their full place in Canada."

To reinforce the importance of this final point, the Liberals proposed a "head start" program for children. "Aboriginal people want to break the cycle of poverty, and a Liberal government will help through an Aboriginal Head Start program. Designed and managed by Aboriginal communities, Aboriginal Head Start will be modelled on other successful head start programs that provide child care and nutritional counselling, and that prepare disadvantaged preschool children for learning." The program would be targeted at three- to five-year-olds and implemented first in urban settings or in large northern communities.

The Liberals vowed they were committed to a new relationship with native people, built on "trust, mutual respect, and participation in the decision-making process." And, once again, they promised to dismantle the Indian Affairs department. Unlike the 1969 situation, however, Ottawa would maintain its federal fiduciary responsibility this time. "We will work with aboriginal peoples to identify where existing federal expenditures for aboriginal peoples, currently in excess of $5 billion a year, can be redirected into more productive uses," stated the document. Regarding treaties, the Liberals promised to "seek advice of treaty First Nations on how to achieve a mutually acceptable process to interpret the treaties in contemporary terms while giving full recognition to their original spirit and intent."

The most significant promise in the Red Book's plan for indigenous peoples, however, was the statement that a Liberal government would conduct itself as if "the inherent right to self-government is an existing aboriginal treaty right."

Of course, all these promises sounded wonderful, but political parties seeking power have been known to change their minds once the election has been won. This time, however, some evidence indicated that the Liberals were working hard to keep their promises to native people even in the face of severe budget constraints. "Native issues have taken a surprisingly high profile early in this new government," reported the *Ottawa Citizen* in the spring of 1994. The new government quickly announced a $10 million expenditure in 1994–95 for the aboriginal head start program for preschool children and their parents; the program would provide community day care and nutritional counselling, and also have a cultural and language component. The Liberals estimated the costs of the program to be $20 million for 1995–96 and $30 million for 1996–97.

According to the 1994–95 edition of *How Ottawa Spends*, overall federal program spending for that period is estimated to rise by about $800 million, with the Indian Affairs department receiving about one-third of that increase ($256 million) due to the growing aboriginal population and the implementation of the Liberal campaign promises. Overall, the funding level for transfers to Indians and Inuit is estimated to continue increasing through the mid-1990s, from $3.8 billion in 94–95, to 4.1 billion in 95–96," notes Michael Prince. In 1995, when the Chrétien government released its second budget and found itself breaking several of its election promises, the Indian Affairs department was one of the few to emerge almost untouched.

It was apparent early in his mandate that Indian Affairs minister Ron Irwin intended to put his stamp on the department. Perhaps this is not surprising considering the history of the man who appointed Irwin and the legacy that Irwin inherited. Jean Chrétien obviously enjoyed his time as Indian Affairs minister. In *Straight from the Heart,* Chrétien says: "Before me the Indians had had seven ministers in seven years. I stayed six years, one month, three days and two hours, and I loved every minute of it....This time was probably the most productive of my career in terms of the number of decisions made and the initiatives taken."

Irwin met the future prime minister in 1969 when Chrétien visited Irwin's home town of Sault Ste. Marie. In 1982, Irwin served as Chrétien's parliamentary secretary during the constitutional talks. Known for his straightforwardness, Irwin declared in January 1994 that the department of Indian Affairs has been "a quagmire of indifference." Not long after, he announced that the government would hold meetings over a six-month period with national and regional aboriginal leaders, provincial and territorial governments, and representatives of the royal commission. Their objective would be to discuss not *if,* but *how best* to implement native self-government. Irwin was working under the premise, as promised, that the inherent right to self-government exists and does not require constitutional recognition. He elaborated that he did not envisage a single model of self-government and expected that "hundreds of different types" will emerge from the process. This view, that no single model will work and that communities will require their own mix of municipal, provincial, and federal powers, removed yet another obstacle that has plagued native self-government initiatives. Then came the announcement that Manitoba's First Nations would become the self-government laboratory, the first group to work out the logistics of native control and the dismantling of Indian Affairs.

Despite such progress, stumbling blocks still remain. When the Liberals first announced that self-government was an existing aboriginal treaty right that did not require a constitutional guarantee, AFN grand chief Ovide Mercredi was not appeased. Mercredi and other native leaders called the proposals a "trust me" initiative: the Liberals provided no certainty that native governmental powers and jurisdictions would ever be protected in the Constitution. When estimates were released indicating that the Indian Affairs department would spend $4 million on consultations to determine how to implement self-government, Mercredi called on Irwin to spend the money instead on discussions between the country's chiefs and the federal government. "The chiefs still insist on constitutional protection for self-government agreements, but they believe it can be achieved without full blown constitutional talks," he said. The chiefs warned against any regional process involving provincial governments and suggested conducting negotiations on the basis of modern-day treaties.

Others have also not reacted with joy over the Manitoba experiment. Freelance journalist and Six Nations Indian band member Jim Moses noted in a May 14, 1994, *Globe and Mail* article that members of his reserve (24,000 hectares north of Lake Erie and south of Brantford, Ontario) reacted warily to the declaration of the self-government experiment. "To them self-government is a two-edged sword: It would make them masters in their territories, but could very well lead to mismanagement of reserve finances by new leaders." Serious questions have been raised by other native people about some leaders' abilities to run native affairs effectively. Traditional leaders speak of the problems of greed and question the validity of gambling and tobacco smuggling as a source of income. High-tech weapons and other communications equipment are also not uncommon on reserves with more radical elements. Does the federal government truly want to give these leaders more autonomy and control? In addition, Irwin's dismantling plan had the provinces asking the familiar question, "Who will pay?" Will this plan mean an increase in provincial responsibilities for native people?

Despite the warnings, significant changes are apparent. "This is the beginning of the end for the Indian Act," said an ecstatic Manitoba Assembly of Chiefs leader Phil Fontaine when the Manitoba experiment was announced. Once again, it is the philosophy behind the plan that is so different than when Jean Chrétien made the same announcement twenty-five years ago. Now, both native and non-native players say the goal is to hand over to native people the true reins of power.

2

Reserves

Pukatawagan is a Cree community sitting along the north shore of the Churchill River in northern Manitoba, 750 kilometres northwest of Winnipeg and a short distance from the Saskatchewan border. Almost 1,900 people call it home. The department of Indian Affairs lists the band's official name as Mathias Colomb, after the chief who settled the band in its present location at the turn of the century. The residents call themselves Missinippi Ethiniwak or the Churchill River people. One of 604 bands across Canada, this community is typical of the 112 bands found in the northern extremes of the country, located so far from the rest of the world that no one bothered to build a road to get there. The only way in or out of the reserve is by air. The community is bordered by dense bush and the wide river. The streets are dirt roads. There are a few trucks and vans on the reserve, but they have nowhere to go. The road ends at the airstrip and a rail line. It is a quiet community, but not a stagnant one. In recent years, Pukatawagan has been undergoing massive changes as the conveniences and comforts of the modern world finally make their way to this isolated post.

In the early 1970s, the news media called Pukatawagan, "Dodge City of the North." Like other reserve communities across the country, Pukatawagan was suffering from heightened tensions triggered by abject poverty. Houses were nothing more than plywood sheds heated by wood stoves. There was no electricity or running water, and few people had telephones. Shooting incidents were common, and drunkenness appeared to be an established way of life. In 1974, band leaders moved to stop the community's downward slide. In an event that has become almost legendary among residents, leaders gathered up all of the guns and threw them into the Churchill River; they banned liquor from the reserve and promised to bring changes. Fourteen years would pass before those promises bore fruit. Today, new homes are being built at a phenomenal rate. There is a new community centre and renewed hope within the people that the coming years will bring many more benefits.

Two hundred kilometres directly south of Pukatawagan and across the Saskatchewan River from the town called The Pas (pronounced *paw*) is the Opaskwayak Cree Nation. This native community is one of the most prosperous in Canada, thanks in part to a 20,000-square-metre shopping mall and the foresight of the band leaders more than twenty-five years ago. In 1968, the band employed three people and had a budget of $20,000; the reserve was just a shanty town. Prosperity and jobs were only found across the river in the non-native community of The Pas. Today, the band is the area's second largest employer, outside of the local pulp and paper operation, with assets worth $21 million and an annual cash flow of $17 million. It employs more than 250 people, native and non-native. Reserve housing resembles any new subdivision found in thriving communities. This reserve, with about 2,100 residents, is typical of the 199 bands across Canada that are situated near urban centres.

The Indian reserves scattered across Canada are the physical embodiment of the native drive for self-government. During the past twenty-five years, changes on reserves have reflected the successes and failures of ongoing attempts by native people to gain control over their lives. The patterns of change have varied widely across the country. Some communities, such as Pukatawagan, have found themselves taking bold steps forward, only to slip back momentarily before struggling forward again. Others have advanced with steady strides.

Former Opaskwayak chief Oscar Lathlin, now a New Democratic member of the Legislative Assembly in Manitoba, says few people could have imagined the changes that occurred on the reserve during the past quarter-century. And no one, he insists, should rule out the potential for similar change and growth in any Indian community. "Twenty years ago our critics could not make any sense of what we wanted to do," Lathlin says. Non-natives predicted the mall would fail, that it would not be able to compete with the stores across the river, and that the non-aboriginal community would refuse to shop there. Although the downtown core of The Pas struggles to survive, the mall, like malls everywhere, is a success, regularly attracting shoppers from across the river and from the surrounding area.

Development of Reserves

The first reserves appeared in Canada in the 1830s. As the Canadian West was colonized, the British government persuaded Indian bands to give up their nomadic lifestyle, assigned them to small tracts of land, and banned the traditional forms of Indian government. Fifty years later, an amendment to the first Indian Act imposed the concept of an elected chief and council on native people.

Indian bands today are still governed by an elected chief and council, which act as the direct link to the department of Indian Affairs and other federal ministries, including the Justice and Health departments. The chief and council administer the funds Ottawa provides for education, housing, and welfare. Until recently, Ottawa alone determined the amount of money to be given to each band and the areas in which it would be spent. Throughout most of the 1970s, when Indian leaders were only beginning to articulate their vision of a new future, band councils functioned merely as government administrators. They were more accountable to Ottawa than to the people who elected them. Moreover, there was never enough money for housing, education, or economic development. People would complain and demand more services; the councils would overspend, increasing their debt, in a pattern that recurred across Canada. Ottawa would chastise them and withhold monies from the following year's budget to cover the debt. Poverty fed on itself in a downward spiral.

Privileges of a Status Indian

Indians living on reserves are considered to be the descendants of North American Indians, who were living in Canada before the arrival of the Europeans. With the passing of the Indian Act, these people acquired a status unique in Canada. They became the responsibility of the federal government and thus were eligible for a wide range of benefits and services. The Indian Act defines an Indian as "a person who, pursuant to this Act, is registered as an Indian or is entitled to be registered as an Indian." Generally speaking, residents of Indian reserves are referred to as "registered" or "status" Indians. Each individual is assigned a status number at birth and given a status card bearing his or her name and number. The Indian Registry, a federal government document, lists each resident's number and membership within a band.

Status Indians living on a reserve are entitled to housing, education, health care, and social assistance benefits, which are paid for by the federal government. Indians and bands do not pay federal or provincial taxes on their personal property on the reserve, including income earned while working on the reserve. Provinces cannot collect sales taxes from a status Indian on any goods that are purchased on a reserve. Some provinces do not collect sales taxes for goods purchased off-reserve that are delivered or used on the reserve. Generally speaking, status Indians who display their status card prior to a purchase are exempt from paying provincial sales taxes. Status Indians are also eligible for the same social security benefits as other Canadians, including the Canada Pension Plan, Old Age Security, the Guaranteed Income Supplement and Family Allowance, unemployment insurance benefits, and social assistance.

Ottawa also pays for education. Elementary education (nursery school to Grade 12) is available on a reserve at schools operated by Indian Affairs or by the band. If enrolment is too low or if programs are not available on the reserve, Indian children can attend provincial public schools. Ottawa provides funds for school construction and maintenance, as well as staff salaries. In addition, Ottawa ultimately pays any tuition fees charged by a provincial school system. Post-secondary education is also available, but on a more limited basis. The government assigns specific post-secondary budgets depending on the band's size, and the council or a designated education committee determines who is eligible for complete tuition and living assistance at a community college, university, or provincially accredited private training institution.

Medical services are comprehensive for status Indians, whether or not they live on the reserve. Most Indians and all Indian organizations consider the provision of a comprehensive medical services program a treaty right, like the other services. However, Ottawa considers on-reserve medical services as a by-product of overall government policy, which can be terminated at any time. The Medical Services Branch of the department of Indian Affairs covers the cost of prescription drugs, dental services, eyeglasses, and medical transportation. For example, an Indian who presents a status card to a pharmacist can obtain prescription medication without charge. The cost is covered by Ottawa. The department of Indian Affairs generally maintains a nursing station on each reserve and covers the salaries of all employees. Doctors, dentists, and eye doctors visit reserves on a regular basis. Again, all costs — salaries, transportation, expenses — are covered by Ottawa.

Membership in a band, in addition to being a qualification for status, has further privileges. Members can vote at all band elections and contest elected offices. If the band has a housing program, and almost all do, members are entitled to a home on the reserve. However, reserve land does not belong to individual Indians. In practice, the land is managed by the band; legally, the land is owned by Canada and held in trust for the band members living there. This situation makes it impossible for band members to obtain a loan because they have nothing to offer as collateral.

Not everyone who lives on a reserve is a status Indian or band member. Non-natives may establish a residence at the permission of the band council, usually because of employment or marriage to a band member. Indians without registered status — who lost it or who never had it because their parents lost it — may live on a reserve with council's permission. Often, non-status Indians are long-term residents. In the West, the site of a remote reserve is sometimes located adjacent to a Métis community or a group of predominantly non-status Indians. For area residents, the legal distinction is generally meaningless; however, only band members can vote in band elections. And only band members can share in royalties accrued to the band or cash settlements stemming from land claims.

Location of Reserves

Almost half of Canada's reserve Indians belong to 435 bands with populations of less than 1,000 residents. Only a handful of bands (fifty-nine) boast populations greater than 2,000. Indian Affairs classifies one-third of the bands (199) as urban, i.e., located within 50 kilometres of a major centre. The department has labelled 112 bands as "special access," which is quaint, considering that they remain inaccessible except by air. Another 267 bands are classified as rural; they are located 50–350 kilometres from a major centre and have year-round road access. The remaining twenty-six are classified as remote; these bands are located more than 350 kilometres from the nearest centre. They are only accessible during the winter months when paths are cleared over frozen lakes and bogs. (This number slowly dwindles as road construction improves accessibility.)

Reserves Today

By its own accounting, Ottawa has spent more than $40 billion on
Indian reserves since 1967–68; a third of that money has been spent
in the last six years. More than 315,000 people or 59 per cent of the
total registered Indian population live on reserves today. On average,
registered Indians are younger than the Canadian population as a
whole. The department of Indian Affairs, using its own statistics and
data from the 1986 and 1991 Censuses, cites that 64 per cent of the
reserve population is under the age of twenty-five, compared to 35
per cent for the overall Canadian population. This trend is expected
to continue beyond the year 2001. What has this $40 billion brought
Indian people?

The average income on reserves is about $8,000, less than half of
the national average. Almost half (47 per cent) of reserve families
live below the poverty line; this rate is three times the Canadian
average. Two-thirds of adults living on reserves (64 per cent) reported earning less than $10,000 in 1990. More than one in ten adults
(11 per cent) reported no income at all for 1990. More than 66 per
cent of Indians of working age are either unemployed or on welfare,
and that percentage is higher on the isolated reserves. However, there
is also prosperity on some reserves, mostly those in the south, which
are close to urban centres: 54 per cent of families live above the
poverty line and 27 per cent earn $10,000 above the poverty line.
Almost 2 per cent of adults reported having an income greater than
$40,000 in 1990. More than one-quarter of reserve residents (28 per
cent) report a Grade 8 education level.

Housing

In 1966, only one in ten reserve houses had central heating; today,
seven out of ten homes have furnaces. Twenty years ago, 12 per cent
of homes had indoor toilets; today, that figure is up to 83 per cent.
The proportion of homes with running water has risen from 14 to 91
per cent. However, more than half of the houses are in need of major
repair even though most were built within the past twenty years.

Ottawa began to significantly improve reserve housing in 1977
when the Canada Mortgage and Housing Corporation (CMHC) became a partner with the Indian Affairs department in providing
programs and low-cost loans to encourage construction. In 1987, the
CMHC conducted a survey to determine the impact of that involve-

ment. The report, *CMHC On-Reserve Housing Programs,* concluded that while the CMHC's financial commitment had been substantial ($1 billion between 1977 and 1987), the results had been mixed. Houses were still crowded, in poor physical condition, and lacking basic amenities. The CMHC report, based on a survey of ninety reserves, found that 36 per cent of on-reserve homes were crowded, compared to 2.3 per cent in Canada as a whole (CMHC defined a "crowded home" as one where parents shared a bedroom with their children, and where boys and girls over the age of five shared the same bedroom.) Forty-three per cent of homes are in need of major repair, compared to 13 per cent throughout Canada. CMHC loans to improve housing conditions (in the $5,000 to $8,250 range) were inadequate, the report stated; the amount would have to be doubled for the loan to become effective. The report predicted that if spending continued at the same rate, housing conditions would not reach acceptable levels until the year 2010. A 1993 Commons committee report on aboriginal affairs projected the need for 40,000 new or renovated homes, with a total cost of $3.3 billion, to raise the standard of housing to an acceptable level.

Even those bleak hopes for housing improvements appeared to have been dashed when Chrétien's Liberal government announced at the end of April 1995 that it was cutting its housing budget in half. CMHC had been building 1,200 new homes on reserves every year, at a cost of $8 million. As a result of the government's attempt to balance the budget, however, the reserve housing funding would decrease to $4 million, reducing the number of new houses to 600 per year.

Living Conditions

In the summer of 1988, Pukatawagan offered hope and change to its residents. The band council had recently opened a $2 million community centre to house the council's administrative offices, a post office, a laundromat, a grocery and general store, a small restaurant, and an eight-room hotel. A southern Manitoba construction firm had built twenty homes the previous winter; another twenty were nearing completion, and thirty more were planned for the following year. These houses are a far cry from the shacks that were built in the past; with five bedrooms, these homes are valued at $80,000 each. They are connected to running water, the sewer system, and hydro and telephone lines. Each one is equipped with four appliances, carpeting, a finished basement, and one-and-a-half bathrooms. Future plans include building a bakery, a gas station, and a tourist lodge to take advantage of the resort setting. However, the signs of progress and prosperity are misleading. The only sources of employment are the band council and the reserve's few band-owned enterprises. As a result, more than 70 per cent of the residents collect welfare. In fact, almost all money on the reserve comes from Ottawa. Salaries for band councillors and staff, programs, and the construction of houses and band facilities are federally funded. Even the salaries and shelter allowances, which cover the rent, originate from Ottawa.

This situation is replayed on most of the reserves across the country. According to the 1991 Census, the number of reserve residents relying on some form of government assistance increased during the 1980s. In 1990, the total number of registered Indians on social assistance stood at 42 per cent, which is 205 times the Canadian average.

Daily Expenses

Life is expensive on an isolated reserve. Since most goods are shipped by rail or air, prices are considerably higher than those in cities; however, salaries and welfare payments remain tied to urban equivalents. The Northern Stores (until recently called the Hudson's Bay stores), the first meeting places for Indian fur trappers and non-natives, retain their monopoly as the only general stores on many remote reserves. A 1993 study by the Manitoba Keewatinowi Okimakanak, which represents twenty-five bands in northern Manitoba, found that food prices were up to 88 per cent higher in some reserve communities than in Winnipeg. A survey of food prices conducted by the *Winnipeg Free Press* in 1994 found that nothing had changed. A ten-kilogram package of flour that sold for $6.99 in a major Winnipeg grocery store cost $12.99 in Shamattawa, a Cree community situated 1,100 kilometres northeast of Winnipeg. To put the pricing situation in perspective, fourteen of Manitoba's sixty-one Indian bands were at least as far away from Winnipeg as Shamattawa. The Sayisi Dene First Nation is the most northern Manitoba Indian community, located at Tadoule Lake, almost 1,100 kilometres due north of Winnipeg. At Tadoule Lake, that same ten-kilogram bag of flour cost $16.50. The same price discrepancies were found for all essential food staples. A two-litre container of milk cost $1.92 in Winnipeg, $4.59 in Shamattawa, and $4.60 in Tadoule Lake.

A kilogram of ground beef cost $3.28 in Winnipeg, $8.24 in Shamattawa, and $7.48 in Tadoule Lake. A loaf of bread cost $1.15 in Winnipeg, $2 in Shamattawa, and $2.75 in Tadoule Lake.

When Manitoba Hydro built a power line to Pukatawagan a few years ago, it wired the entire community and brought with it satellite TV. Almost every house on the reserve, new and old, now has a colour television. Culture from the small box consists of the CBC, a movie channel, and American sports and country music channels. Non-native supervisors who work on the reserve say that many residents, adults and children alike, watch television until three or four in the morning. Since most residents do not work, the day does not start until 11 a.m. or later.

A Violent Existence

The violence that engulfed Canada's reserves in the early 1970s was only one form of the devastation that took hold of Indian communities as a result of Ottawa's attempt to shape Indian people into "acceptable citizens." Welfare programs robbed native people of their self-esteem, and the education and child welfare policies implemented by the non-native administration made them feel ashamed of their heritage. Many turned to alcohol to numb their pain, and the drinking often led to violence. Despite the efforts of Pukatawagan residents to regain control of their lives, drinking remains a problem. The victims of alcohol, those who drink and their often neglected and abused children, are mostly ignored. The overriding feeling in the community is this: if the drunks don't shoot anyone or burn anything down, leave them alone.

From her second-storey office overlooking the main street, Caroline Dumas can see the drunks stumble through town and the children who go hungry and cold because their parents are too inebriated to look after them. Caroline, fifty-four, was hired as an alcohol- and drug-abuse counsellor after she had been sober for a year. She became the co-ordinator when her boss went on a drinking binge and never came back. Caroline was a heavy drinker for eighteen years and, though she has not touched a drop for the past ten years, six of her thirteen children have serious drinking and drug problems; she believes she is to blame. "They don't listen to me when I talk to them. The more I try to help them, the more they try to hurt me. They tell me, 'you don't drink now but you used to be a terrible drinker. You didn't care about us or anyone. You hurt us. So what do you expect us to do?' "

Caroline cannot erase the memory of what changed her life. It was January 1973, and she was thirty-eight. "My husband and I had been drinking all weekend, for four days. I woke up on a Monday morning but I didn't know where I was or what day it was. I wanted to go home and check on my children but my husband wanted to stay because there were five more whiskies and a case of two-four left. When I got home, I found my two youngest sitting on the floor. It was cold, minus forty degrees outside. There was no fire in the house. The two girls were one and two years old then. The youngest one had a bowl between her legs. She mixed together flour, sugar and cold water. She was so hungry she was eating it, even though it was almost frozen."

Many bands have attempted to stem the violence by banning alcohol on the reserve. Bans are easier to accomplish on a remote reserve where the nearest liquor outlet is a plane-ride away. They are impossible to enforce on reserves with easy access to urban centres. Regardless of a reserve's location, someone is always willing to profit from a friend's dependence.

Four years after the famed gun-throwing incident and the declaration of prohibition in 1974, Pukatawagan reverted to being a "wet" reserve. The chief and council realized that their attempts at prohibition only forced people to drink in the bushes, which led to more accidents as revellers struggled home. Band officials say the drinking problem is not as severe as it used to be; Caroline is not convinced.

"Wet or dry, it doesn't make any difference. People have nothing to do here. Especially the young people. There is no recreation program and the school gym is closed all summer. They have no place to go." According to Caroline, the children start drinking at as early as six years of age. They also smoke marijuana or sniff glue, contact cement, nail polish, felt markers, and gasoline. "The kids sleep all day at school because they've been up all night drinking or sniffing."

A non-native group home worker says that bootleggers regularly take the train to Lynn Lake on a Friday night and return the next day with a full boxcar of beer. "They come back Saturday morning with hundreds of cases of beer wrapped in green garbage bags. No one says anything but everyone knows what's inside the garbage bags." A twelve-pack of beer sold for $40 in 1988, and a twenty-four-ounce bottle of liquor cost $60.

Six years later, little has changed for most of Canada's isolated reserve communities. For many young people, some only eight years old, the recreation activity of choice is sniffing gasoline, model glue or paint lacquer. In 1994, the tiny community of Pikangikum First Nation, in northwestern Ontario, grabbed the media spotlight. Between February and June, there were forty-seven suicide attempts requiring medical treatment. In one week alone, there were thirteen attempts. These incidents drew the attention of AFN grand chief Ovide Mercredi, the federal and provincial ministers of Indian Affairs, and the media. They came, they made promises, and they left. The desperate conditions remain.

"It seems that once the klieg lights have dimmed and media attention has shifted to more weighty matters...the governments of Canada and Ontario, and National Chief Mercredi have lost interest in Pikangikum's problems," the band stated in an August 1994 release. "As Canada ignores its treaty promises and Ontario enjoys the use of Pikangikum's traditional territory, the people of Pikangikum mourn in isolation."

People under the age of twenty make up 60 per cent of Pikangikum's population of 1,600. Local officials say gas sniffing and solvent abuse run rampant among young people with nothing to do. "Chief Gordon Peters is concerned about the increasing numbers of younger children who are becoming regular gas-sniffers," continues the statement from the band office.

> In the most recent serious incident, around 11:30 p.m. Friday night, seven youths ranging in age from 9 to 17 were pulled from the lake. They had been sniffing gas and were attempting to swim to an island. Two of the youths were recently discharged from a treatment program for solvent abuse. Their return to gas-sniffing is a direct result of the lack of programs or trained personnel to follow-up. There are many chronic abusers...who are considered beyond hope and have been refused treatment due to their uncontrollable behaviour.
>
> The most poignant example is a young man who has lost the use of his lower limbs due to brain damage. Unable to walk, he is confined to his home where his brothers, also chronic sniffers, bring him gas-soaked rags to relieve his boredom.

Ottawa has labelled northern Manitoba and northwest Ontario as hot spots of native teen suicides. At the Whitedog First Nation, a reserve of 800 people, seventy-five kilometres northwest of Kenora, Ontario, forty-seven people have died of unnatural causes since 1985. In a six-week period starting in April 1995, four young men killed themselves. At the Oxford House reserve in Manitoba, 950 kilometres northeast of Winnipeg, five young people took their own lives between February and May 1995. Turmoil still plagues Pikangikum. During a two-week period in the spring of 1995, there were two suicides and twelve attempts. "From the time we are born, we are always mourning," Louie Cameron, a crisis co-ordinator in Whitedog told the *Winnipeg Free Press*.

Bill C–31

In the 1880s, Ottawa policy makers decided that an Indian woman who married a non-native person should no longer be entitled to the rights enjoyed by other registered Indians. This policy remained in effect for 100 years, until it was challenged by a determined young Micmac woman from New Brunswick. Like thousands of other native women, Sandra Lovelace was denied her right to education, housing, and health care because of her marriage to a non-native man. Rebuffed by the bureaucrats and the courts, Lovelace finally took her case to the UN. In 1981, the Human Rights Committee ruled that Canada's policy was discriminatory and that it denied Indian women and their children rights they were entitled to as native people. Buoyed by the UN decision, native women's organizations intensified their lobbying efforts. Embarrassed by the international condemnation of its policies, the Conservative government of Brian Mulroney amended the Indian Act in 1985 by passing Bill C–31, eliminating the legislation's discriminatory aspects.

Studies conducted by the Indian Affairs department in 1988 estimated that Bill C–31 would result in a 25-per-cent increase in the status Indian population, and that 21 per cent of these people would return to the reserves during a five-year period, adding another 23,000 residents. These figures, which many Indian organizations argued were too low, were higher than Ottawa's original estimates. The impact of the miscalculation stretched the demand for existing services on reserves and created a situation for which Ottawa refused to take financial responsibility. While the total number of Bill C–31 registrants by 1992 had not met federal projections, Ottawa conceded that most of the growth of the reserve population and the accompanying infrastructure problems resulted from these Indians returning to their homes. By 1992, Ottawa had renewed the status designation of 86,000 Indians or 20 per cent of the existing status population. Ottawa is now projecting a further 42 per cent growth in the status Indian population by the year 2005 (from 533,461 to 755,200), most of it attributable to those native people who have regained their status under Bill C–31.

When Ottawa introduced Bill C–31, it promised that additional funds would be provided to prevent any band from suffering due to the impact of an increasing population on already stretched resources. Despite Ottawa's assurances, the bill worsened the situation. Ottawa appeared surprised by the large number of people that applied to regain their status. According to a confidential government discussion paper, which was obtained and released in 1988 by the Canadian Press news agency, senior bureaucrats had given politicians two scenarios of Bill C–31's impact: the registered Indian population would increase by either 10 or 20 per cent. The Mulroney cabinet accepted the lower figures and allocated funds accordingly. Indian groups claimed that the decision to use the lower estimation was an attempt by Ottawa to reduce the extra funds that would be needed for housing, education, social assistance, and health to accommodate the growth in population. They were right.

This confidential discussion paper also predicted that new status applicants living in urban centres would put increased pressure for services on both the Indian Affairs and Health and Welfare departments. Canada Employment Centres would face increased pressure for new training programs, and the CMHC, for greater mortgage assistance. The paper also predicted greater demands for post-secondary education funding. By 1992, the population of off-reserve Indians had increased by almost 50 per cent (from 147,424 to 217,798), a fact that Ottawa attributed to reinstatement under Bill C–31.

Data analysis provided by the Department of Health and Welfare to the *Winnipeg Free Press* in April 1988 confirmed Ottawa's concern over increased costs. The department projected that the increase in the status Indian population caused by Bill C–31 would create serious funding shortfalls in the budgets for native programs, producing a deficit of $1.8 million in 1987–88, which would climb to $73.4 million by 1990–91.

In the spring of 1989, one year after Ottawa released its studies of the bill, Indian Affairs placed a cap on post-secondary education, freezing funding at $130 million annually and effectively forcing thousands of native students to cease or postpone their studies. Yet again, Ottawa showed that it would opt out of its commitments to native people whenever these obligations called for additional funding.

The Nielsen Task Force

In 1985, Indians realized that despite the gains they had made over the past few decades, Ottawa was as willing to stem their efforts as before. The cause of their fears was the Nielsen task force report, the result of a commission appointed by Brian Mulroney soon after the Conservatives came to power in September 1984. The commission's task was to identify all unnecessary spending by the federal government. The authors of the report believed they had found plenty at Indian Affairs. Their recommendations justified the measure of mistrust and suspicion native groups brought to their dealings with the Mulroney government for the next ten years. The report, released one year after the commission's appointment, concluded that financial support of native communities in isolated areas, which would not have survived under normal conditions, did nothing more than drain Indians of all initiative and Ottawa of desperately needed funds. "The net impact of government stewardship over the social and economic development of native people has been frustratingly marginal. Program innovations have produced isolated improvements, but the overall picture remains bleak." The report's solution was to cut spending, cap funds, and force Indians to pay for anything above newly established minimum standards, or let the community collapse. The paper recommended that new programs should encourage young people to move to prosperous reserves with more economic opportunities. The recommendations were never officially endorsed by the Mulroney government, but they revealed that yet another federal party did not fully understand the Indian people.

"The economists believe that you got to go where the market is, that you follow where the jobs are and you never stay in isolated or rural areas because there are no jobs there," says Konrad Sioui, former regional chief of the First Nations of Quebec. "On an economic point of view, that might be true but realistically it has nothing to do with the Indian vision of their territory, their land and their role that Indian people have to play with the land."

The Future: "We Have a Dream"

The reserve, which started as a tool of colonialist power, is now a symbol of Indian independence that epitomizes native self-government aspirations. Most bands are now identified as First Nations, and Indian leaders seek authority over everything within their boundaries. When Ottawa began transferring program delivery to bands twenty years ago, band officials took advantage of the situation to master budgeting and administration. They learned to follow the rules defined by Ottawa. Now, they want to determine their own rules.

"Indian people have survived for 400 years because we haven't given in," says Louis Stevenson, a charismatic Indian leader from Manitoba. "We've held on to those beliefs that we have the right to be ourselves, a right to run our own lives, determine our own future. That is what is going to ensure our society survives."

Stevenson is chief of the Peguis reserve, just north of Winnipeg. He is articulate, and an expert at media manipulation. During the past fifteen years, he has established himself as a national leader, conducting demonstrations in traditional Indian head-dress and moccasins, and several times occupying the Winnipeg offices of Indian Affairs. He gained international recognition in 1987 when he invited the South African ambassador, Glenn Babb, to visit the Peguis reserve. His goal was to clearly link Canada's treatment of its aboriginal people with the apartheid system of South Africa. If the level of media attention surrounding the event was any indication, the ploy worked.

In October 1994, at Stevenson's urging, the Manitoba chiefs held a demonstration on the world stage. The occasion was the Group of Seven (G–7) conference, hosted by Canada in Winnipeg. Again, Stevenson's goal was to embarrass Ottawa for its treatment of native people. "Most of the reserves in this province [Manitoba] are enduring 70- to 90-per-cent unemployment," Stevenson told leaders attending the Annual General Assembly of Manitoba Chiefs in September 1994. "Many of them have a serious housing backlog. There is a lack of adequate education facilities. Our people have the highest mortality rate, the highest suicide rate and our children are more prone to death than any other segment of society. Now we hear the federal government will be hosting a G–7 conference here in Winnipeg to see how the Ukraine can develop their economy. It's very disheartening, discouraging and insulting that our Canadian government can ignore the plight of our people....It's really amazing that our Canadian government can direct its energies and resources to see how it can help another country like the Ukraine develop its economy when they can't even help First Nations develop their local economies here in this country....They should fix things up at home first before trying to solve problems in other countries around the world."

Today, Indian leaders want to assume the same powers other governments enjoy. Many leaders are calling for the right to levy taxes on their people, to take on responsibility for new initiatives in lotteries and gambling, wildlife management, policing and justice, child welfare, and education. They argue that there is no longer a need for support from a mammoth bureaucracy because they are capable of supporting themselves. "When we're talking about establishing self-government, we're not talking about diminishing standards but simply taking control of standards over and rebuilding standards that are culturally appropriate to us," says Joe Miskokomon, former grand chief of the Union of Ontario Indians. "What we're talking about is the utilization of existing resources in a better way."

Canada has held the Indian's hand for over 100 years. It has broken the native spirit with attempts to force assimilation, and used schools and laws to eradicate customs and traditions. But Indians have not forgotten their heritage. Their leaders eventually learned to take advantage of the programs Ottawa offered, to manage multimillion dollar budgets, and to develop and implement reserve programs for housing, road construction, and social assistance. All band governments have taken on the responsibilities of a typical Canadian municipality, and more. More than half of the bands in Canada currently run their own school programs and are preparing to take over health care services. Unlike municipalities, however, bands are unincorporated and still exist only as creations of the federal government. Some communities have resorted to "monster" bingo games to supplement federal revenues. On rare occasions, bands such as the Opaskwayak Cree Nation have convinced Ottawa of the merits of business ventures, the profits of which can be used to provide necessary services in the community. Indian leaders, often with the help of private business, have devised ways to raise money and break their dependency on Ottawa. Now, they want Ottawa to release its grip on their people.

"If we listen to all the scepticism from non-natives, I'm afraid that twenty years from now we're going to be in the same boat," Oscar Lathlin says. Life can change for everyone, he says, and the Opaskwayak First Nation is proof of that. "Each reserve will evolve on its own. I wish we could go to a northern reserve in 20 years and see how far they've come. We have a vision. We have a dream. If we persist, if we don't give up, 20 years from now it's going to be a lot different, a lot better."

3

Urban Indians

They are called "bus refugees." Every year, thousands of native Canadians travel by plane, bus, and rusted automobile from their remote or rural reserves into this country's major city centres; they carry with them their belongings and hopes for a life better than the poverty-stricken one they have often left behind. What they usually find in these concrete jungles is a world where they are unwelcome; where their facial features, accents, hairstyles, history, and ways of thinking keep them apart from other city dwellers; where they exist in a political vacuum, the responsibility of no one in particular and the burden of many.

From the impoverished conditions of reserves, Canada's native citizens move into the city, only to find themselves at the bottom of an even larger heap. Of the 385,800 people who identified themselves as registered Indians in the 1991 Census, about half live off-reserve; this figure is up from 13 per cent in 1960 and 2 per cent in 1950. The numbers are even more striking when one considers that of 737,000 Canadians who identified themselves as being of aboriginal ancestry in the census, only 46 per cent live on reserves.

The 1969 White Paper proposed the abolition of special status for Indians, suggesting that assimilation into the greater Canadian society would result in the elimination of native poverty and discrimination. But in the city centres, where this assimilation theory has been put to the real test, it has become clear that there will be no simple solutions for these serious problems. Though some native people move to the city, find a job, and live happily ever after, their numbers are lost among the thousands upon thousands who do not.

When Indians first started to leave their reserves, not long after signing treaties with the British government in the late nineteenth century, their numbers were small. "Either you had to move to a reserve to receive your rations because the buffalo were gone and there was no food source, or you were forced to urbanize or become civilized by moving closer together," says one urban Indian. Initially, Indians who trekked to the cities were almost entirely absorbed; those who could not assimilate returned home or landed in the underbelly of the urban ghettos.

Social service agencies handled the first trickle of Indian cases that came to their attention. However, as their numbers began to grow, municipal and provincial government programs began popping up as a matter of necessity. Eventually, native friendship centres opened and began acting as meeting places for the growing number of Indians finding their way into the cities.

The numbers of natives arriving began to increase at an accelerated rate during the 1960s. At this time, the issue of who was ultimately responsible for providing services to this group began to emerge as a pressing concern. The piecemeal approach of the past was no longer sufficient, and the chorus of demands for action could not be ignored. "I don't know how they get here," said Stan Fulham, former secretary for the Manitoba Métis Federation and head of a Winnipeg native housing co-operative. "They just end up here." With few work skills in an increasingly technical society, language barriers and different work habits and ways of looking at the world, these native people often end up on skid row. One young native woman told a CBC radio show host in the 1990s that, despite its deplorable and unsafe conditions, the downtown core was still home to her. "Once you're down here...it is where all your friends are." She went on to describe the racism that is familiar to all native people who spend time in the cities.

Stories of racism turned up in dozens of interviews conducted for a special report on Indian issues by the *Winnipeg Free Press* — everything from small daily confrontations to outright abuse at the hands of the police. One native leader, whose husband is a civil servant with a salary that allows a middle-class lifestyle, described several incidents that occurred while she was shopping or eating in a restaurant. In one case, while she was examining a $60 pair of running shoes, a sales clerk asked if she was aware of "just how much those shoes cost." Others shared tales of being followed from the minute they entered some department stores until they left, and of being turned down for apartments because they were native. It is little wonder that many native people avoid racist confrontations by living together in the "ghettoized" pockets mysteriously found in every city. This "ghettoization" begins when the newcomers follow friends or family into the bar and drug scene, a sojourn that often stretches into a way of life with no escape.

The authors of the 1969 White Paper assumed that if the Indian Act and the Indian Affairs department were eliminated, equality for Indian people would automatically follow, and the provinces would take over responsibility for native people where the federal government had left off. The paper's authors also assumed that within thirty years, in time for the new millennium, Indians throughout the country would be assimilated into the largely urban, Canadian mainstream as thriving, tax-paying residents. But during the last twenty-five years, perhaps because of the legislative limbo they have been forced to live in — no specific bureaucracy to co-ordinate services, few leaders to lobby on their behalf, and no legislation to govern them — urban Indians have seen little improvement in their lives. "When you look at the reality, we are far from assimilated," says Lyle Longclaws, a Winnipeg urban Indian leader. "We are very much isolated from the rest of Winnipeg society. You know where Indians live in this city, and you don't go beyond those boundaries when you are native."

Who Is Responsible?

An apt description of the bureaucratic mess that urban Indians face is presented in the book, *People of Terra Nullius,* by Canadian journalist Boyce Richardson, a recognized expert on Canada's native people.

> Because of Canada's rigid system of classifying aboriginals, urban Indians have posed a problem both for governments and for native organizations. The federal government accepts responsibility for the health, education and welfare only of Indians on reserve. Status Indians who move from the reserves to the cities become the responsibility of the provinces and municipalities (although they still continue to hold membership in their band, and are still eligible for education grants). The line of authority of the Assembly of First Nations runs from the chiefs and council of the nearly 600 bands in the reserves, so naturally the Assembly as an organization is concerned mainly with those from whom it derives its authority. In the west, the provincial Métis organizations have recently concentrated more on their locals in small

communities than on Métis in the cities. A third organization, the Native Council of Canada (now the Congress of Aboriginal Peoples), claims to represent the many non-status Indians who have fallen between the cracks of the aboriginal classification system (as well as many status Indians living off reserve). This incoherent system has meant that the needs of urban natives have not been properly met by anyone.

Native leaders point to Canada's treatment of political refugees to highlight the effectiveness of the federal government when it is truly motivated to help immigrants find their way into city life. The example underlines the discrepancies between the treatment of refugees and of native people.

Canada has a well-earned international reputation for its outstanding treatment of the thousands of political refugees who arrive every year. These federally sponsored exiles land on Canadian soil and walk directly into a year-long, all-expenses-paid adjustment program co-ordinated by the federal Department of Employment and Immigration. When the newcomer steps off the airplane, a team of federal employees (including an interpreter) is waiting to help with luggage, customs, and security clearances. The team then takes the nervous visitor to a settlement house, which will be home for several weeks.

This welcoming committee immediately assesses and satisfies clothing needs at tax-payers' expense, and completes all the necessary paperwork for social insurance numbers, health care, etc. Orientation sessions begin on general aspects of Canadian life — how to take a bus, how to use money, and where to shop. When an apartment or house appears suitable, the team determines furniture needs and ensures that the order is filled. The committee offers detailed guidance on how to survive on government subsidies. By the sixth month, the newcomer has begun daily English lessons at one of the local colleges. Upon completion of English courses, the refugee is deemed to be employable. Immigration staff stay in touch, however, offering counselling on everything from solving marital problems to accessing health and other services. Then job hunting and training begin. According to one department official, 90 per cent of refugees spend an average of one year under the wing of the federal government before they find jobs. The 10 per cent who are still searching for work one year after their arrival are then turned over to municipal social services departments. Finally, multicultural initiatives, heavily sponsored by all three levels of government, mean that new Canadians likely find some outlet to express their cultural identities — both the emerging one and the one left behind.

Across Canada, native people often arrive in cities from remote regions as confused as any refugee. But, instead of having one place to start, they are faced with dozens of provincial government departments that might or might not have native programs, a range of municipally sponsored initiatives aimed at the inner-city poor, a growing number of urban Indian associations, housing and health authorities, and native friendship centres. They will discover that they do not qualify for federally funded English-language courses and that even inner-city schools with mostly native populations can offer little help. If they need to use a bus, a friend or family member will have to guide them. In 1993, participants in a round table on health issues, sponsored by the Royal Commission on Aboriginal Peoples, again complained about the lack of urban health initiatives for native people. The participants spoke of "the often piecemeal and buck-passing nature of funding opportunities" for health services development and of how urban natives are "consistently frustrated in their attempts to secure resources from various federal, provincial and municipal sources."

The Numbers Tell a Story

Statistics Canada has gathered data showing that Indians who live off-reserve can expect to become slightly more educated and to make slightly more money than those who live on-reserve. But being marginally better off than their reserve counterparts is little to celebrate. According to the 1991 Census, for the 388,000 aboriginal adults aged fifteen or older in Canada, the unemployment rate was almost 25 per cent; the rate was 10 per cent for the total Canadian population. Of that same native group, 54 per cent reported an income below $9,999, including 13 per cent who reported no income at all during 1990. These figures compare to 35 per cent (income below $9,999) and only 9 per cent (no income) for the total Canadian population. The 1986 Census indicated that dependence on government programs, such as welfare, unemployment insurance, and family allowance, increased for all aboriginal groups between 1981 and 1986. This change included a sixteen-percentage-point jump in the number of off-reserve residents relying on programs, from 25 per cent to 41 per cent.

While detailed off-reserve comparisons based on the 1991 Census were not readily available when this book was revised, the evidence indicates that little has changed. Some areas have seen small positive changes, but little significant improvement has occurred in the last few decades. According to the 1986 Census, the average income for the 134,910 registered Indians who lived off-reserve was $11,000, compared to $9,300 for those living on-reserve. These figures compared to a non-native average individual income of $18,188. The 1991 Census also showed that 42 per cent of registered Indians were receiving some form of social assistance. This figure is 2.5 times the Canadian average.

The situation leaves Indians, regardless of where they live, far behind everyone else. Data compiled by Statistics Canada in 1986 showed that Indians who lived off-reserve had the highest unemployment rate among all aboriginal groups — 17 per cent or more than twice the Canadian rate of 7 per cent.

Education, cited by both native and non-native people alike as the key to a better life for Indians, is another indicator with sobering statistics. Between 1981 and 1986, the number of Indians over the age of fifteen with less than a Grade 9 education remained at twice the national rate. By 1991, that ratio had worsened: 21 per cent of aboriginal people between the ages of fifteen and sixty-four reported having less than a Grade 9 education, compared with about 9 per cent for the Canadian population as a whole. According to 1991 figures compiled by the Canada Research Institute, only 20 per cent of aboriginal children complete secondary school, compared to a national rate of 75 per cent.

Throughout the 1980s, Indian education initiatives, such as band-run schools, appeared to have some impact: the number of reserve Indians with less than a Grade 9 education declined marginally. However, off-reserve figures show virtually no improvement. In 1981, 24.3 per cent of off-reserve Indians aged fifteen or over had less than a Grade 9 education compared to 24.4 per cent in 1986. For the entire Canadian population, these figures were 20.1 per cent and 17.3 per cent, respectively.

Another interesting figure that emerges from various studies is the percentage of young people in the aboriginal population, compared to the Canadian population as a whole. According to data compiled by the solicitor general's office, the median age for off-reserve residents is about ten years lower than that of the Canadian population. For example, in 1981, the average age of non-aboriginal Canadians was thirty, and the average age of aboriginal people was twenty. Only about 7 per cent of aboriginal people were over fifty-five, compared to 20 per cent for the Canadian population. More recent statistics indicate that 38 per cent of the country's urban Indian population is under fifteen, compared to 21 per cent for the country as a whole. As for language barriers, one-tenth of those who identified themselves as urban Indians indicated that their mother tongue was an aboriginal language.

The picture painted by all these numbers is not a surprise for anyone who has walked through any of the slums of Regina, Winnipeg, Vancouver, or even the small towns of northwestern Ontario. On the streets is the reality: young native prostitutes hanging around seedy bars only a few blocks north of Winnipeg's famous intersection, Portage and Main; the overactive soup kitchens of Regina's core area feeding primarily native children; the endless stream of drunk and drugged Indians staggering along the streets of northern Ontario towns.

Eastern Canadians on inaugural trips through the western provinces often comment, with some surprise, at the number of Indian residents, particularly in the city centres. They are also often taken aback by the obvious weight of this group on social service agencies, jails, and unemployment lines. "Indeed, the problems of aboriginal people who have migrated to urban centres include increased alienation and conflict with the law," noted the solicitor general in the 1993 report, *Policing Services for Aboriginal Peoples*. The report explores the impact of the growing urban aboriginal population on the justice system. This "new reality" is described as "a much more complex and varied social landscape, a landscape in which variations in social status are sharper, more distinctive, and less easily mapped. Our urban centres have become less homogenous, and richer and poorer at the same time."

It is in the growth of the aboriginal population, urban and otherwise, where the most striking changes in the past twenty-five years appear. According to the 1991 Census, more than 1 million people describe themselves as having aboriginal origins —Métis, North American Indian, Inuit. Of those, 385,800 are registered Indians. The number of registered Indians living off-reserve was recorded at 186,295, a figure many observers say is, in reality, much higher.

Although the actual numbers of registered Indians are highest in British Columbia and Ontario (77,705 and 70,420, respectively, in 1991), a different picture emerges when the proportion of registered

Indians in a particular province or region is considered. For example, Manitoba and Saskatchewan have the highest proportions of registered Indians (outside of the Yukon and Northwest Territories) with rates of 20.7 and 19 per cent, respectively. Quebec, at 0.5 per cent, has the smallest ratio, followed closely by the Maritime provinces and Ontario, at 0.6 per cent.

In 1991, Saskatchewan's 56,710 registered Indians accounted for 6.1 per cent of that province's total population of 976,000. Manitoba's figure stood at 5.8 per cent. Winnipeg (15,670), Vancouver (12,250), Saskatoon (6,635), and Regina (6,635) have the largest registered Indian urban populations in the country.

In the more broadly defined aboriginal population, about 55 per cent of native people live in the four western provinces, according to the solicitor general's study. At 7.9 per cent, Saskatchewan recorded the highest per capita population of aboriginal people, followed by Manitoba at 7.7 per cent and Alberta at 4 per cent. Edmonton had the largest aboriginal population, 34,500, of any major Canadian city. "It is further estimated," noted the solicitor general, "that in the next two decades the aboriginal population of Edmonton and Winnipeg will double. Within the same time frame, the aboriginal population is expected to triple in Saskatoon and Regina." The reason for the increase, demographers suggest, is the close proximity and thus greater accessibility of these cities to poor reserves.

According to the 1991 Census figures, 63 per cent of Manitoba's estimated 130,000 aboriginal people (including a large Métis population) live off-reserve. At the same time, 63 per cent of Manitoba's status Indians live on-reserve; this figure is roughly the same for Alberta and is one of the highest percentages in the country.

This flow of reserve Indians into major urban centres was predicted in the late 1960s by anthropologist Harry B. Hawthorn in his two-volume study for the federal government, *A Survey of Contemporary Indians in Canada*. "Special facilities will be needed to ease the process of social adjustments as the tempo of off-reserve movement increases," warned Hawthorn. For the most part, Hawthorn's predictions have come true. Between 1966 and 1986, the number of off-reserve Indians jumped 254 per cent — from 47,496 to 158,944 — while the reserve population grew by only 27 per cent. According to the 1986 Census, 38 per cent of Canada's registered Indian population lived off-reserve. Projections to the year 2001 estimate the off-reserve population at 237,400, a number that appears reasonable

AUGUSTANA UNIVERSITY COLLEGE
LIBRARY

considering the 186,295 off-reserve registered Indians recorded in the 1991 Census.

Experts predict that, within 20 years, the aboriginal population will reach nearly two million, accounting for 6.5 per cent of Canada's total population. In Alberta alone, the aboriginal population is expected to quadruple by 2010 to almost 400,000; aboriginal people will then comprise 13 per cent of the province's predicted total population.

In the mid-1980s, when Bill C–31 came into effect, population watchers and observers of federal policy began issuing warnings to Ottawa about ramifications for the Indian population. Bill C–31 followed a 1981 decision by the UN Human Rights Committee that condemned the practice of removing status rights from Indian women who married non-Indian men as discriminatory. Children of the union were also denied registered Indian status. Indian men and their children, however, were not subjected to the same rules if they married non-Indian women.

After Ottawa passed the bill, many Indians were expected to apply to return to the already cash-strapped reserves; the bill was also predicted to cause an increase in the number of urban Indians. As noted in Chapter 2, the total number of Bill C–31 registrants by 1992 had not met the federal projection of a 25 per cent increase in the number of status Indians. Still, 86,000 Indians had obtained their status designation by 1992, and Ottawa was projecting a further 42 per cent growth, to 755,200 people, in the registered Indian population by the year 2005.

Choosing to Stay

As a result of Bill C–31, registered Indians who moved to the cities after losing their status can return home and partake of the already overburdened housing, education, and health services that are extended to all registered Indians. Those who choose to stay in cities, and the majority are predicted to do so, will continue to turn to the federal, provincial, municipal, and Indian governments for services, adding yet more pressure to the already laden bureaucracies. The impact of the bill on western Canada, where roughly 80 per cent of the country's Indian population is concentrated, has been especially profound in the urban setting. In Manitoba, for example, the urban Indian population jumped 330 per cent (by conservative estimates) between 1966 and 1986.

Still, the native migration to cities has not taken the form of a steady tidal wave, and its levels have not met Hawthorn and others' predictions. Improvements to reserve housing, the realization that city life was no picnic, and employment opportunities from successful economic development projects on reserves slowed the rate of migration by the end of the 1980s.

These factors and others have led to the birth of what city planners refer to as a "hypermobile" population. With housing and some possibilities for employment on the reserves, and few opportunities in the urban setting, many Indians have established two home bases. During winter months, home is in the city, where welfare benefits, including heated accommodations and running water, make life at least physically manageable. During the summer, when hunting and fishing can offset meagre welfare payments and the high costs of living, home is on the reserve, with family and friends and the more traditional life.

This "hypermobility" is just one of the reasons why determining the number of Indians, status or otherwise, living within the country's major urban settings, has proven so difficult. In Winnipeg, a city with one of the largest downtown Indian populations in North America, estimates of the number of registered Indians can vary between 18,000, as quoted by various government sources, and 30,000, as determined by urban Indian organizations. This number jumps to 60,000 when all aboriginal people, regardless of official status, are included. According to *Policing Services for Aboriginal Peoples*, the 1991 Census figures for Toronto's aboriginal population are 33,000, or 1 per cent of the city's population. "However, just as in Winnipeg, aboriginal agencies estimate that considering migration patterns and trends, the aboriginal population is nearly 70,000." Even the office of the attorney general of Ontario estimated that 10 per cent of Ontario's aboriginal people live in Toronto.

The fact that no one can determine, with any degree of accuracy, the number of Indians living in Canadian cities highlights what is probably the key urban native issue for the 1990s and beyond — who is responsible for urban native people? At the time of Confederation, there was considerable debate over whether the provincial governments or Ottawa would oversee the needs of all Indians and Indian land. The federal government ended up playing a large role partly because most Indians were forced to live in federal territories to receive their benefits and because few provincial agencies had sufficient expertise or funding to respond to the complex needs of the population.

However, the issue of who should be responsible for natives in urban settings has been debated for decades and remains officially unresolved in the 1990s. "There are responsibilities from the provincial side for supplying the same services to Indian people as they do non-Indians," insisted former Indian Affairs minister Bill McKnight in 1988, echoing a statement made twenty years earlier by then Indian Affairs minister Jean Chrétien. Not so, said newly elected Manitoba premier Gary Filmon. Filmon voiced the opinion of most provincial leaders in the late 1980s, an opinion that was strikingly similar to that of the provincial leaders responding to the White Paper two decades earlier. "I would argue that the federal government still has responsibility for [urban Indians]," Filmon said, adding that providing education, training, and child welfare services for such a needy group would be an expensive proposition. "It will create a massive drain on the provincial treasury." In 1995, federal Indian Affairs minister Ron Irwin had begun discussions with native leaders to launch an urban self-government experiment similar to the one signed with Manitoba's on-reserve leaders.

Needless to say, the debate with politicians and bureaucrats does not end there.

Growing Tensions

Indian leaders across the country are also pondering questions of jurisdiction. On one side of the debate are those native leaders who contend that Indian governments should maintain control over the administration of services to their people, on- or off-reserve. "Urban Indians should continue to come under the jurisdiction of their bands," says Saul Terry, head of the Union of British Columbia Indians. Terry argues that a provincial take-over of services for urban Indians fits too closely with the long-held federal plan to further the involvement of provincial governments, a scheme that must be resisted in the drive for native self-government.

In Terry's mind, band authority should simply extend from reserve to city, with Indian housing and child welfare authorities doing the same work for the urban dwellers as they do for their reserve constituents. "Most of the provinces do not know or understand the responsibilities of the federal government," said Roland Crowe. As chief of the Saskatchewan Federation of Indians between 1986 and

1994, he warned those provincial leaders who expressed some willingness to step into the urban Indian debate: "The premiers feel good
sitting around the table with the big boys, but they'd better think
twice about what responsibility for Indian people means."

On the other side of the debate are Indian leaders who wish to see
the emergence of urban Indian associations that closely mimic band
and reserve structures, but that exist as separate legislated authorities.
"Because we are receiving provincial funding for urban people, we
have to come to an agreement with the province, the feds, and also
with urban governments," said Lyle Longclaws of Winnipeg's Urban
Indian Association in the late 1980s. "That is key, and different from
what the chiefs are pursuing rurally."

Longclaws is convinced that reserves will eventually disappear as
more native people become city dwellers, and that the growing urban
native middle class will eventually predominate. Others passionately
dispute these predictions, saying that the growing power of Canada's
native people will ensure that their lives always stem from the land.
But reserves or no reserves, the number of natives in Canada's urban
centres will grow. "More and more come into the city every day as
bus refugees," says Longclaws. "And they're not going to stop coming." In Longclaws's vision of the urban Indian world, band councils
would initially be responsible for residents who moved away; but
after a period of time, these city dwellers would fall under the
jurisdiction of new urban Indian groups. These associations would
lobby for special legislation that would allow them to govern urban
Indian populations. In this scenario, urban Indian child welfare agencies and educational authorities would be established. Some movement in this direction has already begun. Early in 1990, Winnipeg
native leaders began seriously lobbying for their own school board
and school. Although their reception was not overwhelming, they
show no sign of giving up.

In spite of these tensions, a number of urban native associations
and organizations have emerged. Some groups claim to represent all
aboriginal people within their city's boundaries, while others focus
their lobbying efforts only on the more narrowly defined status or
registered Indians. Throughout the 1980s and 1990s, the building up
and tearing down of urban Indian associations continued with a
vengeance.

In 1970, non-status Indians and Métis united under the banner of
the Native Council of Canada. The stated goal of this new national
body was to represent these two groups, many of whom lived in

urban settings, as well as status Indians living off-reserve. In 1994, facing severe financial hardship, the council became the Congress of Aboriginal Peoples. However, the existence of the Congress has not resolved the questions of jurisdiction. Despite the fact that the AFN assumes its authority from status Indian chiefs, it has often argued that its role is to lobby on behalf of all aboriginal people across the country. Numerous other local native organizations claim to speak on behalf of urban natives. For example, in the early 1990s, the Aboriginal Council of Winnipeg was formed. The council's stated goal was to more fully represent the needs of native people in the city, regardless of status. However, not long after its birth, the organization became the Treaty Council of Winnipeg and allied itself with the Assembly of Manitoba Chiefs, a body representing status Indians. The move upset some native people, who felt they had lost an opportunity to lobby on behalf of all urban Indians.

Although native leaders across the country have emerged during the past few decades with a clearer sense of their common goal of self-government, and despite the growing number of urban native organizations, urban Indians have yet to clearly articulate their focus. When the national urban leadership calls for a demonstration, thousands of Indians across the country respond, but a similar call by an urban association in Winnipeg draws barely thirty people.

Is this lack of focus the result of the associations' contradictory mandates and troubled sense of direction? Or is it the result of extreme poverty? Urban Indians are among the poorest of the poor and may simply be too preoccupied with survival to worry about the intricacies of effective lobbying.

"Natives come in and they are not aware of politics," says Stan Fulham, member of a Winnipeg native housing co-operative. He is referring to the hundreds of native people who land on his doorstep each year seeking aid. "They are disorganized. They require organizations, like the Urban Indian Association, to crystallize their problems and to convey on a continuing basis the story of their economic and social isolation to government."

Like national native groups, urban Indian associations say their primary focus must be education, followed by major economic development strategies leading to jobs for their people. "The various government departments have to start getting a good return for their money," says Calvin Pompana, head of the Urban Indian Association in Winnipeg in 1989. While urban native leaders have some clear objectives, many lack the statistics that will help them gain a better grasp of the size of their constituency and its needs. From this data, they may find the focus they require to lobby for feasible solutions.

New Programs

As one observer noted, urban Indians are barely at the starting gate. Early attempts to solve the urban aboriginal problem were plagued by a mostly non-native bureaucracy that concentrated on short-term solutions to long-term problems. For example, job training programs have tended to undertrain or offer instruction for short-term employment, thus condemning native people to jobs on the lowest rung of the economic ladder. Often, despite such training, native people were not able to find or keep jobs. Thus, the training circuit, complete with an adequate living allowance, became a job in itself for many native people. When one program was completed, another was started.

Many experts say the evolution of off-reserve services has now reached a second stage, characterized by joint efforts such as the CORE Area initiative in Winnipeg and similar long-term federal, provincial, and municipal plans to revitalize downtown core areas in other jurisdictions. These areas, where native people settle, are the focus of much of the programming. After a slow start, in which training failed to solve the problems, a new approach with measurably higher success rates emerged. In one Winnipeg program, native trainees target a very specific job that will be available when they graduate.

In January 1995, *Globe and Mail* reporter Peter Moon documented the growth of urban native service agencies focussed on health care, counselling, and other services, for an estimated 65,000 aboriginal people in Toronto's downtown core. "One sign of the growing success is the suicide rate for natives in the city," wrote Moon. "Nationally, natives have the highest rate of suicide in the country. In Toronto, because of the growing support provided by natives for natives, the aboriginal suicide rate is the same as for the country at large."

Another important development, although still in its early stages, has been the on-the-job, informal education of the city's civil servants to help them understand native Canadian needs. This training has been carried out in the police force as well as in other departments. As part of her job, Sharon Gould, affirmative action director of the city of Winnipeg in the late 1980s, taught non-native employees about native people. This instruction included making workers aware of the reality beyond the clichés, which may form much of their opinion. Her aim was to help these employees understand the needs and goals of a wide range of native people, from the undereducated, struggling to upgrade their formal education and break into the civil service ranks, to the growing native middle class. Gould's program extended to senior management, who, she said, must be more flexible with the kind of resources they provide. Help in finding day care may make the difference in a native woman's getting and keeping a clerical job at city hall, Gould said. Similarly, other trainees may require assistance to deal with spouses who criticize their ambitions or friends who accuse them of selling out in taking a job in the non-native world.

"Native people deal with things holistically," Gould explained, when asked about what she was learning and passing on in the process. "The education we are trying to do [involves teaching civil servants] that there are native people who are professionals and are quite happy on their own. There are native people who need training and support for awhile, and then they are fine. And then there are people who for a whole bunch of reasons don't really want to be here, but they want to come to work for three or four months and then they want to go back to the reserve. And that's fine too." The education of non-native staff also includes the message that there is room for those not interested in climbing the corporate ladder.

Sharon Bertchilde, also of the CORE Area development project, is under no illusion that Winnipeg has solved its native problem. Plenty of evidence attests to the problem's persistence. After twenty-five years of dealing with native issues, city recruitment programs have failed to attract more than a handful of native police officers.

In 1988, the 1,140-member Winnipeg police force listed one officer who gave his nationality as Canadian Indian and a few others, as Métis. Calgary police reported two treaty Indians on their 1,000-member force; Regina boasted seven treaty and Métis officers. The aboriginal population of Regina is estimated at about 40,000; Calgary's is about a third of that. In 1991, the Ontario Provincial Police had sixty-seven First Nations liaison officers who worked with 45,000 off-reserve aboriginal people in the force's jurisdiction. Only one of those liaison officers was of aboriginal ancestry. The same year, Edmonton had eighteen aboriginal officers in its 1,100-officer unit. In 1992, an aboriginal peacekeeping unit was formed in the Toronto police force. It was staffed by three of the force's seventeen police officers who identify themselves as aboriginal (out of about

5,700 officers). Some experts estimate that Toronto's aboriginal population is as high as 70,000.

"I think we have made a whole bunch of little dents but not anything substantial enough to change the way the world is working," Bertchilde says. "Without some sustained effort, what we have done may disappear." She also points out that, even in the short life of Winnipeg's CORE program, the once strict order of responsibility has shifted. "Suddenly the jurisdictional boundaries that have typically been in place are a little fuzzy."

Perhaps these events explain why former Manitoba Native Affairs minister James Downey announced in the late 1980s that his government would launch a program to develop a co-ordinated strategy for assisting the province's urban Indians. Manitoba was the first province in the country to take such a step; other jurisdictions have avoided this action for fear that such interest would signal to Ottawa a willingness to accept financial responsibility. Although the question of who is ultimately responsible remains unresolved, Downey said that he refuses to ignore the plight of urban natives while waiting for solutions. "I think, for too long, the native people have been bounced back and forth between jurisdictions and their lives have not been going on."

4

Self-Government

On December 7, 1994, at the convention centre in Winnipeg, the aroma of burning sweet grass filled the air. Grand Chief Phil Fontaine and Indian Affairs minister Ron Irwin sat cross-legged on a ceremonial red blanket inside the centre. The plaintive, whooping cries of the powwow singers and the sound of their drums echoed throughout the cavernous hall. Hundreds of people had gathered to watch the two men sign a document that heralded the beginning of the end for the department of Indian Affairs and a new beginning for the Indian people of Manitoba. The signing of this agreement to begin the dismantling of Indian Affairs was a key moment in the fulfilment of Indian people's aspirations for self-government.

"This is truly a threshold day for First Nations' peoples in Manitoba," Fontaine said during the signing ceremony. "With this agreement, we can now take the next large and challenging steps forward in restoring our authority and pride as nations, living in co-existence with other Canadians, as originally envisaged by our forebears at the time of treaty-making over 100 years ago." A process was being established to transfer jurisdictional control over a broad range of powers from Ottawa to Manitoba Indian bands. But more than that, the initiative, albeit an experiment restricted to Manitoba, will alter the centuries-old relationship between Ottawa and the several hundred First Nations communities across the country. If the experiment succeeds, Manitoba's Indian bands will be the first to be recognized as individual sovereign governments within the Canadian federal system. "Stepping across this threshold, and seizing this opportunity to be recognized as self-governing nations within Canada," said Fontaine, "is crucial to the future survival and prosperity of First Nations people."

Irwin described the day as unprecedented. The agreement allowed Indian leaders to determine, without restriction, the powers they would assume, at a pace acceptable to their communities. The community members alone would decide the form of their new government. "This initiative will help restore authority, responsibility, and accountability to their leaders to govern their own affairs," Irwin said.

The dismantling agreement marked a radical departure in the relationship between Ottawa and native people. Since the 1969 release of the White Paper, successive governments, both Liberal and Conservative, have commissioned reports and drafted and approved legislation that they believed restored self-government to Indian communities. Their efforts merely highlighted their own ignorance of native culture. Each initiative was always accompanied by the same question: What is self-government? The bureaucrats and politicians wanted a cookie-cutter answer: one model that could be duplicated across the country. It is an answer that Indian leaders have been unable and unwilling to provide. Twenty-five years later, Chrétien has returned to Ottawa as prime minister and while his designate, Irwin, has signed an agreement, that often-repeated question was never asked. Many observers, native and non-native alike, believe that this day marked the start of a new relationship between two peoples.

Manitoba Indian leaders had spent the previous year wrangling not only with federal bureaucrats, but also amongst themselves over the scope and pace of change called for in the document. Although many Indian leaders remain skeptical, they signed the document, hoping to steer their people in a new direction. Despite the agreement, Indian leaders and their people had fresh memories of broken promises and questionable government intentions; they were suspicious that this document would simply be another bitter disappointment.

Before the White Man

Most Canadians know little about the long history of Indian self-government. Before the mass arrival of Europeans in the seventeenth century, aboriginal nations with their own complex institutions of government and society had existed across North America: the West Coast Haida and the Salish of interior British Columbia, the nomadic Blood, Blackfoot, and Plains Cree across the prairies, the Hurons and the Six Nations of the Iroquois Confederacy, the Ojibway and the Naskapi and James Bay Cree of Central Canada, and the Malecite and Micmac of the Maritimes. Linking these different nations was the same mythology: The laws and customs of the people were given to them by a supernatural being, and no one can take those principles away.

In the days before European domination, native people chose their own leaders according to their own traditions and followed rules that defined and legitimized their unique institutions. On the West Coast, tribes governed themselves through the "potlatch," a gathering of people who, during ceremonies involving songs, dances, and speeches, would select their leaders and make decisions affecting the tribe. On the other side of the continent, the Iroquois, also known as the Haudenosaunee Confederacy, governed through what was called the "longhouse": a formalized constitution and a code of laws (which some Mohawk communities in Ontario and Quebec still follow today) that governed the conduct of its people and officials. Male and female leaders were chosen from each family clan, and decisions were reached through consensus. The confederacy was the model that the American colonies would later use for their first union.

The Indian claim to independence is further supported by events in Canadian history. The English and the French formed alliances with the aboriginal nations, first for trade, and then in the fight for control of North America. Following the defeat and withdrawal of the French, King George III issued the Royal Proclamation of 1763, which prevented any further land settlement across North America until the Crown had negotiated treaties with aboriginal people. The revolt of the American colonies forced the English to continue their military alliances with the native people until the end of the War of 1812. After that, Indians were no longer needed; they were just in the way.

Treaties were signed with Prairie native people as a means of allowing peaceful settlement and development. By 1830, the British had introduced the reserve system as part of the treaties. The once nomadic Prairie people were gathered up and settled on reserves. The bands of the West Coast and Central Canada were also confined to small tracts of land. Their systems of government, the longhouse and the potlatch, were banned, and all native people were placed under the wardship of Indian agents. In 1876, the Canadian Parliament passed the first Indian Act, which strengthened the government's control over Indians and the reserve lands, and imposed on them for the first time the concept of an elected band chief and council. It was at this point that the distinction between "status" and "non-status" Indians was first introduced. Status Indians are those registered under the Indian Act, while non-status are not registered. Once free to roam across the continent, Indians found themselves confined to land that they were allowed to use but not own.

Defining Self-Government

Indian self-government has always been a simple and straightforward concept for aboriginal people. It is their right to govern themselves as they decide, sharing power with Ottawa and the provinces. In the predominant aboriginal view today, Indian First Nations should become an integral part of the Canadian federal system, sharing revenues as equals with the provinces and Ottawa, and designing their own social, administrative, and economic institutions. "A lot of people think Indian people are pursuing the goal of independence and that's not the case," says Louis Stevenson, chief of the Peguis band in Manitoba, and a respected voice in the province's Indian community. "I recognize that we live within the country called Canada and its boundaries. So we recognize that Canada is going to be in control over certain matters. We recognize that the province is going to be in control over certain matters. And we recognize that we are in control over certain matters on our own reserves. And where there's overlapping, there's going to be joint sharing of that responsibility with the Canadian or provincial governments."

Political scientist Kathy L. Brock, one of the country's preeminent scholars in the field of the Constitution and aboriginal self-government, notes that the aboriginal approach to self-government negotiations, although alarming to many people, is typically Canadian. In the 1993 book, *Canada and the United States: Differences That Count,* Brock states that today's negotiations are very similar to those that occurred more than 127 years ago during the laying of Canada's foundations.

"The negotiations for powers and jurisdiction [between aboriginal groups and Ottawa] reflect the provincial demands for local control over local affairs which became part of the constitutional deal struck in 1867....More currently, the areas under negotiation parallel the provincial demands for more control over areas such as labour market training, business development, and immigration. Aboriginal land claims are also consistent with this pattern."

The Indian vision would redraw the map of Canada. The twenty-first century would see the country parcelled out into not only the provinces and territories but also as many as 604 smaller, sovereign First Nations communities. The result? A buyer of a new car from an auto dealer on First Nations territory would pay sales tax to that band, not to the provincial government. Police officers issuing speeding tickets would wear a band or tribal council uniform, and revenue from the tickets would go to a First Nations justice system, or motorists would fight the ticket in a First Nations court, before Indian magistrates. Under the new order, Indian children would learn in their history classes of the roles that Harold Cardinal and Elijah Harper played in the struggle of their people.

Financing Self-Government

Federal support of native programs has always fallen victim to the political whims and the economic climate of the day. Indian leaders, however, have no illusions about a magic, bottomless source of revenue upon gaining recognition. Controlling the land and its resources is key to the Indian vision of self-government. The treaties signed between 1763 and the turn of the twentieth century had different meanings for Indians and for the British and Canadian authorities. The governments saw the treaties as a means for relocating the natives, to clear the land for non-native settlement and development. But the Indians saw the treaty as a formal agreement between two sovereign states to share the land in return for certain guarantees. Today, Indians interpret continued government funding as partial payment for surrendering their land. Regaining control of the land is essential to an Indian band's financial future; having authority to determine what occurs on the land is necessary to make self-government complete. However, the land also defines the Indian person. Indian culture and tradition are inseparable from the land. Self-government can only work if the land question — who controls activity on the land — is settled at the same time. "We have our own land base which makes us different than any so-called cultural group in Canada," says Stevenson. "That's part of our nationhood as Indian people. We have a full right to be in control of that territory and all the rights that we have as an Indian nation."

Indian bands that signed treaties with Ottawa, which represent more than half of the registered Indian population of 533,000, claim ownership to large tracts of land that Ottawa has yet to give them. Almost every western band has an outstanding land claim. The 1985 Nielsen task force report, a comprehensive review of all spending on federal programs initiated by the then newly installed Conservative government of Brian Mulroney, estimated the total value of land claims at $8 billion. The task force recommended that Ottawa reach an accommodation with the Indian community on self-government before beginning negotiations to settle the claims. Indian leaders have always viewed the outstanding claims as one way to finance their self-government aspirations and insisted that the settlements be finalized at the same time.

One proposal involves combining land with federal and provincial contracts exclusively assigned to Indian firms. First Nations communities could be established near large urban centres, creating industrial complexes to take advantage of existing federal and provincial projects. Land taxes would be paid to the First Nations government, jobs would be created, and people trained, expanding the tax base of the Indian government. Bands in isolated areas would depend on the natural resources industries — mining, logging, hydroelectricity — to finance their programs. For this means of support to become a reality, native people would have to control development. Under this plan, mining and timber companies would need First Nations approval for their projects. Royalties, which normally go to Ottawa and the provinces, would go directly to Indian governments. "We don't expect anything different than what the rest of society has right now: control over their own lives to control their own future," Stevenson says. "That's what we want." Some bands will never be able to exploit industrial or resource opportunities because of their location. Their future lies with continued federal support. However, unlike Ottawa's present practice of dictating budgets to bands, several aboriginal models of self-government call for continued federal support in the manner that Ottawa deals with the provinces, through equalization payments. This would alter Ottawa's relationship with Indian bands, from ministerial to intergovernmental, removing completely any control or input the federal government has on the allocation of Indian funds.

Devolution: Learning to Walk, Ready to Run

Twenty-five years ago, Ottawa embarked on a devolution policy as its response to native demands for self-government. Under this policy, Indian Affairs gradually allowed Indian bands to administer their own programs, beginning with education, housing, and social assistance and later adding child welfare and policing. But the local band officials, who were responsible for looking after their own people, received little in the way of administrative training by Ottawa. As a result, they frequently had problems fulfilling their new duties. To compound the situation, program content and budgets were still dictated by Ottawa. Devolution thus created a cadre of untrained band officials who found themselves unable to do any more than carry out government orders on the reserve. Budget deficits and service delays became routine. However, band administrators did learn from their mistakes in the ensuing years. Today, many native leaders run efficient, municipal-style administrations. In 1980–81, Indian bands administered 41 per cent of the department's program funding. By 1991–92, this proportion had increased to over 77 per cent. To facilitate this transfer, bureaucrats in the department's finance branch developed two new initiatives in the mid- to late 1980s: alternative funding arrangements (AFAs) and flexible transfer payments (FTPs). The AFAs gave selected band councils lump sum payments covering a five-year period for a determined range of programs. Unlike bands who operate under annual budget plans, the AFA bands were given greater discretion in determining community priorities; they were allowed to transfer funds to other areas where necessary. The FTPs enabled other bands who rejected or did not qualify for an AFA to reduce their annual financial reporting requirements. In contrast to more conventional program administration where all surplus money is returned to Ottawa, bands with FTPs retained surplus program funds from year to year. Despite these gains, Ottawa or the provinces still determined the programs — including crucial areas such as education, child welfare, justice, health, and economic development — to be delivered to Indian people and the amount of money available for those programs.

As Indian bands and Ottawa soon discovered, administering program funds did have its disadvantages. Writer Michael J. Prince, in the 1994–95 edition of *How Ottawa Spends,* concludes that Indian Affairs bureaucrats often took their own initiative in developing these new funding arrangements. "The last 10 years can be seen as a period of experimentation in the funding arrangements: a period of testing and stretching the bounds of the Indian Act in expanding the scope of First Nations' decision-making authority." Bureaucrats and band officials paid a price for all this experimentation. Prince notes that the office of the auditor general (OAG) has remained concerned over this free-wheeling approach to the development of Indian financial policy. Between 1979 and 1991, the OAG voiced the same concerns: How can the minister of Indian Affairs be held accountable to Parliament for department funds when over 77 per cent of the funds are administered by band or tribal councils? In fact, the department has no controls in place to assure Parliament that money is being spent as intended. The reports continue to state that there is no legislative mandate for the AFAs, that much of the department's evolving role has not been defined by legislation, and that specific policy and program objectives are absent. Prince also suggests that AFAs are illegal because they delegate the determination of Indian policy to band councils.

The concerns of the auditor general have been borne out by recent financial troubles on many Indian reserves. Many Indian leaders found that having the power to spend money did their people little good when the amount of money was insufficient. Given the extent of poverty on most reserves, band leaders have been unable to restrict their spending to what Ottawa gives them. As a result, many bands ran up serious deficits, some to the point at which administrators could not be paid. An Indian Affairs audit of band finances released in January 1995 found that one-third of the country's 604 bands in 1993 had accumulated debts totalling more than $537 million. Indian leaders, interviewed by the *Winnipeg Free Press* upon release of the audit, said that the debt situation worsened during the Mulroney years, particularly between 1988 and 1993. During that time, many communities used band funds to oppose both the Meech Lake and Charlottetown Constitutional Accords. In addition, some bands met with financial difficulties when they could not pay expenses associated with conducting research into fighting Ottawa over land claims. Indian leaders attributed the debt situation not to their inability to manage their own financial affairs, but to Ottawa's decision to underfund key program areas and outright refusal to fund other initiatives.

The New Agenda: Self-Government

Between 1970 and 1994, Ottawa spent more than $40 billion on a variety of Indian programs, yet the overall living conditions of Canada's aboriginal people have shown marginal improvement. A new agenda is needed to end the wasting of both resources and lives. Indian leaders recognize Ottawa's problems as a lack of political will and dwindling financial resources; thus, taking control of their own programs and funding sources, they argue, is the only way to change conditions. For Indian leaders, the next step after devolution is self-government, with Indian governments setting their own priorities and spending accordingly. "When we talk about self-government, we mean the capacity to control our own affairs," says Konrad Sioui, former Quebec regional chief. "We don't only mean how we can transfer some authority from the federal or provincial governments."

The National Strategy

Between 1980 and 1993, constitutional recognition of aboriginal self-government has been the goal of Indian leaders. Only with this acknowledgment, they argued, would they know that Canada has recognized aboriginal peoples' right to govern themselves without the involvement of Ottawa or the provinces. The concept, raised repeatedly in negotiations, has left federal and provincial levels of government cautious. During this period, Ottawa and the provinces had given tentative support to the notion of self-government; however, on the whole, they had refused to implement the concept until Indian leaders could define a single model applicable anywhere in Canada. Furthermore, they had demanded a specific timetable for the transfer of powers. Indian leaders refused both demands; hence, negotiations between Indian leaders and federal and provincial bureaucrats proved frustrating. With wide variation in Indian traditions across the country, native leaders demanded the right to adapt their customs within the framework of self-government. Under the Indian proposal, some bands would immediately assume control of their lives. For others, whose development of economies, infrastructures, and governing agencies lags decades behind, self-government would follow at a much slower pace.

Finding an acceptable definition for self-government has been the major stumbling block to federal and provincial governments accepting the notion. There has been widespread concern at both levels over elevating the status of Indian reserves from city-style, self-administering communities to sovereign governments. Until now, Ottawa and the provinces have claimed that they alone held the authority to make laws and to establish institutions to implement those laws. All powers exercised by Indian bands have been handed down by Ottawa and approved by provincial governments. In areas such as native policing, education, and child welfare, Ottawa agreed to the transfer with the qualification that Indian organizations agree to subjugate themselves to provincial authorities. But Indians argue that they do not need anyone's permission to run their own lives. With the exception of the past 200 years, they have lived as sovereign nations for thousands of years. During that 200-year period, first Britain and then

Ottawa manipulated Indian lives and produced only disastrous results. "They took control of our lives and with the conditions that are prevalent here today, it's quite obvious they failed miserably," Stevenson says. "There was an outright attempt to wipe us off the face of this country and they failed at that too."

Ironically, recent political initiatives and judicial rulings have largely promoted the concept of self-government. The Liberal government first raised the notion of Indian self-government during the political wrangling of the early 1980s, as Trudeau led the country on his personal agenda to repatriate the Canadian Constitution. Initially, there was no mention of aboriginal people in the Constitution. The term "aboriginal" first appeared in the Constitution Act in 1982. Upset at being omitted from the country's constitutional document, Indian leaders went to London to lobby British MPs and the Queen to block re-patriation. In a last-minute bid to win greater public support for the initiative, Trudeau relented. Section 35 of the Constitution Act of 1982 recognizes and affirms the existing and treaty rights of the aboriginal peoples of Canada. However, the act does not define those rights. For the newly identified aboriginal people — Métis, status Indians, non-status Indians, and Inuit — those rights include the inherent right to self-government. Four FMCs between 1983 and 1987 and two failed constitutional accords have been unable to produce an acceptable definition of self-government.

Brock, in her paper, "The Politics of Aboriginal Self-Government: A Canadian Paradox," writes that for aboriginal leaders, entrenchment of the inherent right to self-government in the Constitution would accomplish two key objectives: it would allow aboriginal communities to expand beyond non-native political arrangements that stress individual rights, welfare, and municipal government structures; and it would expand the powers and authority traditionally exercised by aboriginal communities, thus allowing for the establishment of new forms of aboriginal government. During the FMCs, Brock says that aboriginal leaders were not asking the provinces and Ottawa to give them this right or to delegate authority to them. "They were demanding that the federal and provincial governments recognize a pre-existing and unconditional right....Had an amendment been achieved, then three orders of government would have been entrenched in Canada: the federal, the provincial, and the aboriginal." Brock notes that opposition to the Indian position concentrated on four main points: First, the provinces wanted a definition of self-government, which aboriginal leaders were unwilling and unable to provide. Second, the provinces were reluctant to give self-government status to such a small population base; they were wary of the political and legal ramifications associated with the sovereignty status that would be attached to the First Nations. Third, the provincial premiers considered themselves to be representatives of all citizens and aboriginal leaders to be essentially lobbyists for a very small, very narrow, special interest group. Finally, some premiers felt that if the notion of self-government was left undefined, the courts would eventually determine the definition; they weren't willing to allow the courts to settle the question and possibly impose costs they could not afford.

According to Brock, the series of FMCs did not result in the recognition of the inherent right to self-government in the Constitution. The process worked against the goals of the aboriginal leaders because, in part, they were too focussed on one issue. They had no other issues with which to make concessions or threaten a veto in their negotiations with the provinces. However, the conferences did have two important benefits: "They mobilised and focused Aboriginal organizations," Brock says in *Canada and the United States: Differences That Count.* "Second, the discussions had introduced the Canadian general public to the concept of self-government and placed the item squarely on the table for governments to deal with in the future."

The frustrations felt by Indian leaders during the political negotiations have been somewhat offset by key successes achieved in the courts. In 1990, the Supreme Court of Canada made three rulings that bolstered the Indian community's claims to self-government and that will one day form the legal building blocks for their aspirations. In the *Guerin* case, the court ruled that Ottawa has a fiduciary duty to Indian people to act in their best interests and when that trust has been violated, Ottawa can be held accountable. In the *Sparrow* case, the court stated that Indian rights take priority over all others, even government claims of overriding priorities in the public interest. Rights assigned by treaty are entrenched by the Constitution. Where no treaty exists, traditional rights are assumed and can only be narrowed through fair bargaining. In the *Sioui* case, the court concluded that Ottawa could not apply a narrow, literal interpretation to treaty rights in order to define what obligations must be fulfilled today. Taken together, the three cases will shape all future negotiations on self-government. Provincial concerns that Ottawa is giving too many powers to First Nations will be silenced by the *Sparrow* case. Indian leaders will cite *Guerin* to fight any attempts by Ottawa to reduce or stop funding of programs as they are transferred. If Ottawa disagrees over the range of powers being claimed by the new First Nations governments, federal negotiators will be faced with the *Sioui* case. And, if the Chrétien or a future government reverts to the traditional tactic of refusing to negotiate, then Indian leaders can use these three cases when they return to the Supreme Court to be granted the legitimacy that is being denied to them. Indian leaders in the United States took this route in the 1830s, when the Supreme Court ruled that American Indian tribes must be recognized as "domestic, dependent nations" with a broad range of powers and separate jurisdiction.

Self-Government Models

Much of the debate on aboriginal self-government during the FMCs and the failed Meech Lake and Charlottetown Constitutional Accords has been shaped by the Penner Report, the landmark paper released in 1983. Although it did not meet all of the aboriginal community's expectations, it has remained the benchmark for all subsequent legislation, models, and initiatives on Indian self-government.

As previously mentioned, in 1983, a special House of Commons committee, chaired by Liberal MP Keith Penner, released a report strongly urging Ottawa to recognize aboriginal self-government in the Constitution. The all-party committee had spent the previous year holding hearings and reviewing submissions from native individuals and aboriginal organizations across Canada. The report contained the first recommendations from a government body advocating recognition of Indian First Nations, or Indian bands as they had been known, as a distinct level of government, instead of mere municipal bodies with expanded powers created by Ottawa.

The Penner Report urged Ottawa to immediately include the right of Indians to self-government in the Constitution and to pass legislation that would enable Indian bands to achieve that goal. As First Nations, the report said, bands have the right to determine their own membership and powers, whether they act alone or formally join with other bands sharing the same traditions and language. The report concluded that various Indian tribes were, in fact, nations of people who shared a common history, culture, and language. And, like the authors of the White Paper before it, Penner called for the dismantling of the department of Indian Affairs. The reasons, of course, came from different viewpoints. Whereas the White Paper's assimilation plans would make Indian Affairs redundant, Penner's plans consisted of replacing the department with a smaller ministry to ensure that Canada's obligations to the distinct First Nations would be maintained. Ottawa would establish both a tribunal to settle disputes between the emerging First Nations and other governments, and a commission to determine when bands were ready to assume their new status. Finally, the report recommended that Ottawa finance the new First Nations as it does the provincial governments, with equalization payments.

Yet, Indian leaders disliked much of the Penner Report. The document insisted on liberal, democratic institutions as the basis of Indian government, ignoring native traditions and customs, which dated back thousands of years. It based Indian government on individual band councils, again circumventing any attempts by native people to re-establish traditions they had followed before the Europeans arrived. There was some flexibility, however, since the report allowed bands to determine their own future direction; band members could form a government more closely resembling their historical roots. The rights of non-status Indians and status Indians living in urban centres were not addressed.

Even with its faults, many Indian organizations applauded the Penner Report. The paper provided a starting point for negotiating a new arrangement between status Indians and Ottawa. Indian leaders believed the flaws could be overcome.

The Penner Report had little impact on the first FMC in 1983; however, it did prompt the Liberal government to introduce its own legislation in 1984, and it may have played at least a small part in what has been heralded as the first Indian self-government legislation, Bill C–46, which was also passed that year.

Bill C–46, the Cree-Naskapi (of Quebec) Act, became part of the James Bay Agreement. The bill, accompanied by similar provincial legislation in Quebec, represented the culmination of a series of negotiations that began nine years earlier involving land claims and cash settlements, and that allowed for the construction of the mammoth James Bay hydro project in northern Quebec. The legislation was passed as a compromise, to win the Indian community's support for what was seen as a lucrative project for the province. The Indian community had threatened legal action that could have delayed indefinitely or eliminated the project. Under the legislation, the government bestowed land, cash, and a degree of self-government upon eight Cree bands and a Naskapi band. The bands were removed from the control of the Indian Act and given a wide range of powers. Ottawa then incorporated the bands and legally created band councils, with elected chiefs and councillors. The councils possessed the right to formulate laws affecting land and natural resources, use of buildings, band funds, community development and charitable projects, and the cultural and traditional values of the Cree and Naskapi people. The 1984 legislation prevails over all other acts of Parliament, and provincial laws do not apply when they conflict with the Cree-Naskapi Act.

During the final days of the Liberal government in Ottawa, then headed by Trudeau's successor, John Turner, the first piece of self-government legislation for all Indian bands was introduced in Parliament. But Bill C–52, as the legislation was known, would once again show that Ottawa was not listening. Ottawa showed no indication of accepting First Nations as a third and equal level of government and offered no hope for constitutional legitimization of aboriginal aspirations.

Bill C–52

The Liberal government moved unilaterally with Bill C–52. Without native input, and by completely dismissing most of the recommendations in the Penner Report, Ottawa formulated a framework for all future Indian self-government settlements. The Liberal government was prepared to give an even broader range of powers to Indian communities than was offered in the James Bay Agreement. These powers included the regulation of all land use, laws to govern public order, and control over the environment, including renewable and nonrenewable resources, wildlife, and agriculture. The new policy even covered control over the administration of justice on Indian land. For the first time, Indians would be allowed to establish judicial and quasi-judicial bodies with jurisdiction over Indian laws, to create their own jails, to set up Indian police and prosecution authorities, and to determine family law for all permanent residents, affecting marriage, separation, divorce, adoption, and child welfare.

However, Bill C–52 still subjected all Indian laws to Ottawa's final approval and the Canadian Charter of Rights and Freedoms. Predictably, the Indian community condemned the legislation. They argued that Ottawa had only one concept of government — a liberal democracy that had no room for aboriginal customs and traditions. The legislation limited Indian jurisdiction to on-reserve residents. It remained silent, however, on the right of any Indian authority to represent and care for band members living in urban centres, which is a goal of some Indian leaders. Indian communities would remain, despite Ottawa's claims, mere instruments of the federal government, carrying out only those functions assigned to them. Bill C–52 died with the defeat of the Liberal government that year.

The Mulroney Years

September 1984 saw the election of Brian Mulroney and the Conservative government. One of his main objectives over the following ten years was to find accommodation for Quebec within the constitutional process. Like Trudeau before him, Mulroney tried to broker public acceptance of a wide range of constitutional proposals by trying to appease everyone, including aboriginal people. During this ten-year period, the FMCs were held, as required under the new Constitution Act, and the Meech Lake and Charlottetown Constitutional Accords were introduced. In addition, the Mulroney government embarked on a series of community self-government initiatives that drew strong criticism for being very expensive, time-consuming, and, ultimately, unsuccessful.

The Mulroney government's first attempt to reconcile the Indian problem was contained within the recommendations of the Nielsen task force report. Appointed soon after the Tories came to power, the task force examined all federal government programs. Its recommendations for resolving the self-government question fell far short of the aboriginal vision of the future. The task force saw no room for a constitutional accommodation of aboriginal people. Instead, the report stated that self-government should remain merely an administrative structure with local Indian functionaries carrying out duties that Ottawa agrees to transfer under provincial supervision. Although Ottawa did not officially endorse the task force findings, subsequent legislation led Indian leaders to conclude that the recommendations were in fact being carried out.

The Sechelt Model

Near the end of the 1986–87 fiscal year, the Mulroney government began a series of community self-government negotiations. These talks followed the end of the FMCs and were considered complementary to the high-level constitutional negotiations over inclusion of the right to self-government in the Constitution. The only positive outcome of this process was the Sechelt Indian Band Self-Government Act, Ottawa's second piece of self-government legislation.

Many of the same powers that had been given to the James Bay communities two years earlier were also given to the Sechelt, located on the British Columbia coast, west of Vancouver. The Sechelt were also given the right to create a constitution establishing the authority of the band council and its powers. However, the constitution had to be approved by Ottawa before it became official. Several months after Ottawa passed the Sechelt act, the British Columbia government also passed its own Sechelt legislation. It recognized the band council as the governing body of the area, thus allowing the band to exercise all powers granted by the province.

Unlike the case of the James Bay communities, there was no land claims settlement with the Sechelt. Although the federal legislation takes precedence over most federal laws, the Sechelt band is still subject to two key pieces of federal legislation governing natural resources: the Indian Oil and Gas Act and the British Columbia Indian Reserves Mineral Resources Act. In addition, the band does not have the authority to control lotteries and gambling within its borders.

Political scientist Brock says that a federal audit of the community self-government initiative, conducted in February 1993, was critical of the program. In the seven years since its inception, Ottawa had begun negotiations with 400 bands; at the program's conclusion, only fifteen talks were still in progress, three communities had reached tentative agreements, and one other community in Alberta had signed a self-government agreement. The other negotiations were abandoned. The total cost of the program exceeded $50 million, with $30 million of that sum transferred to individual bands to cover their negotiating costs.

From a non-native perspective, the James Bay and Sechelt agreements, along with the community self-government initiative, appear to fulfil the aboriginal goal of self-government. Ottawa and the provinces of Quebec and British Columbia have created working examples of municipal-style governments, giving the First Nations communities broader powers affecting culture and natural resources. The bands have proven themselves capable of carrying out their new responsibilities.

Despite the success of the agreements, many Indian leaders across Canada oppose them. They say that both pieces of legislation imposed a western-style, liberal democracy on the First Nation communities. The traditions and customs of the Sechelt and the Cree were ignored. The powers now exercised by the Sechelt and the James Bay Indians were delegated by Ottawa and the provinces. The legislation reinforces the view that Indian governments are the tools of Ottawa and the provinces, administering only those functions allocated by the senior levels of government. The legislation is a denial: Indian people should not have to bargain for these rights.

The Charlottetown Accord

Belief in this open-ended approach to self-government led the majority of Indian people to vote against the 1992 Charlottetown Accord. For Mulroney, the accord accomplished what Trudeau had not been able to do: it brought Quebec willingly into the Canadian Constitution. For Canada's aboriginal people, the agreement was also seen as a breakthrough document. It recognized aboriginal people as the first people to govern the country and, finally, entrenched the inherent right to self-government in the Constitution. The accord also guaranteed aboriginal people representation in a reformed Senate. But the element that would ultimately prove unacceptable to many Indian people was the five-year time frame over which leaders of the aboriginal groups, Ottawa, and the provinces would negotiate appropriate forms of self-government. During this period, existing federal and provincial laws would apply. The accord postponed any discussion of special native courts or a native justice system to another series of FMCs slated to begin four years later. It also postponed the controversial topic of continued financing to the next round of FMCs.

The accord was held up as a victory for all aboriginal people, and for status Indians in particular. Brock described it as a historic agreement. "The right to self-government had gone from being a disputed item in 1983 to an accepted direction of policy and negotiated constitutional clause in 1992." But reserve residents across the country overwhelmingly rejected it. Brock cites findings from an Elections Canada report, *Federal Referendum: Unofficial Results in Specific Aboriginal Communities,* from October 1992: she notes that more than 62 per cent of reserve residents voted "no" to the accord. (A breakdown of reserve residents showing how aboriginal and non-aboriginal groups voted could not be provided.) Brock, in *Canada and the United States: Differences That Count,* states that opposition across the country came from conflicting forces within the aboriginal community, including native women's groups wanting greater protection in the Charter, treaty reserves wanting greater assurance of their treaty guarantees, and other band chiefs fearing a loss of funding through the accord.

According to Brock, the leaders of the four aboriginal groups at the Charlottetown talks were the first to achieve unanimous agreement on self-government. However, this consensus was reached by compromising on key issues. The accord itself violated many of the principles Indian leaders had been advocating for more than ten years. The Indian community rejected the agreement because it still forced native people to accept conditions of self-government imposed by Ottawa and the provinces. In addition, Indian leaders want each individual band to determine the timing of its own independence and the range of its powers of jurisdiction. If the right to self-government was accepted, it should not be denied to any band, regardless of when Ottawa or any other power judged it ready.

The Return of Jean Chrétien

Within the Indian community, the Charlottetown Accord and the ensuing debate destroyed the fragile consensus on a national agenda for achieving self-government. The defeat of the Mulroney Tories and the return of the Liberals under Jean Chrétien in the fall of 1993 brought new players to the self-government game and provided new opportunities for the Indian community. The election outcome was also to widen the split between some Indian leaders. While Ovide Mercredi, grand chief of the AFN, continues to push the original strategy of entrenching self-government within the Constitution, others, such as Phil Fontaine of Manitoba, see a chance to achieve their dream without dealing with eleven first ministers and their bureaucratic entourage.

The Liberal campaign promised to change the relationship between the Indian community and the rest of Canadian society. "The role of a Liberal government will be to provide Aboriginal people with the necessary tools to become self-sufficient and self-governing," the party's pre-election Red Book stated. The document acknowledged that the "inherent right of self-government is an existing Aboriginal and treaty right" and committed a Liberal government to dismantling the Indian Affairs department while maintaining Ottawa's financial fiduciary responsibility to Indian people. The dismantling agreement signed in Winnipeg roughly one year after the Liberals came to power was the partial fulfilment of that election promise.

The document is a radical departure for Ottawa. For the first time, Ottawa accepted the notions that Indian communities would decide the nature of self-government and that the approach could vary from community to community. Ottawa committed not only to the dismantling of Indian Affairs in Manitoba and to the transfer of jurisdiction of all department programs, including education, social services, and fire protection, over to band councils, but also to the transfer of jurisdiction held by other federal departments, including the Ministry of Health. Transfer of authority for specific programs to individual communities would not occur without a thorough review and consensus within each community. The agreement does not jeopardize existing treaty rights and it commits both Ottawa and Indian leadership to defining treaties in contemporary terms. Ottawa agreed to finance the initiative, at a total cost of $5.4 million over a ten-year period. The document calls for the agreement to be reviewed after the third, sixth and tenth years, to ensure that it is meeting the expectations of all involved.

Brock, in *Canadian Government and Politics,* writes that the Liberals came into office with three policies on self-government. They would, for a time, continue the community self-government initiatives, and they would continue talks with national aboriginal groups on entrenching the inherent right to self-government in the Constitution. But their top priority was the dismantling experiment in Manitoba. Indian Affairs minister Irwin abandoned the community initiative within six months of being sworn into office, having agreed with the federal audit that it was too expensive, too time consuming, and unproductive. Talks with national leaders appear to have been put aside. Chrétien is reluctant to reopen constitutional talks, for Quebec or aboriginal groups. The government's position leaves national aboriginal leaders with little to do but observe the Manitoba experiment. Brock notes that Ovide Mercredi remains opposed to the Manitoba experiment because it does not include constitutional recognition of the right to self-government. He fears, she says, that dismantling could be challenged or stopped in the future unless it is accompanied by constitutional protection. In addition, he is leery of involving provinces in such discussions because the traditional treaty discussion format limits participation to Ottawa and individual bands.

The Manitoba agreement is clearly an experiment. There are no guarantees that similar open-ended arrangements will be extended to other Indian bands or aboriginal groups. In fact, during negotiations for this experiment, Ottawa continued with its policy of tripartite agreements, calling for Indian bands and the Saskatchewan and New Brunswick governments to sign documents for the sharing of power over natural resources and health care. Many Indian leaders across the country remain skeptical. Ottawa has long had a "divide-and-conquer" policy toward the status Indian community; it has attempted to break the solidarity of national organizations by enticing smaller bands with token offers. Just weeks after the December 1994 signing of the dismantling agreement, cracks in the new relationship began to appear.

The first attempt to extend the dismantling initiative to other federal programs backfired on both the Manitoba Indian leaders and Ottawa. An agreement was to be signed in mid-February 1995, transferring the control of the federal native health care system to Manitoba's Indian bands. But Health minister Diane Marleau refused to sign the document, literally at the last moment, because the chiefs were insisting that health care was a treaty right while the prime minister's office insisted that the provision of health care was simply a matter of government policy. The difference in views is critical. Under the government's policy, health care for natives can be abandoned at any time, and funding for the dismantling initiative can be reduced or eliminated. But with health care as a treaty right, Ottawa would be held responsible for financing the program even if it was under First Nations control. "We discovered at the last hour that the federal government negotiated in bad faith," Fontaine told reporters during a hastily called news conference in a downtown Winnipeg hotel. "We discovered at the last hour that their word is not good. That we cannot trust them."

A month later, on March 22, 1995, Ovide Mercredi accused Irwin and Ottawa of backtracking on their commitment to self-government; he announced the discovery of federal briefing notes that mentioned limitations on the extent of self-government powers. Irwin said he had been meeting with individual chiefs, elders, and provincial governments to produce a policy paper for the cabinet. Mercredi was incensed. He had previously been distrustful of the dismantling initiative and the Liberal's promise to pursue self-government without constitutional protection. Now it appeared that Irwin was reversing himself on government policy to allow First Nations communities to decide the form of self-government, and he was doing so by excluding Mercredi and the national Indian organization. "Who appointed him God?" Mercredi was reported as saying by the Canadian Press news agency. "[The government] tries to reverse history and undo the progress we made."

Many uncertainties remain, even within the Manitoba aboriginal community, on the dismantling initiative. Although the agreement covers all sixty-one Manitoba bands, only forty-five chiefs attended the ceremonies and signed the document. A lawyer who advises several Manitoba bands comments that, of the chiefs who did not sign, about half of them were too busy attending matters in their communities; the others opposed the accord. Apparently, many chiefs remain skeptical of Ottawa's intentions, believing this to be yet another scheme to eliminate a $4-billion-per-year bureaucracy. Chief Louis Stevenson believes that most communities will approach the initiative cautiously. He said that no concrete steps would be taken unless provisions are made to continue current funding levels and to ensure that their own treaty rights are not jeopardized. Stevenson predicted that the appearance of real sovereign First Nations might not occur for another ten years, if ever. The *Winnipeg Free Press* reported that many individuals, including women and elders, opposed the deal because they believe that their communities are not ready to accept the responsibilities associated with self-government. Many women's groups feared that the dismantling initiative would entrench the abusive male-dominated élite that controls some reserve communities. "The existing structures have not worked for women and children...and I fear this is happening too fast," said Winnie Giesbrecht, a well-known woman in Manitoba's aboriginal community, to the *Winnipeg Free Press*. "A great deal of women are very afraid of self-government," comments Kathy Mallett, of the Original Women's Network. "They don't know what it means to them."

It is not certain how Canadians will respond to the dismantling initiative once its implications are known. Several public opinion surveys have shown support for the notion of Indian self-government. But it is unknown whether the public will support an initiative allowing a band with as few as fifty status Indians to become a sovereign government, free to legislate hunting, gambling, development, and taxes, which might conflict with provincial or federal laws. Two constitutional accords aimed at recognizing Quebec as a distinct society failed to gain public support, yet Ottawa is proposing to give the same status to every Indian band in the country. Canadians have repeatedly stated that they are not willing to continue the practice of the past 200 years and condemn the aboriginal community to further misery. But are they prepared to accept the alternative, which offers Indian people an opportunity to find themselves and their place within Canada? The country must decide soon.

5

Economic Development

Today there is the growing danger that a majority of Indians...may become a more-or-less permanently isolated, displaced, unemployed or under-employed and dependent group who can find no useful or meaningful role in an increasingly complex urban industrial economy.

— Harry B. Hawthorn
A Survey of the Contemporary Indians in Canada

In 1966, Harry B. Hawthorn thus summed up his assessment of Indian conditions in Canada's first comprehensive review. Hawthorn, as the editor and director of the report, attempted to expose the widespread poverty and despair of native people and to find an acceptable way to integrate natives into Canadian society while still retaining their distinctive culture and traditions. The study was commissioned in 1964 by the Indian Affairs Branch (later to become a department of its own) of the Ministry of Citizenship and Immigration. The study's findings and Hawthorn's own observations comprised a warning to the government and to the people of Canada about the possible demise of the Indian community if appropriate actions were not taken. The fact that deplorable conditions still exist today on Indian reserves and still face Indians in urban settings across Canada is damning evidence of the failure of Ottawa's policies to meet the challenge issued in the Hawthorn report.

Between 1968 and 1988, Ottawa spent more than $2 billion in social assistance for Indian bands across Canada and almost $2.5 billion on Indian economic development programs. With those expenditures, Ottawa created a national policy that pulled native people in opposite directions; the results were predictable — conditions did not improve. The 1991 Census found that, on average, more than 68 per cent of Indians of working age living on reserves are either unemployed or collecting welfare. On isolated reserves and in some urban centres, the figures reach 80 to 90 per cent. How could billions of dollars be spent with nothing more accomplished than the realization of Hawthorn's nightmare? There is neither a simple answer, nor a single villain. Economic development was one of the few items specifically targeted in the 1969 White Paper. The authors of the new Indian policy set aside $50 million to launch native economic development initiatives, while Ottawa created a new ministry, the Department of Regional and Economic Expansion (DREE), to reduce regional disparities across the country. A year later, the policy created to foster native economic development initiatives was officially withdrawn. Civil servants, still faced with the task of implementing the Hawthorn recommendations, were told to develop those initiatives in conjunction with DREE. Over the next twenty years, the government would spend billions of dollars futilely, trying to heed Hawthorn's call for revival of the economically depressed native community.

Policy of Welfare

Many experts believed that Ottawa failed to improve conditions due to the lack of a policy direction that might have ensured the long-term economic viability of Indian communities. "As political enthusiasm waned and new priorities came into vogue, Ottawa officialdom brought DREE 'into line,' " one federal official was quoted as saying in a consultant's report that examined Ottawa's native economic policies. "Throughout, it has lacked clear, accepted goals and increasingly, a coherent driving force." The native economic initiatives, which were devoid of any concise policy on future direction, yielded programs that simply handed social assistance to natives, stunting their economic development.

Ottawa's inability to solve the Indian reserve problem has fostered the attitude amongst many politicians and bureaucrats that there is no alternative lifestyle for these communities. Indian Affairs has labelled most of the northern and isolated reserves as economically unviable, targeting them only for social assistance. Former Indian Affairs minister Bill McKnight said in a 1988 interview that welfare must remain in place for Indians living in those areas. "What would you suggest in an isolated locale, without markets, without resources, without an industrial base, without economic opportunities. You try as best you can to provide a social safety net, as we do to all

Canadians." Such a statement appears to reject alternatives that could lead to native self-sufficiency, at least in the reserve setting, and begs the question of what happens when severe cuts are made to the social safety net.

Indian Affairs continually refuses to reconsider its spending priorities for the country's 604 reserves. To Ottawa, welfare is a safety net for the 315,000 people living on reserves: to Indians, it is a crippling disease. Social assistance has been a way of life for several generations, and it has become a cycle that is almost impossible to break. "Our welfare budget is $2.7 million and our economic development budget from Indian Affairs is $52,000," Louis Stevenson, chief of the Peguis band and one of the Manitoba Indian leaders, said in 1988. "If we had full control over those revenues, we could reverse that arrangement where economic development is a priority. Why couldn't we have $2.7 million at our disposal to create jobs and to promote business and establish an economic base on the reserve instead of pissing it down the drain on welfare? You don't get a return on money from welfare. Once that $2.7 million is issued, it's a one-way flow."

Six years later, with the return of Jean Chrétien and with a new Liberal federal government promising self-government for native people, the safety net philosophy remains enshrined as government policy. At the Annual General Assembly of Manitoba Chiefs in September 1994, Indian leaders heard once again that this policy would remain in effect. Brenda Kustra, regional director general of Indian Affairs for Manitoba, told the chiefs that while Ron Irwin, the minister of Indian Affairs, encouraged his staff to convert social assistance dollars into funds for economic development initiatives, no mechanisms exist to allow this to occur. To no one's surprise, Ottawa is not planning to investigate this option. "I am not aware of any overall initiatives targeted at looking at the economic situation and self-sufficiency of First Nations in Canada in a national forum," Kustra answered in response to repeated questions on why there was no such policy. However, she added that developing such a strategy remains a priority for the government. She was unable to reconcile that statement with an earlier admission that the region's economic development funds had been slashed in the previous year's budget. The chiefs refused to accept this bureaucratic double-talk. "Your department is concentrating on getting our people to rely on the department for social hand-outs and welfare," charged Felix Antoine, chief of the Roseau River First Nation. The other chiefs agreed. "We are now entering fourth and fifth generations of our people who depend on welfare, with no end in sight," added Stevenson, still chief of Peguis. Kustra's only response was that Irwin was urging the continuation of localized, pilot projects that, if successful, could be duplicated on a national scale. Given Ottawa's track record in such areas, Indian people were pessimistic.

Gambling: The New Buffalo

During the past two decades, economic development and the Indian vision of self-government have become interdependent. Two hundred years of dependency have devastated the aboriginal community. Now, Indian leaders say that real improvement can only be achieved by ensuring that political changes accompany economic initiatives. For many Indian people, the new route to their future lies with gambling. Like the buffalo hunt that, centuries before, provided Indian people with food, clothing, and a way of life, gambling, many Indian leaders say, will give their people the wealth and power that have eluded them for so many years.

The success of native-run gambling casinos and bingo halls in the United States provides some inspiration for Indian leaders in Canada. In the United States, native gambling has become a $6-billion-per-year operation, fuelling the construction of homes, schools and seniors' residences, paving and lighting streets, creating new jobs for thousands of native people and providing annual royalty cheques for band members. Some American Indian tribes have used the profits to purchase non-native businesses. Gambling became a reality south of the border with the 1988 Indian Gaming Regulatory Act. The legislation gives Indian tribes a broad range of powers for gambling purposes, provided gambling is legal in the tribes' home state or a special agreement has been negotiated with state authorities. States that currently allow Indian gambling include Michigan, Wisconsin, North and South Dakota, Washington, Minnesota, California, and Arizona.

In Canada, many Indian leaders see gambling as both the fastest, most effective way to finance self-government and a visible declaration of self-government authority. While Indians are a federal responsibility, gambling is a provincial matter. Like disputes in the fields of child welfare, education, and justice, gambling has become a jurisdictional issue; like these other matters, provincial governments take their own approaches. However, there is one common theme: the provinces insist on regulating and authorizing all gambling ventures. In Saskatchewan, the provincial government wants to form a partnership with bands and share profits from the establishment of two possible native-run casinos. In Manitoba, the provincial government has refused repeated requests to open native-run casinos. In Ontario, the NDP government accepted the concept of the native casino, and invited bands to submit bids for operating rights. Indians throughout the province will share the profits. Maritime governments have approved bingo halls, but not casinos.

The responses of the various provincial governments have infuriated many Indian leaders, who see gambling on their own reserves as falling within their legal entitlement. Native leaders have challenged the provinces' authority, by setting up illegal casinos and bingo halls on reserves. Police raids in Saskatchewan and Manitoba shut down these operations. Other bands, often supported by American gambling suppliers, have announced similar plans. The confrontations are part of a deliberate Indian strategy to force the courts to examine the laws. Indian leaders hope to win court rulings that will allow them unfettered casino and gambling operations.

The issue has, however, divided the Indian community. Some Indians do not see gambling as a panacea, believing that it will bring a host of social problems. There is also a concern that it will attract organized crime. Most of the casino suppliers are from the United States, and some native people have had troubled relations with state gaming authorities and police. Other natives are simply upset because of the willingness of their leaders to co-operate with provincial governments in establishing the casinos. These Indians argue that they need no special permission to conduct their own affairs on sovereign Indian land.

The gambling dispute between provinces and Indian leaders is similar to other conflicts over authority. However, the provinces also fear losing billions in much-needed revenues if Indian casinos become a reality. In Canada, casino and lottery revenues are used to supplement programs in health care, education, and social services. In the United States, state government involvement in those areas has always been minimal: few tax dollars were allocated to those areas, so gambling profits were seen as revenues that did not belong to the government. In Canada, provincial governments have been using lottery money to subsidize their ever-growing budgets. Provinces that have, or are considering, casino operations see these ventures as another way to supplement those budget expenditures. Indian leaders say they want the revenue for most of the same reasons and claim that the provinces' position is yet another attempt to undermine their sovereignty.

Ottawa's Failed Programs

Ottawa's attempts over a twenty-year period to revive the native economy have been a disaster. A survey of several such programs that existed across the country between 1968 and 1989 found them often to be nothing more than short-sighted, temporary job-creation plans. A study of seven Indian-run economic development agencies conducted for the 1983 Penner Report showed that Indian bands believed that Ottawa's efforts to launch native economic initiatives had actually been counterproductive. Government programs proved to be too bureaucratic and time-consuming, and they did not accommodate high-risk ventures. On reserves with little economic activity, every business venture becomes high risk. Repeated assessments have concluded that government funding proved undependable and sporadic, and actually hindered long-term development.

Analysis of federal studies obtained through the Access to Information Act not only confirms the Indian assumptions, but also shows that the programs were, in fact, destructive to many communities. A succession of key federal-provincial programs aimed at improving the economic viability of Indian reserves in western Canada did little more than build roads, which led Indians away from their homes. The studies, which examined program effectiveness in Alberta, Saskatchewan, and Manitoba, show that although overall incomes and living standards have increased on reserves, the socioeconomic gap between native and non-native people has widened, and more Indians than ever before are dependent on welfare. The repeated failures of the programs prompted one consultant to speculate that federal and provincial governments never intended to improve conditions for native people; the entire exercise was just an expensive public relations gesture. Unable to lay the groundwork for a viable economy and the stated objectives of the various programs, Ottawa and the provinces found it much easier to simply build things for Indians.

Northlands Agreements

It would be impossible to assess all of the programs devoted to economic development. Thus, discussion here is limited to studies of "northlands agreements," which Ottawa and the three prairie provinces signed between 1974 and 1989. These initiatives have been chosen because they were promoted as innovative and successful by the federal and provincial governments. The length of the programs also allows independent assessments of effectiveness.

The northlands agreements were initiated by DREE, which in later years became the Department of Regional Industrial Expansion. Total funding exceeded $460 million. All agreements were aimed at eradicating the disparities in the northern areas of the three provinces through the implementation of economic development strategies. A review of the independent studies shows that all of the programs, regardless of when or where they were introduced, failed to accomplish their goals. However, the consultants reports of the government-funded analysts repeatedly glossed over the findings with an overly positive, generalized introduction that often misled the reader: "Agreement represents a good application of public funds," noted the consultants who evaluated one of the three Saskatchewan agreements. The analysts then went on to outline in great detail the program's massive failings.

Saskatchewan

Between 1974 and 1989, Ottawa and Saskatchewan committed more than $212 million to three separate economic development initiatives. The three programs comprise the Canada/Saskatchewan Northlands Agreement (1974–79; 1979–83), and the Northern Economic Development Subsidiary Agreement (1984–89). Analysis shows that the programs failed to improve conditions for native people. The government spent millions of dollars on capital improvements, including housing, recreation centres, telephone systems, and roads, but made no attempt to establish a local economy that would lead the residents to some level of economic independence.

The Canada/Saskatchewan Northlands Agreement Evaluation (1982) and the Mid-term Review of the Canada-Saskatchewan Northern Economic Development Subsidiary Agreement (1986) reached similar conclusions: despite the efforts and funding, northern Saskatchewan suffers many of the same problems as a developing Third World country — staggering population growth, coupled with an absence of economic activity. At best, the agreements were able to provide training and jobs for a few people, but they proved totally inadequate for the majority of the northern native population.

Provincial officials bypassed the co-ordinating components and long-term aims included in the agreements, and instead opted for what was easier to accomplish in the short term: a massive construction campaign. Although this approach offered temporary economic relief for northern conditions, it made a mockery of the agreement's objectives of laying a foundation for real economic change in the north. "Unfortunately, other elements that make a community self-sustaining are still missing, including an economic base to provide permanent jobs for local residents and a tax base to operate and maintain the new facilities," the consultants wrote.

An evaluation of Saskatchewan's Northern Economic Development Subsidiary Agreement shows that the program failed after two years; it was destined to remain a failure. This program did not meet its objectives of economic planning, nor did it create local jobs or provide facilities for permanent employment. Although it did offer job training, no jobs awaited the graduates. This program appears to be another example in a long line of government initiatives that raised expectations, only to deliver short-term opportunities.

This study was also critical of the federal and provincial governments' efforts to promote the agreement. Despite the program's budget of $25 million, the government made no effort to publicize the availability of funds. This neglect calls into question the motives of both governments: did they intend to actually spend the money or was the entire program created just to appease the concerns of southern residents? Statements made to the consultants by field staff and participants about the unavailability of funds support the view that there was little real commitment.

The study concludes that the multimillion-dollar agreement would have minimal impact. "There is no clear political priority placed on northern development by either federal or provincial governments," wrote the authors of the study. "Given its scope and the very limited amount of 'new money' available to it, [the agreement] will never have more than a marginal impact in the context of all government programming aimed at economic and human resource development." The litany of sins cited in Saskatchewan were being replicated across the country.

Alberta

The authors of another federally sponsored analysis, the Canada/Alberta North Subsidiary Agreement Assessment, paint a depressing picture of governments' efforts to improve northern Alberta native communities between 1975 and 1982. "One of the basic stated goals of the Alberta Government is to diversify and decentralize economic development in the province," the consultants noted. However, they added that they could not see how this particular agreement and its programs could have lessened regional disparities either within the north or between northern and southern areas of the province.

In this case, the government targeted more than $48 million to improve conditions in the northern communities; however, like the government officials of their eastern neighbour, the Alberta bureaucrats found it easier to spend on services and facilities than to launch a true local economy. Although this approach did improve some living conditions by constructing new housing and other facilities, the expenditures in these areas ended up working against the long-term objectives of the program. The study quotes a federal official: "You can spend as much money on hard services and infrastructure as possible. In this province it is a bottomless pit. With this particular project area (transportation agreement), it seems to be the emphasis of the (provincial) government to provide access roads to remote communities so that the residents can leave the community." Native and other observers have long suggested that a lack of real economic development has simply made it easier for natives to use the new roads to relocate in more established communities.

Manitoba

In Manitoba, analysts reviewing the Northlands Development Agreement (1982–89) came to the same conclusions reached by consultants in Saskatchewan and Alberta. Ottawa and Manitoba pumped more than $200 million into the northern part of the province during the seven-year period. In the end, only one thing had changed: more native residents were collecting welfare. Total welfare payments by Indian Affairs to reserve residents increased 30 per cent by 1986, from $20.5 million to $26.7 million. The analysts were left with the impression that the only people to benefit from the native programs were non-natives from southern Manitoba who moved north to take advantage of the construction activity.

On Their Own: Business Success

Ottawa's negative attitudes towards reserves, typified by the comments of former minister McKnight and others, stem from frustration over the inability to improve conditions. Many Canadians who share this attitude believe that reserves are nothing more than a drain on national resources. Others, who recognize Ottawa's failings, see that these communities are opportunities waiting to be developed. Every native community needs an infrastructure of grocery and hardware stores, repair shops, and clothing outlets, but in most cases these stores have been created and operated by non-native business people. The success rate of Indian entrepreneurs shows that, when left to manage their own affairs, they can and do thrive: The Quebec Cree own an airline, Creebec Air. The Pas band in northern Manitoba is the area's second largest employer, operating a successful multimillion dollar shopping complex across the river from The Pas, a non-native community. Alberta Indians operate Peace Hills Trust, a trust company in western Canada. The Squamish Indians of British Columbia have turned lucrative land holdings adjacent to Vancouver into a multimillion dollar operation. Indian leaders offer these ventures as proof that, with control of funds, they can survive and thrive without welfare or Ottawa's misguided and wasteful programs.

Indian entrepreneurs have also increasingly turned to the private sector for both funding and advice. Canada's business community is slowly responding, having long ago concluded from its own experience that Ottawa lacks the expertise to implement its big-budget programs. "I don't mean this in any negative way but government is highly expenditure oriented," Cliff Boland, former president of the Canadian Council on Native Business, said in 1989. "What do they know about making profit, retaining earnings and re-investing back into the business?"

The council is a coalition of the country's top business leaders who feel obligated to help natives starting out in the business world. The list of the council's supporters includes the chairs and chief executive officers of many prominent businesses in Canada, such as Northern Telecom, General Foods, Brascan, Cadillac Fairview, Nova Corp, Xerox Canada, Shoppers Drug Mart, and IBM Canada. Since 1984, the council has been working with native entrepreneurs, offering advice and contacts, but not financial support. The organization also operates an internship program, placing native people with firms to learn business skills they can later apply to their own companies.

According to Boland, Ottawa's efforts have concentrated only on short-term job creation and training projects. "Native people don't lack for the amount of government-oriented training. One of our success stories had gone to eight different training programs. She's one of the best educated people I've ever met. But she's never been shown how to set up a business or how to manage." Native people interested in entrepreneurial business have no guidance for starting out or avoiding mistakes. "We don't want to change their culture or tradition. We want to share with them our skills and our business network that they don't have."

A guilty conscience has prompted more than one business leader to join the council. "So long as we have this Third World in our own country, we have a soft underbelly in society that has to be addressed," says Don Noble, former executive vice-president of Northern Telecom and past chair of the council. "On top of that, we all have deep down within us some feeling of a need to put something back and we're better [able] to do that with native people who've been too harshly disadvantaged over the years."

Nontraditional Financing Methods

The 1983 economic development study prepared for the Penner Report suggested that Ottawa believed most of the Indian projects would fail, leaving federal bureaucrats less than enthusiastic about lending support and money for new ventures. This attitude places budding native entrepreneurs in a bind, because they need Ottawa's financing. The Indian Act prevents Indian land from being mortgaged, which in turn makes it impossible to mortgage a house sitting on that property. As a result, Indians have next to nothing to offer a lending institution as collateral for raising the kind of capital needed to launch a business. They need access to private capital to finance their ventures. Some native people favour the creation of an Indian bank that provides risk capital and investment experience. In Toronto, Martin Connell and Linda Haynes have shown Ottawa and the Canadian business community that such a venture can work, by starting their own lending institution, Calmeadow.

The initiative by Haynes and Connell, president of Conwest Explorations Inc. and former chair of Toronto's Skydome, stems from a deeply held belief about sharing their good fortune with Canada's disadvantaged people. Calmeadow (formerly, the Calmeadow Foundation) borrowed its operating principles from an experiment first carried out in Bangladesh twenty years ago. In this scenario, a "loan circle" is established among a small group of individuals who need financing to start their own businesses but do not have the necessary collateral. Five to seven people vouch for each other's character and commitment to repay each loan they receive. The first two people obtain a small loan, and if the repayments are made, the next two individuals are given loans. The process is repeated every two months. In 1987, Calmeadow became the first such institution in North America to use the "peer group lending" model, working exclusively with individuals on Indian bands who wanted to start or expand a business. Calmeadow provides funds for the initial loans, and that money is lent out again in subsequent loans. If someone misses a payment, the "circle" is broken, and the loans stop until repayment resumes.

In 1990, Calmeadow separated itself from the daily loan operations and left those issues in local Indian hands. The organization now works with established and aspiring entrepreneurs on reserves, who become the founding members of a loan fund. The fund members administer the loans and encourage the formation of smaller loan circles. By the end of 1994, the Calmeadow experiment was clearly a success story. Loan funds are operating in eleven Indian communities from Ontario to British Columbia and in Iqaluit, Northwest Territories. A total of 319 individuals had received loans, as of October 1994, with a payback rate of 95 per cent. The typical loan is about $1,200; no loan exceeds $3,000. The cumulative amount loaned since 1987 is more than $500,000. As of October 1994, $80,500 is tied up in 111 active loans.

The typical loan applicant on an Indian reserve is often a woman operating a craft venture. Calmeadow's statistics reveal that 57 per cent of loan applicants are women. Phyllis McLeod used her first loan to purchase a heavy-duty sewing machine, which allowed her to offer custom sewing and alterations in her community of Merritt, British Columbia. McLeod is a member of the Sunrise circle in Merritt; she receives its administrative support from the Skikiy Loan Fund, located in Nicola Valley, northeast of Vancouver. McLeod is a 1989 graduate of the Nicola Valley Institute of Technology with a diploma in Fashion Design.

In southwestern Ontario, Rhonda Longboat wanted to start a riding stable operation, but she lacked the funds. Longboat formed a circle with three other people from the Walpole Island First Nation reserve and obtained a $1,000 loan from the Three Fires Development Loan Fund; she used this loan to finance a larger government loan that allowed her to purchase paddock fencing for her horses. Longboat and her family now operate Pottowatomi Stables with five horses.

The success of the loan funds and their loan circles on Indian reserves prompted Haynes and Connell (who is also chair of the Canadian Centre for Philanthropy) to establish similar groups in Toronto (1994), Vancouver (1992), and Nova Scotia (1991), which are open to any disadvantaged group or individuals. To date, including the native program, almost $1 million has been loaned in such a manner to 595 individuals. Calmeadow is also working overseas, with local credit partners; it is helping more than 700,000 self-employed people in Bolivia, Colombia, Kenya, South Africa, Bangladesh, and the Philippines.

The Calmeadow approach could be one key to developing basic infrastructures on reserves. If reserve residents were to spend their money — obtained from welfare or wages — on reserve businesses, cash would stay within the community, instead of leaving the reserve and supporting non-native business.

Set-Aside Contracts

Indians living in major cities and on reserves close to urban centres see the potential of another concept called "set-aside contracts." For several years, Stan Fulham in Winnipeg and Joe Miskokomon in Toronto have been promoting this approach to native economic development, which has already proved successful in the United States. In this model, government contracts awarded to private industries must contain a subcontract for part of the work to go to native businesses.

"If General Motors is going to be making light tanks in London (Ontario), then a certain amount of it has to be contracted out to light industry on reserves," says Miskokomon, former grand chief of the Union of Ontario Indians. He believes that Indians on reserves can compete in the business world if they are given help to get started. Ottawa and the provincial governments must help bring the Indian community into the Canadian mosaic, according to Miskokomon, and reserves should also be seeking ways to act as suppliers for larger, well-established industries in neighbouring urban communities. "The economics of Indian communities is not big enough to sustain business. You have to attract it. You either attract it into the community or you manufacture something that will be produced for someone outside in a bigger industry."

Fulham maintains that the set-aside contract model would also work in cities where a mall or industrial park is owned and operated by native entrepreneurs. Small businesses, such as a barber shop or shoemaker, could survive alongside a larger "anchor tenant." On the scale of a supermarket or light industry manufacturer, the anchor tenant would act as the beneficiary of government contracts and ensure the financial stability of the mall. "We can manufacture anything you can think of...salt and pepper shakers, pencils, whatever," says Fulham, head of a nonprofit, native, co-operative-housing venture in Winnipeg and former secretary of the Manitoba Métis Federation. "The native community would have something they can identify with but it wouldn't only be supported by native people. It would be supported by the community as well." Businesses in the mall would share costs and management skills to help each other succeed. "Basically what it is, is an incubator. You incubate small native businesses."

The years of lobbying by Miskokomon and Fulham for set-aside contracts may soon bear fruit. Such a concept was a component of the Liberal Party's Red Book in the 1993 federal election. Though the Liberal government has yet to enact any of those promises for Indian economic development, its election campaign included changing federal procurement policies to stimulate the growth of native businesses, which is key to the introduction of set-aside contracts. Thus, before Ottawa purchases goods or services from any supplier, that supplier would have to ensure native participation in the project. In addition, the Liberal campaign of 1993 promised to explore new ways of obtaining financing for Indian business ventures and community development projects, including the creation of National Aboriginal Development banks. The Liberals believed that such institutions would be financed by the Canadian corporate community and wealthy Indian communities. This bank would be allowed to issue bonds, which Canadians could purchase to finance Indian ventures. More than a year into its mandate, however, the Liberal government has yet to make those changes to federal procurement policies or develop new banks.

Twenty-five years ago, Canada's native people embarked on a new path, intent on regaining complete control over their lives within a self-government framework. Tremendous strides have been made in local administration, child welfare, education, and housing. But economic development, the area that was to have financed all the others, has suffered repeated setbacks under Ottawa's guidance. Ottawa's achievement of only marginal improvements in overall living conditions has kept the majority of Indian people trapped in Hawthorn's world of misery, poverty, and violence, and slowed progress in other areas. Worse still, the wasteful spending of billions of dollars on programs that were bound to fail has led many non-native Canadians to believe that it is time to curb any further spending and cast the Indian community off to fend for itself.

Despite the obstacles Ottawa has thrown in their path, Indians still harbour the desire and hope to end their dependency on welfare. There remain, however, many uncertainties; for example, will gambling become the new buffalo? Will the Chrétien government fulfil its 1993 election promise to finance Indian business ventures? The wealth, and subsequent power, generated by casinos could solve all of the problems facing the native community, or it could make them worse. The Chrétien government has raised expectations and, at the very least, signalled that Ottawa is willing to break from a past reliance on failed policy initiatives. Long-term success may still lie with the development of an entrepreneurial class within the Indian community, a group of people with the imagination and will power to create the necessary wealth and jobs. Indian business success stories across the country grow in number every year, becoming models for the community and offering proof that native people can survive in the business world. Surprisingly, they are thriving with advice and financial support from the Canadian business community. Canada's business leaders, unlike many federal and provincial politicians and bureaucrats, have concluded that with careful guidance, native people can effect real change within their communities.

6

Health Care

For more than a generation, the federal government has stated that its goal is to raise the standard of health of Canada's aboriginal people to the general level of well-being enjoyed by most other Canadians. But the bulk of available evidence indicates that federal government expenditures, the billions spent for Indian health care since the late 1960s, and all of the accompanying bureaucratic and medical goodwill have been far from sufficient. In 1961, the life expectancy of Canada's aboriginal people stood at sixty-one years, a full decade less than that of other Canadians. In 1991, that discrepancy had not changed: according to the Canadian Research Insitute, the life expectancy for aboriginal women was 60.2 years compared to 76.3 years for non-aboriginal women.

Most health care statistics show this discrepancy. Throughout the 1960s, health studies and information provided by medical field workers painted a distressing picture: Native infant mortality rates stood at more than double the national average. Sexually transmitted diseases, accidental and violent deaths, alcohol abuse, and teenage pregnancies were all serious problems in aboriginal communities that the government had targeted for special attention. Tuberculosis, which was rare in the general Canadian population at the time, and respiratory diseases were wreaking havoc in the impoverished native population. To add insult to injury, noncompetitive salaries and arduous, sometimes violent working conditions were causing chronic nursing staff shortages, particularly in remote regions, leaving those in the field — native or non-native — overworked and frustrated.

Not much has changed since the sixties. Infant mortality rates and the incidence of diseases such as tuberculosis, which are linked to substandard living conditions, have improved somewhat, but even these rates remain well above national averages. "Infant mortality rates are generally considered to be a powerful reflection of underlying disparities in socioeconomic conditions and health care services," John O'Neil, a researcher with the Northern Health Research Unit, Department of Community Health Services at the University of Manitoba, told the Royal Commission on Aboriginal Peoples in 1993. Between 1984 and 1988, the infant mortality rate in Canada stabilized at 7.8 deaths per 1,000 live births. This figure compared to rates of 19.9 per 1,000 for the Inuit and 17.7 per 1,000 for the registered Indian population. In November 1993, the *Globe and Mail* reported on Statistics Canada figures showing that status Indians were forty-three times as likely to contract tuberculosis than non-aboriginal people born in Canada. The rate of tuberculosis was reported to be 81.3 cases per 100,000 for status Indians in 1992, compared with 1.9 per 100,000 for non-aboriginal people born in Canada. The figure for all aboriginal people stood at 60.8 per 100,000; the rate for Canadians as a whole was 7.4 per 100,000.

Despite the depressing figures, probably the most frustrating trend for those working in the field of aboriginal health is that the few gains that have been made have been offset by problems elsewhere. In fact, health officials point out that, after twenty-five years of non-native medical intervention in the native community, old health problems have simply been replaced by new ones.

By the 1990s, cancer and cardiovascular disease, rare among native people at the turn of the century, had become the second most common killers. Diabetes, once unheard of among Indians, had reached epidemic proportions in many communities, with levels more than three times the national average for people living off-reserve. According to the 1991 Census, the disability rate for aboriginal people stood at 31 per cent or 117,090 people, more than double the 15 per cent reported by other Canadians. For Indians living on reserves, the rate was even higher at 33 per cent. For aboriginal people between the ages of fifteen and thirty-four, the rate was three times the national rate.

Sexually transmitted diseases are out of control, with some estimates putting their incidence at ten times the Canadian average. Studies presented to the royal commission's 1993 round table on aboriginal health estimated that eight out of ten aboriginal women had experienced some form of sexual abuse. This statistic has raised fears in the medical profession about the devastating impact AIDS will have on remote communities, once it is introduced. Fetal alcohol syndrome, the result of alcohol abuse, has also become a lethal health problem.

"Participants indicated that current rates of alcohol abuse and sexually transmitted diseases will likely result in epidemic conditions for AIDS and fetal alcohol syndrome," notes the commission's final report on the conference. "If this occurs, the service needs will far exceed the resources currently available to aboriginal communities that have assumed responsibility for delivering health services on behalf of the federal government."

Furthermore, death rates among the registered Indian population in 1991 were two to four times the Canadian average. Violence, including suicides and accidents, remains the number one killer of Canada's aboriginal people, and is closely linked to alcohol and drug abuse. According to 1991 figures compiled by the Canadian Research Institute, accidents, poisonings, and violence accounted for more than 33 per cent of aboriginal deaths, compared with 9 per cent for the Canadian population as a whole. Aboriginal people die in fires at a rate that is seven times that for the rest of Canadians. John O'Neil told the commission that "while diseases of the circulatory system (heart disease and stroke) and neoplasms (cancer) are the major killers of most Canadians, aboriginal people die primarily from injuries and poisonings, causes that are clearly related to socio-economic conditions and, hence, preventable." The royal commission was also told that, in 1984, the suicide rates among aboriginal people stood at 43.5 per 100,000 compared with 13.7 per 100,000 for the Canadian population as a whole and that suicide was especially prevalent among aboriginal youth between fifteen and twenty-four years of age. As high as these rates are, they show a substantial decline from the 64 per 100,000 recorded in 1981. The figures are even higher among aboriginal people between the ages of fifteen and twenty-four. In addition, an earlier study notes that, between 1974 and 1987, one-quarter of all family-related murders in Canada involved native people.

If there is one signicant outcome of the past twenty-five years, it is that frustrated health officials throughout the country are speaking as one; they are insisting that native people are dying from diseases linked to self-destructive lifestyles, poverty-stricken environments, and the legacy of intervention by non-native society. None of these illnesses will respond to improved medicines or other medical interventions. "The further message that comes through," notes Louis T. Montour in his written introduction to the commission's round table report, "is that no health or social issue can be 'cured' if the problems are approached in a piecemeal fashion. Health issues must all be addressed as part of a systematic understanding of the links between oppression and self-destruction."

The sentiment that native health cannot be viewed from the narrow prism of disease rates has echoed throughout dozens of major health studies and initiatives since the 1960s. Still, little has changed. The 1991 Census, for example, found that 50 per cent of native Canadians lived in crowded conditions, a rate far higher than in the rest of the country, and that 20 per cent of native homes were in need of repair, compared with 8 per cent for the country as a whole. Tuberculosis has long been linked to crowded living conditions. Employment rates were also depressingly low for aboriginal Canadians. The cure, medical officials say, is beyond their jurisdiction. The solution can only be found in the political realm and in the wholesale acceptance of native self-determination and control.

Jurisdiction for Health Care

Like the equally complex issue of native justice, Indian health was not specifically mentioned in the 1969 White Paper. While the government's new philosophy would have some impact on all aspects of native affairs, the departments of Indian Affairs and Health and Welfare were expected to carry out their work separately, with only a nodding acquaintance. At the time, the two departments communicated through an interdepartmental committee. This process was a sore point for many who had long complained that clearer lines of communication might help to eliminate duplicated services or to ensure that everyone was working on common goals. The familiar question of federal versus provincial jurisdiction also entered this debate. The issue of Indian health is a strange animal in the world of federal responsibility for aboriginal people. While Ottawa has for centuries accepted its legal liability (based on treaty agreements) for education, social services, and other basics, the question of who is responsible for the delivery of health services has been unresolved.

Health care is a provincial responsibility in Canada. However, Indians have argued since the signing of the treaties that Ottawa is also responsible for overseeing and funding their health services. As proof, native people point to Treaty 6, signed in 1867, between Canada and the Crees of the provinces now known as Alberta and Saskatchewan, which refers to the provision of a medicine chest "at the house of each Indian agent for the use and benefit of the Indians at the direction of the agent."

Despite native insistence, Ottawa long argued that the provinces were ultimately responsible for native health care. However, the federal government accepted most of the burden of administrating Indian health services on an "interim basis" on "moral grounds," because they recognized that most provinces were ill-equipped to handle the complex needs of the residents of remote communities. As a result, native health care carved its own path, outside of the Indian Affairs portfolio.

The maturation of native health — specifically who controls the administration and related services — has lagged about a decade behind the development of other native issues in Canada. In 1945, the department of Indian Affairs handed over responsibility for the delivery of Indian health services to Health and Welfare Canada. A reorganization of field services in 1962 resulted in the creation of Health and Welfare's Medical Services Branch. The branch has continued to serve as native health overseer for the delivery of both treatment and public health programs in remote areas ever since.

In August 1969, the health services consulting firm of Booz Allen Hamilton Canada Ltd., commissioned to study Indian health operations, released its report detailing for the first time the abhorrent conditions native people faced. The report's recommendations fell into two categories: short-term proposals dealing with the acute inadequacies of services and environmental conditions leading to disease, and long-term proposals highlighting the need to change the socioeconomic conditions of Indian life. "To improve health services without making concurrent improvement in living conditions is analogous to treating the symptoms rather than the disease," stated the report. "In the long run, the provinces and Indians themselves should assume the responsibility for providing health services to Indians." The report envisioned the provinces taking over the major role in Indian health care within a decade.

After the Booz Allen report, federal authorities continued to espouse their long-standing policy of refusing to take responsibility. "Despite popular misconception of the situation and vigorous assertions to the contrary, neither the federal nor any other government has any formal obligation to provide Indians or anyone else with free medical services," stated the 1969 Health and Welfare annual report. That view was reinforced the same year by then Native Affairs minister John Munro, speaking at a federal-provincial conference of health ministers. "There is no contract on health services between the Indians and the federal government," he said. While Ottawa had delivered services "up to now," the government said that, "where there are good facilities, as there are in the southern parts of the provinces, the federal government felt that the provinces should be asked to assume the same responsibilities for Indians and non-Indians alike."

The Delivery of Health Care Services

Like Indian Affairs, the Medical Services Branch has struggled with the daunting task of delivering services to the widely dispersed and diverse native population. And, like Indian Affairs, the branch has for decades often responded to the multitude of practical problems — from chronic staff shortages to the sheer logistics of delivering services in the remote northern regions — with an almost arrogant self-confidence.

No one disputes the sometimes heroic efforts made by many in the medical profession to improve the lives of native people. However, there is also a plethora of research outlining a litany of sins, from the rejection of traditional Indian medicine by medical services, to the removal of children needing medical treatment from their home communities for months and even years at a time, with little explanation to the families. Some evidence also suggests that medical intervention throughout the 1970s bordered on criminal activity. In 1977, for example, a Jesuit priest working with the Inuit on Holman Island questioned what he perceived to be a government program aimed at sterilizing Inuit women.

Aboriginal birth rates have long been an issue of study for medical experts. Until the mid-1940s, the birth rates for both status and non-status Indians remained stable at about 40 births per 1,000 people. This number climbed until the 1970s, when it dropped from a high of 47 to 29 per 1,000, a figure which was still almost twice the national rate. Medical experts point to a multitude of reasons for the sharp decline. Improved health services for the native population meant that women who wanted sterilization or needed hysterectomies because of problems related to multiple births and sexually transmitted diseases were more likely to receive that care. As well, the branch's educational programs had some impact on the use of birth control. But there were also indicators that at least part of the decline was the result of an overzealous pro-sterilization policy. The rise in birth rates in the late 1980s and early 1990s (to three times the non-aboriginal rates) calls into question more innocent theories.

One medical expert in Manitoba described the reaction in the mid-1970s when he and his staff first arrived in the north and found a thriving operating-room business. "When we got involved we were surprised to figure out how on earth some of those [operating rooms] were kept open two and three days a week in reasonably small communities," recalls Brian Postl, head of Manitoba's Northern Medical Unit, which oversees the delivery of health care to Manitoba's remote native communities for the federal Medical Services Branch. "A very common procedure of those [operating rooms] was hysterectomies. No question. And we stopped that." While he has never seen any data to prove that a written or unwritten sterilization policy existed between doctors and the government, Postl says rumours were circulating among medical experts. "Certainly, anecdotally, that's something we have all heard about and [it] probably did go on." Compounding these events were all the smaller sins committed by a non-native medical profession trying to impose its will on a people who had survived for centuries on its own.

According to John O'Neil, such events, coupled with a devolution policy in Indian Affairs, led to the introduction in the 1970s of a handful of initiatives that began the transfer of control over health services to native people. In 1975, the federal and Quebec governments signed an agreement with the James Bay Cree and the Inuit of Nunavik to create the first aboriginal health and social services boards in Canada. The same year, native leaders took over the federal National Native Alcohol and Drug Abuse Program. Still, the idea of handing real control over health services to native people was not very popular and would take much longer to be realized.

In 1979, however, an event occurred that appeared, in some ways, to set the administration of Indian health care on an entirely new path. At the opening of a native-run facility called the Battlefords Indian Health Centre in northwestern Saskatchewan, an official of the Medical Services Branch delivered a speech outlining a new federal policy, "The Three Pillars," on the question of native health.

This policy set a new direction for future native health services, and, among other things, comprised what appeared to be a sudden, unwavering admission of federal responsibility for native health care. While the NIB (today known as the AFN) had been pressuring the government to re-examine its stance, few leaders were aware that a new policy was to be announced that day. "Policy for federal programs for Indian people (of which the health policy is an aspect), flows from constitutional and statutory provisions, treaties and customary practice," stated the two-page document. "The Federal Government recognizes its legal and traditional responsibilities to Indians, and seeks to promote the ability of Indian communities to pursue their aspirations within the framework of Canadian institutions."

What a difference a decade makes. Ten years earlier, the Medical Services Branch was reluctantly agreeing to administer Indian health services on an "interim" basis. Suddenly, in 1979, with no advance warning, but with Indian demands for greater control growing across the country, the branch appeared to suddenly admit responsibility, and more. "The Federal Indian Health Policy is based on the special relationship of the Indian people to the Federal Government, a relationship which both the Indian people and the Government are committed to preserving." This "special relationship," according to the policy's second pillar, would be strengthened by "opening up communication with Indian people and by encouraging their greater involvement in planning, budgeting and delivery of health programs."

With the announcement, the bureaucracy of the Medical Services Branch, once engrossed in providing health services and gathering statistics measuring disease and mortality rates, slowly began to focus instead on the creation and implementation of a complex, multistep transfer plan, which would have to be adopted by Indian bands before any degree of control was relinquished.

The most important pillar underwrote all other changes: it stated, in nonspecific terms, that health improvements must be built, first and foremost, on "community development, both socioeconomic development and cultural and spiritual development to remove the conditions of poverty and apathy which prevent the members of the community from achieving a state of physical, mental and social well-being." This refrain, repeated for decades, is as much in vogue in the 1990s as it was in 1979, or in 1969.

For those people at the Battlefords Centre that day, it appeared, at first glance, that the Medical Services Branch had done a complete about-face. However, a closer look at the Three Pillars showed that, ultimately, change would be neither easy nor quick. Despite the total rejection by native people a decade earlier of Chrétien's White Paper and government assurances to Indian leaders that those policies were not being implemented, the Three Pillars announcement of 1979 served notice that the federal bureaucracy was still attempting to persuade the provinces to assume a larger piece of the administration of Indian services.

The third pillar specified the administrators and their responsibilities in the complex framework of the future Indian health care system. The federal government would oversee "public health activities on reserves, health promotion, and the detection and mitigation of hazards to health in the environment." The provinces would participate in the "diagnosis and treatment of acute and chronic disease and the rehabilitation of the sick." This role greatly increased the provinces' responsibilities, both financially and administratively. And native people, listed last and given the least to do, were to be responsible for the promotion of health and "adaptation of health services delivery to the specific needs of their community." Despite the contradictions and political infighting that have plagued the relationship between the native community and the government for decades, the document included no plans for the elimination of the Medical Services Branch once transfer was accomplished. Like Indian Affairs's dealings with the native community throughout the 1970s, the branch's "special relationship" was to be fostered for all it was worth.

Searching for a Cure

In 1980, Justice Thomas Berger of the British Columbia Supreme Court was appointed head of a federal commission to, once again, study and make recommendations on Indian and Inuit health services. The familiar refrain reverberated across the country: native health care could no longer be treated in isolation. "The matter of Indian health care is critical," wrote Berger in his final report. "The reason is that so many of the causes of Indian ill-health lie beyond the fact of the illness itself, and the remedies lie beyond the mandate of the [Medical Services Branch]." He recommended, among other things, that a national conference on native health be convened. It never materialized.

Cynics also suggest that the 1979 Three Pillars policy was, in fact, little more than a thinly disguised manoeuvre to guarantee the survival of the Medical Services Branch by forging a new role for the federal department in the midst of all the transfer confusion. "Transfer does not mean goodbye," Health minister Jake Epp told Indian delegates at a 1987 conference on health transfer in Montreal. "It means a new relationship between two partners, both equally dedicated to improving the health and quality of life of your people." Regardless of the underlying motives, plenty of evidence shows that the all-important pillar of the new health policy did not trigger the necessary massive federal initiatives, financial or otherwise. No pro-grams surfaced to attack the diseases that were claiming Canada's native people and contributing to such poor health statistics. Instead, most of the energies of the key players were devoured by the details of transferring authority for health care to often ill-prepared native bands under the umbrella of growing self-government initiatives.

Throughout the 1980s and 1990s, the system was caught in the "pre-transfer stage," according to the Medical Services Branch; in-dividual bands were given funding to prepare a feasibility study on assuming the responsibility for health care services. The sheer com-plexity of the transfer plans eventually devised by the Medical Serv-ices Branch, as well as some of the negotiating tactics, indicates that the branch was mimicking several aspects of Indian Affairs's model of self-government initiatives in the transfer of control to Indians; native leaders have long held up these tactics as evidence of the lack of true intentions.

First of all, the branch essentially agreed to transfer a non-native bureaucratic system, including all notions of decision making and the hierarchy found in the current system. The plan was devoid of any native cultural component, and it offered little room or opportunity for such accommodation. Indian leaders have argued that, if transfer was truly being conducted with the ultimate goal of self-government, then both the control being transferred and the process itself were so restrictive as to guarantee failure. For example, only mandated pro-grams were being offered for transfer, with no option of moving funds from one program to another. Therefore, services that might have offered surplus funds because of effective preventative pro-gramming or simple underutilization, such as dental care and trans-portation, were being tendered out to private contractors and were not on the transfer block.

Second, the government was not offering any new funding, despite Health minister Jake Epp's admission in 1987 that it would cost Indians more to administer the same services Health and Welfare has been struggling to handle on limited resources for decades. Epp also warned that once they assumed control, Indian bands would be solely responsible for any deficits they incurred.

Third, fear, on the part of native leaders and bureaucrats, played an important role in the process. Like others before them, branch officials were apprehensive about the ability of Indian leaders to handle everything from managing their own programs considering the political realities at the band level, to the deterioration of pro-

grams deemed imperative under Indian control. Thus, Indian bands
looking at transfer proposals were, and continue to be, faced with a
barrage of rules, including spending restrictions, non-negotiable programs such as immunization, and negative attitudes about everything
from traditional medicine to home births.

During the 1987 National Indian Health Transfer Conference,
organized by the AFN, Health minister Jake Epp discussed the problems plaguing the transfer process. While he noted that bands and
tribal councils were managing 25 per cent of the national Indian
health services budget in 1987, he admitted that the restrictions on
the allocation of funds and the choice of programs to be offered were
the source of numerous difficulties.

Epp's remarks echoed evidence given to a 1982 parliamentary
committee, chaired by Liberal MP Keith Penner. As in other entan-
glements with Indian Affairs, native leaders complained that transfer
was an illusion. "Indian witnesses were quick to point out that the
devolution of health programs did not include transfer of control,"
reported Penner. "Real power remained with Health and Welfare."
The leaders referred to Epp's vision of the branch's role after transfer. Based on the view that Parliament is ultimately accountable for
tax money, Epp stated that, in its new role, the branch would serve
as a watchdog, and review annual financial and community planning
reports to ensure that money was being spent according to the transfer agreement. As well, branch staff would serve as technical and
teaching advisors for the bands.

It is within this context that bands considered the issue of power
transfer. In 1993, the Royal Commission on Aboriginal Peoples held
a round table on native health care. During the three-day conference,
participants expressed their frustration over the evaluation procedures the department of Health imposed on the transfer process.
Alma Favel-King, executive director of the Health and Social Development portfolio for the Federation of Saskatchewan Indian Nations,
spoke of native communities that had taken advantage of new funding and the transfer plans:

> This funding initiative has enabled First Nations to test
> their own ability to manage programs and to remove cul-
> tural and language barriers to health care services. The
> services controlled and delivered by First Nations are
> more acceptable to people and have in many instances
> resulted in an increase [in] demand. The limited resources

available through the initiative do not allow flexibility to meet the increased demand for services, however, particularly with respect to mental health programming. The federal government has consistently refused to consider funding activities they consider to be 'program enrichments' through the Health Transfer program. This has seriously hampered the ability of First Nations to fully address their specific health priorities within the confines of historical spending by the government and forced them to spend valuable resources to develop proposals and lobby for funding from other sources.

The commission heard complaints that improvements in native health care were also being held up by a lack of communication at the federal level. Restructuring in both the Indian Affairs and Health and Welfare departments, in response to government attempts to streamline the bureaucracy, had not been conducted with the needs of native people in mind, charged Favel-King. "The restructuring...has not resulted in improved communication and co-ordinated planning between the two federal departments but rather has left many key regional staff scrambling to identify what their roles and responsibilities are under the new structures. Again, the needs and goals of First Nations do not seem to be reflected in these organizational changes," noted Favel-King.

"Vented in this context was the lack of consultation and co-ordination among federal departments, such as Indian Affairs and Health and Welfare, and particularly among Health and Welfare and provincial departments of health," stated the commission's report on the round table. "While some communities understand funding strategies and are able to exploit opportunities, other communities are ill-informed about the various protocols in place and often miss out on program opportunities because of an overall lack of co-ordination on the part of...funders."

Despite the problems, many bands had been moving ahead with transfer plans, believing that control, even of a troubled, underfinanced bureaucracy, is better than no control at all. The first Health Program Transfer initiative was signed in 1988 (with Montreal Lake). By 1990, eight transfer agreements had been reached, and sixty-seven pre-transfer initiatives had been launched, according to information submitted to the royal commission. To some native leaders, however, these agreements simply added too little money and limited control to the still unanswered question of who, ultimately, is responsible. These bands refuse to become the "administrators of [their] own misery." They argue that these transfer initiatives are traps, similar to those set by Indian Affairs in other fields — intricate plots to renege on both the federal government's obligation as legal trustee and the accompanying financial burdens, by shifting the responsibility onto the shoulders of provincial governments and Indians themselves.

Despite Ottawa's claim of responsibility in 1979, some critics point out that the federal government has never admitted to a "treaty right" to health. "The question is," Favel-King told the royal commission, "if First Nations are agreeing to transfer, are they in fact defining their treaty right to health in the future?" Specifically, Favel-King worried that native rights to health could be defined by the transfer agreements signed with the government and not by any recognized treaty right. "It can be argued that the treaty right to health is being defined by various policies being instituted and enforced by bureaucrats within the federal government," she said. For example, she noted a contract Medical Services Branch signed with Blue Cross to administer some services within the branch. The contract resulted in a marked limitation on the drugs available to aboriginal people. Native leaders have had little power to stop this kind of contract, or to stop other changes occurring within the Medical Services Branch. "What is apparent, in fact," added Favel-King, "is that the treaty right to health is being defined by economic conditions of the national and regional government, not by an understanding of treaty obligations."

Some Indians believe that the Battlefords Centre and the handful of bands that wrestled a degree of control in the late 1970s and early 1980s, long before transfer became the *cause célèbre* of the federal government, are the lucky ones. "There wasn't a whole heap of planning," said Charlotte Johnson, a Manitoba director of the Medical Services Branch, about the dozen bands who ventured into the control quagmire in the 1970s. "I'm not sure anyone knew what the consequences were. And there were certainly people working on this side of government whose attitude was 'let's transfer.' It's their problem now. There were a lot of growing pains, but I think the programs, by and large, have come out in ten years time to be pretty decent."

The bands that have taken control of health care may have been hampered by a certain naiveté about the complexity of the system, say the envious ones, but they were not hindered by a massive bureaucracy focussed on exactly what and how much was being given up. Certainly, the Battlefords Indian Health Centre and the few others like it offer some insight into what happens when the federal government finally cuts the strings and allows Indians to find their own way.

The Battlefords Centre began with a simple philosophy — to provide culturally appropriate programs for native people. The original directors decided to concentrate on preventative programming, not on the provision of clinical services, since they did not at the time have the expertise at hand. Spending of the centre's $1.5 million annual budget is directed by the chiefs of the eight Saskatchewan bands, who gather for monthly board meetings in the two-storey, modern, cement structure located in the economically depressed area of North Battleford, Saskatchewan. "We don't have a lot of dealings with Medical Services or the federal government," explained then Battlefords Centre director Alma King in 1989. "We're funded by them. But our formal relationship is that we don't report on detailed program activities except for an annual report. And we provide monthly financial reports to them."

Native-Run Health Care

Several issues became apparent after more than a decade of operation. First, and foremost, staff believed they were able to respond to the needs of their communities more effectively than the decentralized Medical Services Branch. The centre was also living proof that fears about pet programs, staff instability, or even program deterioration were groundless. For example, once the need for immunization was explained, band chiefs became active advocates on their reserves, according to Battlefords staff. "Native people are often very scared of different pills and needles," said Larry Wuttunee, chief of the Red Pheasant band and chair of the centre's all-chief health board. "We didn't know what they were before. Now the CHR [community health representative, who is usually native] and the nurse will clearly explain."

The centre's staff, from nurses to community health representatives, are interviewed and hired by the board of chiefs, and the programs are designed with input from the band chiefs; hence, respect grew for the personnel and programs. As a result, the employment environment is more stable than that which existed under federal directions. The vast majority of the staff, 70 per cent of whom are native, have been with the centre from the beginning. "Our people [the centre's staff] have empathy for Indian people," said Jonas Semaganis, chief of the Little Pine band. "That's what makes us unique from other services."

The Battlefords Centre also found that its separation from the Ottawa bureaucracy resulted in a more holistic approach to health, one that often resulted in staff responding not only to the acute health needs of its clientele, but also to some of the underlying causes of native health problems. "If someone comes in off the street for treatment and mentions they are looking for a job but have no resumé, we take the time out and help them write a resumé," says Joanne Lucarz, the centre's community health director in the late 1980s. "That's going to make them healthier. What we try to do here is never say no, that's not our area. And none of the staff say that. That is what is different about Indian organizations. One Indian person will not say to another, 'No, that's not my job.' "

The centre also provides a liaison with the non-native medical establishment. One employee helps smooth interactions between native patients and Battleford-area hospitals. Lucarz, who often finds herself in the role, says the liaison may be called on to translate a doctor's orders into Cree, or to explain traditional native medicine to often impatient and disrespectful hospital staff.

Although Favel-King and Lucarz believe the centre has successfully carved out its own niche, they fear that, if the federal government continues to pay only lip service to the causes of native ill health, the sheer weight of the assignment will destroy the Battlefords Centre and others like it across the country. Lucarz has been told recently by federal officials that, if they had been in power in the 1970s, the centre would not exist. "When you say the feds want Battlefords-type centres to happen, I disagree," Lucarz says. "They don't want a powerful organization like this developing in too many places. Because it is really easy to pick off a band, band by band, but it is really hard to pick off eight bands."

Furthermore, despite the inroads the centre has made in ten years, there are no illusions among the staff that they have cured what ails Indian people. Alcoholism, chronic unemployment, violence, diabetes, and other diseases continue to plague native people here, as they do elsewhere in the country, but there are no specific statistics in Ottawa to support this. "In the first years, I was collecting a lot of good stats, but the other zones weren't," explains Lucarz. "We looked real bad. So we stopped counting."

"It has occurred to many folks here for a long time that we should stop counting the diseases the Indians are worse at, that we have reached the point of knowledge that we know they are in big trouble in terms of health," said Brian Postl of the Manitoba Northern Medical Unit in 1989. The unit, connected with the University of Manitoba, is under contract with the Medical Services Branch to provide health services to twenty-five northern Indian communities in the province. "We can get more and more specific and we can do more and more studies defining another disease that they have more trouble with, but at some point we have to take the step to link health status with socioeconomic conditions, social pathologies, alcohol and drug abuse. Health becomes an economic development issue." In northern Saskatchewan, at the Battlefords Centre in 1989, director Alma King talked about the 80 per cent unemployment rate in the bands her centre serves, the alcoholism, and the federal government's approach to the problems. "I think Ottawa is more concerned with what its jurisdiction is and not getting involved in other things because it would be setting a precedent."

Another statistic that has shown depressingly little improvement over the last twenty-five years is the number of native people who have entered the health profession. Unlike the growth in the number of aboriginal lawyers, the numbers of native doctors, nurses, and other health care professionals have almost remained stagnant. According to Health and Welfare figures, in 1983, 200 health care professionals out of 325,000 across the country were of native ancestry; this number included sixteen doctors, four dentists, and one pharmacist. In 1993, there were fifty-one aboriginal physicians, one physical therapist, and one speech pathologist. The burden on this small group was immense, and burn-out had become a serious issue by the time the royal commission held its hearings in March 1993. Even improvements in salaries and working conditions have failed to cure chronic nursing shortages, making the erratic delivery of programs — by natives and non-natives — almost a disease in itself.

In 1989, Brian Postl felt that any support on the native health care issue from the Canadian Medical Association (CMA), similar to the endorsement given by the Canadian Bar Association for a separate native justice system, would be years away. He argued that the legal profession comes face to face in the courts with the failure to take action; however, in health care, only those professionals directly involved with Indians can clearly grasp the situation."I wouldn't say the Canadian Medical Association is unaware. But most folks don't spend much of their time dealing with or being involved with issues relating to Indian health."

Postl was being overly pessimistic. In December 1993, the CMA appeared before the Royal Commission on Aboriginal Peoples to announce that the degree of ill health among natives is unacceptable. It also argued that the solution was not as simple as finding more cures for the various illnesses of native Canadians or finding better ways to provide those services. The answer, the CMA said, lies in the political and legal realm and the resolution of self-government initiatives and land claims. These ideas were echoed by the eighty participants in the March 1993 round table on health sponsored by the commission. *The Path to Healing*, the final report of the round table, noted that few of the participants had spent much time discussing medical statistics; they had already accepted that such analysis had little to do with solutions.

The causes of the problem were repeatedly identified as the "need to secure access to traditional lands and...resources, as well as self-government structures that remove the yoke of colonialism which has damaged the spirit of many aboriginal people," wrote John D. O'Neil, rapporteur for the session. "The participants shared a sense of frustration with the inability of various levels of government and the health care system to respond adequately to the desperate needs in some aboriginal communities," said O'Neil. "This frustration also extended to the round table process, in that many participants felt that further discussion and study on the issues was not moving us closer to solutions."

The panellists also issued warnings against accepting lip service in place of demands for a more pluralistic, integrated, multidisciplined and multisectoral approach to native health care. "Some participants emphasized...that the Euro-Canadian concept of holistic health care, while an important development within Western society, is only a pale reflection of the holistic approach to health that characterizes aboriginal traditions," wrote O'Neil in his overview. "These traditions, which emphasize the multi-dimensional nature of people as physical, mental, emotional and spiritual beings, must inform aboriginal health development."

Concerns were also expressed over the "buck-passing nature of funding opportunities for health development," as well as the failure of aboriginal organizations, "from the band to the national level," to make health services a priority. "Several participants described the sometimes chaotic administrative structures at the band level that inhibit healing and social program development..."

In February 1994, federal and provincial health ministers decided to forge a joint aboriginal health policy. They agreed to twenty recommendations, most of which were simply statements of general principles. No firm commitments were made. "What seems so disturbing," Gary Bohnet, a spokesman for the Métis National Council told the Canadian Press at the time, "is that neither level of government seems willing to tackle the problem head on." A year later, the policy had not materialized.

In spite of critics who have said that native health will never improve in isolation, recognition that native self-government will some day be a reality has been growing in Canada. And, while they may still be out of step, changes in health service delivery for aboriginal people have begun to mimic the advances being made in the political realm. Since the late 1980s, the number of native-driven health initiatives, particularly in Ontario and Quebec, and provincial policy changes that recognize the distinct nature of native health has grown. In November 1994, Ontario Health minister Ruth Grier announced a new policy that included, among other things, an infusion of money and official recognition of traditional forms of aboriginal medicine. As the *Globe and Mail* reported: "The new policy endorses the use of traditional healers, medicine people, midwives and elders." This NDP government initiative came in response to a growing insistence on the part of native leaders over the years that aboriginal methods must be an integral part of native health programs. As well, Grier announced that the native health care budget would increase from $2 million annually to $20 million over five years. "This will include the financing of ten new aboriginal health centres, three new hostels to treat aboriginal patients in Kenora, Timmins and Toronto, and five new youth and family substance-abuse treatment centres and healing lodges." (With the June 1995 election of a Conservative government bent on severe program cuts, there was little hope that the NDP plan would materialize.) In Quebec, programs have been introduced in the past few years that view housing, education and mental health care as components of a broad native health strategy.

"Indian people are becoming more assertive in vocalizing what their needs are," Alma King maintained in 1989. "I think they are becoming more vocal about telling professionals what their needs are instead of being told that this is good for you." "I think their self-destructive tendencies are turning around," said Rita Dozois, a retired

Medical Services Branch nurse with twenty-nine years of experience both within the bureaucracy and on Ontario and Manitoba reserves, in an 1988 interview. "I think Indians are starting to realize they are the only ones who can stop it. But it will take a long time and that's something we modern whites don't have much of. When you stop and think that from the time we reached this country to the time we reduced them to nothing, it took over 200 years. Why do we think they have to recover in ten?"

Meanwhile, the native health care debate rages on, as Brian Postl and other professionals in the field continue their day-to-day fight against disease in native communities. While they labour for major changes, they see examples of both successful native-run centres across the country and others that struggle. They see slow movement towards self-government and the sense of pride native people have in their cultural heritage. And they watch reluctant bureaucrats and apathetic Canadians who allow things to continue as they have in the past.

Postl argues:

> It is entirely in the political purview. We can talk specific disease rates and death rates, but the bottom line ends up being a Cabinet decision. Whether or not to make the commitment to provide every Indian house on a reserve with running water and waste disposal. Whether or not to allow the economic development of some of these communities to proceed....If you look at the areas that are most open to intervention or prevention, you're looking at injuries, accidents, alcohol, violence. Those are all issues of social structure chaos, and social economic development. If we did nothing else but look at those particular areas, we could do more for the health of native people than by almost any other function.

Brian Postl also believes that the final solution rests with the initiative and energy of the native people themselves. The main source of frustration for Postl, however, is that Canadians, for the most part, act as if the native problems do not exist. Following the recession of the 1990s, Canadians seemed even less open to pushing for help for the dispossessed. They unite for injustices elsewhere in the world, argued Postl, but somehow ignore their lack of knowledge and concern about injustices facing their own country's indigenous people. "This is all a very large political issue that the general public doesn't sense is important enough to force action. And until that happens, I think politicians will do enough to make sure that there's nothing of huge embarrassment or scandal. It is really left to the Indian people and their lobbies to influence decisions, and I think they are getting really good at that," says Postl. "If there's despondency, it is that our society as a whole, despite having a huge social system of mores, doesn't trigger into Indian people. Now, is that racism? I think it has to be. It is an ugly word, but it may be. It is a racism of omission."

7

Education

For the staff at the Indian Affairs department, the days of spring and summer of 1989 were unlike any they had seen before. Starting in early March, Indian protestors began occupying every available space in the corridors and reception areas of department offices across the country. Skeptical staff initially viewed the demonstrators with humour. But within a matter of days, the situation escalated into the largest peaceful Indian demonstration in more than twenty years. As the number of protestors increased, the bureaucracy ground to a halt. To keep the office functioning, the police were called in; hundreds of protestors were arrested in offices in Winnipeg and Thunder Bay. In response, several demonstrators started hunger strikes, some of which lasted longer than thirty days. In April, hundreds more, beating drums and bearing placards, gathered at Parliament Hill. In May, the Catholic bishops announced their support for the native demonstrators.

The cause of the disturbance was a decision by then Indian Affairs minister Pierre Cadieux (under the Conservative government of Prime Minister Brian Mulroney) to place a cap on the department's post-secondary education budget, limiting spending to $130 million annually. The Indian community was furious. Just as native children were finally, though in small numbers, taking advantage of all available educational tools, Ottawa was trying to restrict the number of students attending university and college. In keeping with Ottawa's devolution policy, Cadieux's decision meant that band councils would now face the unpopular task of determining which students would receive school funding. Those individuals not chosen would have to seek provincial student loans; more likely, they would not go at all. Of course, Ottawa's decision did not account for the thousands of Indians living in urban centres, who had no band council to approach for funding. With this decision, Indian Affairs violated its own objectives of increasing the number of Indian students attending post-secondary institutions.

To the Indian community, Cadieux's decision was another attempt by Ottawa to frustrate native progress. Aboriginal people have been slowly recovering from the devastation caused by 100 years of government-controlled educational programs, which systematically eliminated their language and culture and ignored their place in history. Having finally gained control of many of their own grade schools and high schools by 1989, Indian leaders had realized the importance of higher education in the revival of their communities. Cadieux's move was a slap in the face to their demands for greater self-determination. They saw no other option but to plead their case before the Canadian public. At stake was an integral component of the future of native people — unrestricted access to post-secondary education. However, in this struggle with Ottawa, the Indian community would ultimately lose.

Just as a record number of young Indian people began to consider university or college education as a real possibility, Ottawa became obsessed with controlling its spending. Before 1989, Ottawa did not have to worry about the cost of the Indian post-secondary education program, because that cost was relatively insignificant. Then, Ottawa imposed a budget, based on enrolment levels, and severe criteria for continued funding support. Although the federal government increased subsequent post-secondary budgets, it was determined to control costs. In that summer of 1989, Cadieux rationalized the cap as a prudent budget measure, and it remains in place today.

Academic Achievement

Native people used to think that reaching university, much less graduating, was an impossible goal. Finishing grade school was often the highest academic achievement for most students, and on some isolated reserves, the situation has not changed. In the twenty-five years since the release of the White Paper, Ottawa has spent more than $7.6 billion on native education with minimal results. Indian students continue to show higher drop-out rates, poorer test scores, and a greater number of grade failures compared to national and provincial averages. The 1986 Census revealed that 37 per cent of the adult Indian population, almost double the national average, was considered illiterate or had less than a Grade 9 education; 5 per cent of Indians graduated from high school, compared to 13 per cent of all students nationally and only 1 per cent of native people were university graduates, when 9 per cent of all Canadians had a university degree. The 1991 Census showed marginal improvements: 28 per cent of the adult Indian population was considered illiterate or had less than a Grade 9 education, and 1.3 per cent of native people were university graduates. Without consulting census material, the department of Indian Affairs would not know the numbers of Indians attending and graduating from university; it stopped collecting that data in 1985. While the level of Indian education has gradually improved since the 1960s, the large discrepancy between the native and non-native communities remains unchanged. In twenty-five years, Ottawa's expenditures on Indian education produced nothing more than a generation of students that are only slightly better educated than their parents.

How could a government spend billions of dollars with little real benefit? Indian leaders blamed a bureaucracy that insisted on hiring non-native instructors from urban centres to teach children who could not speak English. Some bureaucrats blamed the Indians. Other govenment officials appeared blind to classroom reality; they were satisfied simply with the fact that spending on education had increased.

Residential Schools

The federal government's extremely poor record regarding native education has a long history. At the turn of the century, Ottawa struck an agreement with church missionaries operating schools on some reserves. In exchange for boarding an even larger body of Indian students, Ottawa agreed to finance the construction and operation of these schools. Amendments to the Indian Act were passed, authorizing churches to take Indian children from their homes and force them to attend the notorious residential schools. Church leaders, with Ottawa's support, took it upon themselves to "civilize" the Indian children, to give them a "proper" Christian upbringing. For ten months of the year, native children lived at these schools, where beatings and sexual assaults were not uncommon. The children were forbidden to speak their native language or practice their traditional beliefs. Thus began one of the darkest periods in the relationship between Indians and non-native society.

Indian leaders believe that Ottawa deliberately used church institutions to destroy their culture. The high incidence of abuse, which has been cited frequently, is too well documented to be dismissed simply as isolated occurrences or the exaggerations of a few angry individuals. "I personally attended Indian Residential Schools for eleven years and on leaving it took me another eleven years to mentally undo the devastation perpetrated therein by religious and other fanatics," wrote William Clarence Thomas in 1982, a former superintendent of an Indian-run school board in Manitoba. "No one ever hugged us or told us they loved us. We were mere numbers. Strappings, beatings, hair cut to baldness, being tethered to the flag pole, half day school with unqualified tutors, and slave labour the other half were commonplace."

The devastation caused by the residential schools was widespread and enduring. Claims by Indians that these experiences have been the cause of many of their problems today have been supported by clinical studies. Residential education created several generations of people without parenting skills or moral direction. It spawned a multitude of social problems that are now only beginning to be resolved. Peter Hudson, a professor and former director of the University of Manitoba School of Social Work, ties most of the emotional and psychological problems of the native communities — violence, drug and alcohol abuse, child abuse — to the residential schools. "One of the biggest impacts of the residential school system is there are now three generations of kids who are now adults who did not experience a close, normal, family life. Where do we learn how to parent? In the family where we are raised. Yet three generations of kids were raised in institutions. What would they know about parents, family life?"

Hudson says that the trauma of the residential school experience is one of the factors contributing to self-destructive violence. "People in residential schools tell stories about scrubbing themselves for hours to remove their brown colour, of any trace of being Indian." He says that Indians often came to believe that they were worthless, and they started hating themselves. "Some of these people, their lives are a total mess. The inward violence takes various forms. There are no taboos any more. Everything comes up for grabs. It could take the form of child sexual abuse, spousal abuse, alcoholism, delinquency, vandalism. The violence becomes all pervasive. I suggest the violence is there as a result of the thought process, of being thought of as worthless and having no pride in who you are and what you are. The violence follows from that."

Provincial, Federal Schools

Demands from Indian leaders in the late 1940s prompted Ottawa to distance itself from residential schools. A special joint committee of the Senate and the House of Commons held hearings across the country between 1946 and 1948. The hearings became forums for Indian leaders to articulate their displeasure with the residential schools and to demand changes. As a result of the hearings, Ottawa signed formal agreements with individual school boards and provincial education departments for the integrated schooling of Indian and non-Indian children; native students were usually bussed to a neighbouring school in a non-native community. Where such distances were too great, Ottawa began building schools on reserves. The improvements, however, were marginal. The schools offered a "white" education which failed to recognize Indians as human beings. Indian communities had little or no involvement in the "white" school boards or in the operation of the schools on their own reserves.

Oscar Lathlin, former chief of the Opaskwayak First Nation and now a New Democrat member of the Legislative Assembly in Manitoba, comments that, faced with those obstacles, the children of his generation never had a chance. "If you would tell a child right from birth that he's no good, that he's a drunk, that he's not able to hold onto a job, that he's lazy, that he's a welfare bum, that he's just plain no good and you tell him that over and over and over again, by the time that child becomes 16 years old, he actually believes that he's supposed to be lazy."

Lathlin, now forty-seven, has beaten the odds. He graduated from high school, finished one year at university, and spent some time working for Indian Affairs before returning home and entering band politics. He retired as chief of the province's most prosperous band in 1990, turning to provincial politics and winning the seat in the sprawling northern Manitoba riding that encompasses his home. He was re-elected in the 1995 provincial election. Lathlin, like all Indian leaders, believes that education is one of the keys to his people's future. But for education to benefit his people, Lathlin asserts that Indians must take control.

As part of its reaction to the White Paper of 1969, the Indian community began pressuring Ottawa to transfer control of education to native hands. In 1972, the NIB presented its paper, *Indian Control of Education,* to then Indian Affairs minister Jean Chrétien. In line with Ottawa's devolution policy on native affairs, he promised to fulfil Indian demands.

In a speech to provincial education ministers in Regina that same year, Chrétien stated that control of the curriculum, teaching staff, and parental involvement, would be key to the department's devolution policy: "When Indian parents ask that the curriculum recognize their cultural values and customs, their language and their contribution to mankind, do not make a mistake, they are not asking for the moon. Their request is legitimate and reasonable." The new approach, he maintained, would ensure that adequate funds would be provided to upgrade facilities, that teachers would have proper cultural training and continued support, and that culturally relevant material would be added to the classroom curriculum. "Unless we make such provision," he said, "we can expect nothing more in the next twenty years than we have reaped during the past twenty years."

More than twenty years have now passed, and Indian control today amounts to nothing more than administering a service approved by Ottawa and the provinces. "Ottawa sets the formulas, they set the [funding] guidelines," says Joe Miskokomon, former grand chief of the Union of Ontario Indians. "The province sets all the curriculum and Indian people write all the pay cheques and that's about the extent of [our] involvement in education." Ottawa provides a per-pupil grant to operate the schools and cover staff salaries. The teaching staff usually work from a provincially approved curriculum guide, using specified texts.

True transfer of power would give Indians more than the right to sign a pay cheque; it would give them the right to hire administrators and staff, set budgets, and incorporate native curriculum — powers every non-native parent has through school boards. "We're not talking about reducing the quality of education but enriching it by putting in cultural components that we feel are important, like our language," Miskokomon says. "We're not talking about eliminating the sciences, the maths and English. The [Indian] people going to compete in the world have to have those things but at the same time, they should not lose where they've come from. They should have the understanding and the foundation of where they've come from and why they are here."

Ottawa has followed through on its policy of transferring control, at least by its own definition. More than 100,000 status Indians are enrolled in schools across Canada; 49 per cent attend the 353 band-managed schools, another 5 per cent attend federal schools on reserves (a dwindling number as transfers to Indians are completed on a yearly basis), and the remainder (46 per cent) attends provincial schools. More than half of the country's Indian bands have assumed control of the federal schools. In some instances, the bands have relinquished this authority to native education committees, which usually operate like school boards with elected representatives from the reserve community. In theory, these bodies are responsible for hiring academic and support staff, co-ordinating curricula, and drafting budgets. In reality, the extent of their control is determined by Ottawa's willingness to support them.

Education Policy

Indians complain that their ability to direct their own education is severely curtailed because of legislative inadequacies and lack of funding. Policy in this area, as in others, has been developed ad hoc. Sections 114 to 123 of the Indian Act give the department of Indian Affairs the authority to operate schools and enter agreements with provinces and territories to provide for education only on reserves. No other decisions are supported by legislation. The federal government has no legislative right to allow for the creation of Indian education authorities. There is no national Indian education act. Academic standards are set by each province. The entire framework of Indian education is the creation of cabinet orders and Treasury Board guidelines. Without a legislative framework to prescribe education programs and without federal funding, Ottawa offers only programs that it deems necessary or that it is pressured into providing. Policies covering the creation of kindergarten classes, devolution, and even the existence of Indian education authorities, are set by the government of the day. And policy, as the Indian leadership has discovered, changes with public opinion and partisan political priorities.

Indian school authorities have no alternate means to raise funds for their budgets. Unlike non-native school boards, native education committees cannot levy taxes on reserve residents. Even if they could, few could afford to pay. Bingo games, while a source of income, help recreational programs and nothing else.

Education spending has always accounted for most of Indian Affairs's budget, but in recent years, there has been no rational link between student enrolment and funding. While annual spending grew from $70 million in 1968 to $433.6 million in 1982–83, subsequent budgets have fluctuated wildly even though on-reserve school enrolment increased by almost 40 per cent during the same time frame. Funding reached $539 million in the 1986–87 fiscal year, dropped to $476 million by 1988–89 and started to rise again the following year to $487.7 million. By 1992–93, the allocation for education had reached $683.7 million. Indian authorities complain that long-term planning is impossible because the budget fluctuates so much from year to year. When money does arrive, it often arrives late, which forces authorities to borrow funds and incur interest charges that Ottawa does not cover.

Uncertainty over the budget comes at a time when Indian student enrolment is growing substantially. In 1975, almost 72,000 Indian students were attending on-reserve schools. Ten years later, more than 82,000 students were in classrooms. By the fall of 1992, more than 100,000 students were enrolled at on-reserve schools. Indian leaders now need more funds to develop culturally relevant classes and offer teachers cultural training, but the financial support is not there. Statistics and studies show that the money spent in the past was poorly managed. The Indian leadership has finally reached a degree of sophistication at which it can manage its own affairs; however, Ottawa now refuses to provide the funds for proper training in the education field.

Federal Schools

The federal government's devolution experiment in Indian education produced results no better than those of the residential schools. The failure of federal schools has been documented several times, mostly by the staff. In 1978, Indian Affairs released *Education of Indians in Federal and Provincial Schools in Manitoba, Evaluation Report,* which compared school records of Indian students for the previous four years in federal schools with student records from schools operated by the province's Frontier School Division. The report concluded that there was little difference between the performances of Indian students in the two systems: the drop-out rate was high; 30 per cent of students were behind at least one grade; the number of high school graduates was small; absenteeism was common; and parental involvement was rare. The department of Indian Affairs, as usual, did nothing.

In 1982, the department released a scathing internal report that clearly blamed the bureaucrats for the poor academic record of Indian students. According to the *Indian Education Paper, Phase 1,*

Ottawa's policy for transferring control of education had been flawed since Chrétien introduced it ten years earlier. As Indians have always maintained, Ottawa essentially transferred control of a faulty program to people who were not trained to administer the system and who lacked the skills and experience to correct its failings. "This policy emphasized both the need to improve the quality of Indian education and the desirability of devolving control of education to Indian society," the author of the paper states. "The problems which now face Indian education were all either existing in 1973 or can be traced back to inadequate policy definition and inadequate devolution preparation and procedures."

The paper clearly details the problems of the department's policy. In the name of devolution, Ottawa reduced its funding for curriculum development, teacher and student support, and the monitoring of standards. Indian education authorities were not given the assistance necessary to deliver a quality education system. Flaws in the federal system were transferred along with the control. Essentially, no one had defined "Indian control." Among the issues facing Indians were a curriculum that did not reflect an Indian child's history or circumstances, inferior school facilities, and a teaching staff characterized by high turnover, inadequate training, and low morale — problems that Chrétien promised to solve.

Ottawa did very little following the release of its *Indian Education Paper* in 1982. In an interview in 1989, Indian Affairs assistant deputy minister John Rayner said that the department wanted to hear from the Indian community once again, before taking any corrective action. Indian response would not come for six years. To avoid implementing changes, Ottawa deftly bought that time by funding a multimillion dollar study launched by the AFN, the new national lobby of Indian bands formed in 1981. The AFN surveyed all band leaders to identify the problems of the existing system and possible solutions.

The Indian Plan

In the spring of 1988, the AFN repeated what Indian people had said sixteen years earlier in the NIB paper. The AFN's three-volume report, *Tradition and Education: Towards a Vision of Our Future*, stated that education programs in federal and provincial schools were inadequate because of the refusal to acknowledge aboriginal languages, culture, and spiritual beliefs. The paper calls for education to become a cornerstone of self-government and for aboriginal languages to be given official status. "Education, as a force in human development, lies at the base of achieving effective self-government," the paper's authors wrote. "Self-knowledge, self-confidence, self-respect and self-sufficiency must be developed in order for any people to attain a healthy society, a stable culture, and self-government."

The paper revealed that Indian people had not reached consensus on details such as whether the language of instruction should be English, French, or native; or whether teaching staff should be only native, only non-native, or a mix of both. The report concluded that each band has the right to answer those questions on its own and within its own time frame. "[Native people] are saying we want to have control of our lives, our own children, to direct our own future," Joe Miskokomon adds.

The paper also calls for Ottawa to relinquish its administrative and policy functions and remain only as a funding agency. Instead of demanding adaptation of various provincial curricula to include native culture, the paper calls for an integration of the two elements, with flexibility for individual bands or organizations to develop a program that meets their own people's objectives. Instead of adding a daily class on native culture to the curriculum, Indian leaders want to start over, to ensure that all of the lessons reflect traditional customs. "Learning must be associated with spiritual, physical, and emotional growth, as well as academic growth," the paper states. "Traditional First Nations methodology of teaching and learning must be considered. It is imperative that First Nations use the strategy of placing education into culture rather than continuing the practice of placing culture into education."

The federal government's response to the paper has been further delay. Despite the two policy papers from Indian organizations and the department's own studies in the past twenty-five years, Ottawa says it needs more time to develop the appropriate strategy. Meanwhile, it continues its policy of administration by bureaucracy. In 1989, Rayner said Indian Affairs was developing another policy position on education to address the issues identified by the AFN paper, but he gave no date for when that policy would be produced. "We're working on an overall document on objectives and policy. We have to be sensitive to the needs of Indian people. It's their education. If they don't buy into it, we can't deliver it." Five years later, the Indian community was still waiting.

Classroom Realities

The inadequacies of the present education system extend far beyond Ottawa's delaying tactics and policy blunders; the conditions of the system are also shaped by the realities of the day. Many reserves offer a bleak existence to their residents, who connect with the affluent outside world through satellite television and occasional trips to urban centres. There is also a suspicion among many Indians who have had negative experiences within the education system that makes them unwilling to offer encouragement to their children.

Sandy Lindsay, a retired superintendent with the education branch of Indian Affairs, believes that Indian parents must shoulder some of the blame for their children's poor academic performances. "Maybe parents feel school isn't meeting any of their basic needs. The three Rs are still the total program today. [Schools] are preparing students for university and jobs in the technological south yet they're living in a community where there are none of the jobs available based on the kinds of training they are getting and they have no intention of leaving."

On a desk in Lindsay's home is a stack of course studies he prepared for northern native schools. While still with the department, he found that many students knew little about the wildlife and vegetation in their surroundings. He aimed to teach the students what their parents may have forgotten, but the department never approved the courses. Bureaucrats decided that an education program designed for a student in Toronto was adequate for an Indian child. Lindsay charges that this kind of education program, coupled with the Indian child's perception of the outside world, creates unrealistic attitudes. "Our surveys indicated kids want to stay in the north but they want inside jobs where it's warm and comfortable, a desk job, and they expect the kinds of wages that would give them a good living without hunting or fishing."

According to a northern Manitoba band school principal, despite the efforts to establish a more culturally relevant curriculum, to expand language instruction, and to hire native teacher aides, academic performances remain poor. "Up to Grade 6, attendance is very good. After Grade 7, attendance drops off. When the older kids hit Grade 7, they stay up all night shooting pool. There are four pool halls [on a reserve with a population of slightly more than 1,000]. If they come in at all, they sleep at their desks. We tried almost everything to encourage attendance, including giving out prizes and cash awards." In 1988, the band council provided $5,000 in gifts and cash to encourage attendance and reward students; bicycles, televisions, stereos, and $20 gift certificates for the best academic records, and $10 gift certificates for best improved record. The incentives did not work.

"Part of the problem is the lack of support from the families. Parents encourage children only up to the grade they reached. After that they do not care," the principal says. "The biggest problem is alcohol. It affects both the parents and children. The reserve went dry two years ago but the problems are worse now. We offer counselling for drug, alcohol and sex abuse and if we could get rid of the alcohol we'd get rid of a lot of problems." According to Lindsay, the problems encountered by the school principal can be overcome with community leadership. Indian leaders cite several examples where parental involvement and encouragement have boosted attendance records to levels comparable to those of non-native urban schools. Attitudes towards school on reserves are changing. Surveys from the 1991 Census show that 72 per cent of elementary-aged children on reserves reported having aboriginal teachers, and almost half (48 per cent) used an aboriginal language in the classroom.

Ottawa has signed agreements with the provinces to send Indian students to provincial schools, usually for the high school grades. These schools are often located in rural areas. Provincial authorities and Indian leaders have found it difficult to convince children to leave their reserves for higher education. Indian students are intimidated by the world beyond their reserves; this fact partly accounts for the high drop-out rate. The 1991 Census shows that almost 30 per cent of adult Indians dropped out of school before Grade 9. The 1986 Census revealed that only 5 per cent finished high school. The 1991 Census no longer reports the proportion of high school graduates, noting only that 46 per cent of native people have attended high school. Many of these students come from poor families that cannot afford to spend money on such things as trendy clothes for school. Other students find the racist attitudes of their non-native classmates disturbing.

"We're talking about proud people," says Konrad Sioui, a hereditary chief from Quebec. "They don't want to go to schools to be laughed at because they look too poor. Our kids are no different than others. They all want to succeed but when they get into these melting-pot schools, the children are pushed away, treated as second-class citizens, discriminated against, sometimes even by their own teachers." Those not strong enough to face the pressure, Sioui says, retreat to the reserve. "They say, 'if that's the way I'm treated outside, why should I go, try to do my best?' Inside the reserve [we] might be poor but at least we're able to have some relations and respect between ourselves and that is sufficient for me."

Even the success stories can have less than optimal endings: most of the children who do stay in school go elsewhere to find a job. "That's one of the tragedies," says a provincial school official. "The communities need as many qualified people as they can get. The sad part of it is, because there's such high unemployment, young people will set their sights somewhere else." But Oscar Lathlin says that keeping children in school takes top priority, even if they decide to work off-reserve after graduation. "I don't care whether those university graduates come back to the reserve. What I care about is now they're in the position to make some choices."

Education as a Treaty Right

When former Indian Affairs minister Pierre Cadieux announced in March 1989 that Ottawa would cap post-secondary education spending, the statement was made in typical federal fashion, without Indian consultation. More importantly, Indians considered the cap to be a violation of their treaty rights. Indians have always chosen a broad interpretation of the education rights given to them under the treaties, while Ottawa has held a narrow, literal reading. To Indians, education covers kindergarten to university. Ottawa says it is bound only to provide primary, elementary, and secondary schools on reserves; anything beyond that it considers extra.

"We know for sure that if you would interpret a treaty and you want to test it in any court, any judge would say, yes, post-secondary is included in that treaty," Konrad Sioui says. "You've got to adapt what is written in a treaty to what it means today and any judge would do that. We've always said that education is a fundamental right. The treaties said that the Indian would be educated as the white man are."

Cadieux's decision echoes government policy, a tactic used by many other departments when dealing with Indian issues. Since post-secondary education was not mentioned in the treaties, Ottawa considers funding at this level voluntary. Cadieux's announcement also marked a reversal in Ottawa's commitment to increase native enrolment in post-secondary institutions. In the department's 1985 paper, *Post-secondary Education Assistance Evaluation Study, Final*

Report, one of the goals was to achieve a participation rate in post-secondary education at least equal to that of the non-native Canadian population. In that same year, Ottawa stopped recording the number of Indian students attending university. After that, Ottawa lumped together figures for enrolment in university, community colleges, and college entry programs. The 1991 Census shows that only 1.1 per cent of adult reserve residents have a university degree.

Although post-secondary education remains tied to a budget plan, funding, even under the Conservatives, had increased to more than $227 million by the end of their tenure, with an average increase of almost $20 million over that five-year period. The Chrétien government increased that amount to $247 million for 1994–95 and made a commitment to the Indian community that funding would continue to increase at the rate of $20 million annually. However, Cadieux's decision highlighted the two main concerns of Indian leaders today regarding Ottawa's ad hoc education policy: the program is based on the whims of the cabinet, and the funding is inadequate. When faced with budget restraints, Ottawa will try to avoid its responsibilities.

In a letter to all chiefs and band councils dated March 20, 1989, Cadieux sent this ominous message: "The [post-secondary] program will have to live within its annual allocation which may mean that a small number of students will temporarily have to seek those sources of support available to other Canadians. The challenge now is to ensure that the substantial funds already in the program are used as effectively as possible to produce graduates with qualifications that will assist communities in moving towards self-government and improved economic growth." The period since the imposition of the cap has been difficult for the entire Indian community. The situation increased stress on students, families, and band leaders. With the majority of reserve residents young people, Ottawa was effectively cutting off one of their routes to a better future.

To non-native outsiders, Cadieux's message made sense, but to the band councils, who administer the loans, it presented a dilemma. Bands need professionals to ensure their own growth and development but Indian students may opt for a life outside the reserve. According to the 1989 directive, students admitted to band-controlled post-secondary education programs must tailor their studies to meet the goals of self-government and economic growth; only those interested in becoming chartered accountants, lawyers, planners and professionals need apply. Others — those wanting to study art, music, history, political science, or languages — would have to apply for provincial loans.

The guideline changes were introduced at a time when Indians were beginning to take advantage of the program, in numbers that Ottawa did not anticipate and was not prepared to fund. In 1969, Ottawa spent $250,000 on post-secondary education; less than 500 Indians were attending university or college programs. By 1982, almost 7,000 students were enrolled in post-secondary classes. When the cap was imposed, 6 per cent of status Indians (15,000 individuals) were attending university compared to 20 per cent of all Canadians. By 1992, the gap had widened even further. More than 21,000 Indian students were attending university or community college, a figure representing only 4 per cent of all status Indians.

"It was easy to put that old policy in place because there were very few of our people that would get a university degree," Sioui says. "So, in the eyes of the world, of the Canadian people, that looked very sharp. It was a very nice policy. Now that we're arriving at that stage, now that we have some chance to bring some of our people to the post-secondary level, Ottawa says we can't. Where is the rationale? Where is the logic?" Sioui says demonstrations and sit-ins were an attempt to show Canadians what was at stake. "That policy is a threat to our youth that we will always reject. Just the fact that they would even talk about putting that in place unilaterally is a sign of how they want to treat us, how they want to keep us second-hand, not wanting us to get higher degrees and higher jobs and to become more self-sufficient."

To some native leaders the policy change supports predictions that Ottawa will never endorse self-government and will continue, despite repeated denials, to shift a greater burden of responsibility onto provincial governments. The only way to have bridged the gap in 1989 between natives and non-natives in post-secondary enrolment (6 per cent versus 20 per cent, respectively) would have required tripling the $130 million budget. By 1995, Ottawa was spending more than $247 million, yet the gap between Indians and the rest of Canadian society had widened. The prospects are bleaker still for the next three years. The Liberal government is planning massive cuts in transfer funds to the provinces; these shortages are expected to double or triple the cost of post-secondary tuition. It is unlikely that the same federal government would approve substantial increases in funding for the Indian post-secondary education program to match this sudden rise in tuition costs. The message Indian leaders received regarding policy change from the Conservative government in 1989 is the same as that delivered by the Liberal government in 1995: the provinces, and Indians themselves, will have to make up the shortfall.

Most Indians are unemployed and only a small number can expect to have full-time jobs. Few would risk a loan without the security of a reserve or Indian organization job waiting for them after graduation. If an increasing number of Indians are forced to borrow to fund their education, the majority of them simply will not go.

According to Oscar Lathlin, only within an Indian-controlled, Indian-directed education system will native children regain the identity stolen from their parents and grandparents decades before. "The trick is to maintain your roots while getting an education. You can get your Masters in science or get a Ph.D. or become an electrical engineer and still be an Indian. That's the kind of programming that we need but was never delivered by Ottawa." With education comes the opportunity to exercise choice. "Before we had no choice," Lathlin says. "Whether we stayed on reserve and were dirt poor, living on welfare and actually believing that's our culture. Or we come to [Winnipeg's] North Main. Or we go to jail. That's not much of a choice."

8

Child Welfare

In no other area did federal bureaucrats and professional social workers wreak so much havoc in so little time as in the field of child welfare. During the period from the early 1960s to the early 1980s, many Indian communities across Canada lost an entire generation of children, scooped up by professional workers who claimed to be working in the best interest of the child. Parents never saw their children again. These children often grew into troubled teens and adults — tortured by a past they could not reclaim, psychologically twisted from living in a world where they did not belong. Many turned to alcohol and drug abuse, ending up in psychiatric institutions and prisons, and many more chose suicide as their escape. In a 1985 report on native adoption and foster placements, Edwin C. Kimelman, associate chief judge of the Manitoba Family Court, accurately described the situation as the routine and systematic "cultural genocide" of Indian people.

When Ottawa, at the insistence of the Indian community, began phasing out the hated residential schools in the 1960s, it returned children to parents who had themselves endured the same experience. For these parents, the concept of a family life had been destroyed during their own stay in these schools. As a consequence, they felt lost and confused about their new parenting roles. They could not turn to their own parents because that generation, devastated by the same experience, had no advice and could not act as role models for their children. These new parents turned to alcohol and drugs to deal with their own pain, and their children often became victims of physical and sexual abuse.

Ovide Mercredi, chief of the AFN, explains that Indian communities had their own support systems for child abuse before non-native society intervened.

In the past there had always been support in the community to look after families. If a parent or parents were
neglecting or abusing their children, someone would
come forward, not necessarily a chief, but someone they
respected…maybe an elder, a relative, a friend…someone
who would talk to them, tell them to straighten themselves
out. If they didn't correct the situation, the chief or others
would step in and remove the child from the family and
place him with relatives or friends. The parents had no
choice. Even if they objected, they could not get the child
back until they turned themselves around.

For the past ten years, Indian communities have been obsessed
with regaining control of their children's lives through native-run
child welfare agencies, seeing success in this instance as proof of
native people's ability to govern themselves without outside interference. But for many of the scarred survivors of the "cultural genocide," attempts to re-establish the family component in their
traditional way of life have only continued the cycle of tragedy.

In 1951, Ottawa amended the Indian Act to allow provincial
agencies to extend child welfare services onto reserves; however, the
government did not provide any funding to allow the provinces to
become actively involved. The result was a patchwork of service
delivery that developed over the following thirty years. While some
provinces did provide limited services, others did nothing, except to
intervene in emergency situations. With the growing dependency on
welfare, the placement of children in the care of parents who often
lacked emotional stability and the necessary skills, and the loss of
the traditional way of life, emergency situations quickly became the
norm on reserves. Problems became so widespread that the traditional safeguards were overwhelmed.

"[Parents] turned to drinking and that led to other things," Mercredi says. "They became very irresponsible. They didn't look after
their children. More than one family had the problem and the community could not respond."

With inadequate support from Ottawa and the provinces, Indian
society slowly crumbled. Native people struggled with problems
such as an ill-defined identity and a severely crippled sense of self-
worth. Their only escape was an alcohol- and drug-induced numb-
ness. The norms of acceptable social behaviour broke down. Over

the years, life for many individuals became a downward slide into oblivion. Indian agents and provincial social workers found the situation horrifying, but instead of trying to deal with the underlying cause, they simply removed children from their parents and their communities.

Writer Patrick Johnston, in his book *Native Children and the Child Welfare System,* coined the phrase "sixties scoop" to describe the removal of children from their homes during this period. In British Columbia in 1955, of the 3,433 children in foster care or group homes, less than 1 per cent (twenty-nine), were native. By 1964, native children represented 34.2 per cent (1,446) of the total number of children (4,228) in care. The passage of time only compounded the horror. In every province across Canada, a disproportionate number of native children were in care. By 1980, 4.6 per cent of all registered Indian children were in care across Canada, compared to less than 1 per cent of all Canadian children. By 1985, the numbers had climbed higher: 6.4 per cent of all status children were in care, while the overall Canadian rate remained at 1 per cent. The situation was worse in Ontario and the four western provinces.

In 1980, in British Columbia, native children accounted for 36.7 per cent of all children in care, but only made up 3.5 per cent of all children in the province; in Alberta, 29.7 per cent of all children in care were native, but only 2.9 per cent of all children in the province were native; in Saskatchewan, native children accounted for 63.8 per cent of all children in care, but only 8.3 per cent of all children in the province; in Manitoba, 32.1 per cent of all children in care were native, but only 7.7 per cent of the province's children were native; and in Ontario, native children accounted for 8 per cent of children in care, but only 1.1 per cent of children in the province.

Worse still, these children, once placed in care, often never returned home. For non-native children, placement in foster homes was usually a temporary situation. In contrast, for the majority of native children, the new living situation became permanent, as they were shuffled among foster homes for years or permanently adopted. Furthermore, most of these placements were with non-native families. An Indian Affairs study of placements between 1971 and 1981 revealed that Indian children placed for adoption usually went to non-native families. Many believed these children would be better off — removed from the impoverished, life-threatening conditions on reserves — but time has shown that, for many of these children, life did not improve.

Experimenting with Children

Carla Williams and Cameron Kerley are two of the most publicized cases of Indian children placed in non-native homes. Both were born on Manitoba reserves and taken out of the country to live, Cameron to the United States and Carla to the Netherlands. Both were physically and sexually abused by their adoptive fathers, and both returned home, but under different circumstances.

Cameron was eight years old when his father was murdered in 1972. He and his three sisters were placed in foster homes by the Children's Aid Society. His mother died two years later from alcoholism. A year later, when Cameron was eleven years old, he was adopted by American Dick Kerley, a bachelor, and taken to Kansas. Soon after, Cameron became a problem child; he skipped school and often ran away from home. He started drinking and taking drugs. No one knew what had triggered this behaviour.

At nineteen, Cameron killed Dick Kerley with a baseball bat. He pleaded guilty to second-degree murder and, in 1983, was given a life sentence. It was only then that Cameron told the world about his nightmarish life with Dick Kerley — a horror story of physical and sexual abuse, which he ended with the swing of a bat. After serving two years in an American prison, Cameron was transferred to a Manitoba penitentiary to serve the remainder of his sentence, which by then had been reduced to a twenty-year term. He became eligible for full parole in May 1990 but proved incapable of coping with limited bouts of freedom. In late May 1991, while on a day pass to attend an Alcoholics Anonymous meeting, Cameron failed to return to prison. The next day, in a highly dramatic turn, he called in to a Winnipeg open-line radio show and surrendered to authorities. He escaped again one year later, this time fleeing from a halfway house after attending an emotional family reunion. Police apprehended him days later on a highway in Saskatchewan, in a car driven by an older brother. By the summer of 1994, Cameron, then 30 years old, was behind bars at the Stony Mountain Penitentiary, north of Winnipeg.

Carla Williams's parents were Ojibway Indians, from a southern Manitoba band, who had moved to Winnipeg. They both suffered from alcoholism, and their heavy drinking prompted the Children's Aid Society of Eastern Manitoba to seize their four children in 1968. Their youngest son, Carl, who was born a year later, was also taken by society officials.

Carla was four years old when she was placed with a non-native foster family. Three years later, her natural father hanged himself. The following year, in 1972, Carla was placed for permanent adoption with a Dutch couple, who then moved back to the Netherlands. Carla did not see her brothers and sisters again for seventeen years.

The adoption was dissolved within a year, but Carla was unable to escape the nightmare her life had become. Her adoptive father pursued her through a succession of foster homes. A prominent physician, he obtained visitation rights and used those opportunities to sexually abuse her for the next seven years. At the age of twelve, four years after her initial adoption, Carla tried to kill herself; she was placed in a psychiatric institution. She remained under psychiatric care as an outpatient for another three years. Carla gave birth to two children during that time, each fathered by the abusive physician and seized by local child welfare authorities. She married at nineteen and was forced into prostitution by her new husband. Over the course of the next four years, Carla would have two more babies, each by different men, and again, each seized by child welfare authorities.

When Carla was twenty-three, a chance encounter with Canadians travelling in the Netherlands led to contact with a Manitoba Indian child welfare agency, which would help her to reunite with her family in Winnipeg. In the fall of 1989, at the age of twenty-five, Carla returned home to a tearful reunion with the brothers and sisters she had not seen in almost twenty years. By then, she had remarried and was pregnant with twins; she also had cancer — doctors said she would live for another six to eight years. In the late summer of 1994, Carla's cancer was in remission and she was living on an Indian reserve in northern Manitoba.

The stories of Cameron Kerley and Carla Williams are not isolated accounts. Following protests from Indian leaders, the Manitoba government stopped out-of-province adoptions of Indian children in 1982 and asked Judge Kimelman to examine the issue. Kimelman's 1985 report, "No Quiet Place," was a detailed list of horrors — an exhaustive compilation which concluded that the damage to Indian children had been real, frequent, and widespread.

Kimelman quoted the work of a Minneapolis doctor who had extensively studied Indian children who had been adopted or raised in foster homes. Those investigations indicated that Indian children placed in non-native homes would, as teenagers, often suffer emotional problems and turn to drug abuse and suicide. "All available information would indicate that the Indian people were correct in their assertions that once their children entered the child care system they were not likely to ever be returned to their own families," Kimelman wrote. "The evidence would indicate they were correct in their claim that not only were those children lost to their own communities, the lives of the individual children were seriously and permanently impaired."

By the late 1970s, Indians were becoming aware of the destructive nature of the non-native child welfare system. As part of their self-government aspirations, they demanded their own agencies, which would be administered and staffed by Indians and held accountable to their own people. Today, that dream has been partly realized. Almost 4,000 Indian children, 40 per cent of all Indian children in care in Canada, are the wards of Indian-run agencies. In all instances but one, these agencies have replaced the Children's Aid Societies. They are staffed by Indian care workers, with Indian supervisors and directors, and they are accountable to a board of directors chosen from the community or consisting of band council representatives. However, the agencies remain under the jurisdiction of provincial legislation.

Ottawa has refused to enact national Indian child welfare legislation, which could give the ultimate authority in this field back to the Indian communities. Instead, the federal government has relied on tripartite agreements, with bands and provincial governments, that assign this authority to provincial jurisdiction. The capacity of the Indian agencies to apprehend children and offer protection and prevention services is mandated by provincial law, and these agencies remain ultimately accountable to a provincial authority.

A Return to the Past

The only exception to the above regulations is the child welfare program of the Spallumcheen band in British Columbia. This is the only Indian band that has succeeded in achieving complete autonomy in the area of child welfare. Like the others, this agency is funded through the department of Indian Affairs. Unlike the others, however, this agency was created by a 1979 band by-law, which asserts its own jurisdiction and replaces that of the province of British Columbia.

A federal review of the Spallumcheen agency's service between 1980 and 1986 verified what Indian leaders across the country have long been saying: Indians can achieve results using traditional methods. The Spallumcheen program has reduced the number of children taken into care and, more importantly, increased reliance on the extended family for the care of children.

The 1987 Indian Affairs study, *Indian Child and Family Services in Canada, Final Report,* concluded that the Spallumcheen band alone had realized the Indian dream of replacing the formal, non-native institution with the traditional, extended family approach. Other bands had merely replaced non-native agencies with their own organizations, which were staffed by Indians, but which functioned in the same manner as the previous agencies. The Spallumcheen restored the traditional safeguards to the community members. Instead of relying on a native agency modelled after a non-native institution, members of the Spallumcheen band turned to their families and elders for help. "The Spallumcheen initiative has sought to re-institutionalize the function within the extended family," the study concluded, and the strategy worked. A band-funded study in 1986 found the same results. Children placed in non-native homes were returned to the band, and services are now provided within the community to children who need protection. Unlike the situation elsewhere, the number of children needing care has been reduced. The accessibility of child welfare services to band members has increased, but the cost of those services has been reduced. Most important, the community has accepted the services.

The Manitoba Experiment

With both the federal and provincial governments recognizing the jurisdiction of the Spallumcheen band, Indian bands and tribal councils across the country aspire to emulate its example. Despite the improved conditions of the Spallumcheen community, however, Ottawa considers this case to be only a pilot project. The department of Indian Affairs prefers to cite the Manitoba example, in which tripartite master agreements — between Ottawa, the province and tribal councils — outlined procedures for the creation of five Indian child and family service agencies. These organizations are staffed and managed by Indians and funded by Ottawa; daily operations fall under provincial jurisdiction. Results of the model have been mixed. Manitoba remains the only province where more than 60,000 people, 90 per cent of reserve residents, are served exclusively by Indian agencies. Yet some of the agencies have been overwhelmed by internal and external problems and unable to duplicate the Spallum-cheen success. The agencies discovered that the number of emotion-ally troubled and abused children was greater than they had anticipated; and workers reluctantly placed more children in foster homes. Problems facing the agencies include a shortage of funds, a lack of programs for dealing with sexual abuse, and an overworked and undertrained staff.

When the Manitoba Indian leaders negotiated the master agree-ments in the early 1980s, their objectives were similar to those of the Spallumcheen band: they wanted to look after their own children using traditional methods, to reduce the number of formal placements by keeping children in extended families, and to reclaim, or "repatri-ate," as they called it, children who had been adopted into non-native homes. Ten years later, the successes of the Manitoba model are often overshadowed by the battle for control of these agencies. Chiefs and band councillors repeatedly challenge the authority of the provincial government and interfere with the day-to-day operations of the agen-cies; these actions are all defended under the guise of self-govern-ment. The victims, once again, are Indian children.

There were early successes in adoption and repatriation programs in Manitoba. Between 1983 and 1987, the number of adoptions dropped from thirty-four to seven, with almost all children being adopted into native homes. Repatriation was a minor success, with twenty-one children returned to their homes by 1987. A difficulty in this area arose when Manitoba refused to disclose where Indian children had been sent, claiming that its confidentiality laws pre-vented such action. Repatriations were only possible when adopted children told their natural parents that they wanted to return home, or when natural parents were notified that their children, previously placed in foster care, were being considered for adoption.

Though unaware of the serious problems the Manitoba Indian agencies would soon encounter, Judge Kimelman wrote in 1985 that the organizations were better suited, in theory at least, to serve the needs of their communities than were the child welfare societies, which, he concluded, offered little value to either the non-natives or natives. Quoting from a 1984 report to the province, Kimelman noted that "...none of the agencies — except the Indian ones — showed sufficient sensitivity to the special cultural patterns and charac-teristics of the people served."

According to Kimelman, the non-native agencies wrongly as-sumed that the norms and rules of their society should be embraced by everyone. "The cultural bias in the system for the past 40 years has made Native people victims. That must cease." For example, these agencies would demand that single native mothers live on their own if they wanted to regain custody of their children. "This demand goes against the native patterns of child care," Kimelman says. "In the Native tradition, the need of a young mother to be mothered herself is recognized. The grandparents and aunts and uncles expect the demands and rewards of raising the new member of the family. To insist that the mother remove herself from the support of her family when she needs them most is unrealistic and cruel."

Manitoba Indian leaders and their agencies used Kimelman's condemnation of the status quo as a shield for their own excesses. The fatal assumption of the Manitoba model, which Kimelman apparently accepted, was that stable, sound, and healthy communities would serve as the backdrop for the traditional approach. To everyone's horror, the communities where the new agencies operated were as dysfunctional as the families in need of assistance.

The Manitoba agencies failed in their delivery of child welfare services. Nationally, the number of Indian children in care between 1976 and 1987 dropped steadily in every province except Manitoba. Since 1983, the number of reserve children in care in Manitoba has nearly doubled. The agencies did not expect the complexity and severity of the problems they encountered, nor were they prepared to deal with solutions. "Originally, these (child welfare) committees set out to do prevention work but really all we did was protection work — apprehend children," says Mercredi, who, before his election in 1990 to the post of grand chief of the AFN, was a key child care negotiator in Manitoba. "We were, in essence, doing the same thing that we opposed in the first place." One consultant's report on the work of two southern Manitoba agencies stated that case workers were under pressure to fulfil traditional expectations and still comply with provincial legislation, which was not possible. Between 1983 and 1987, as the five Indian agencies came into being, the number of registered Indian children in care increased by 81 per cent, from 863 to 1,563. Almost 1,200 of those children had been placed by the five agencies. Meanwhile, the tripartite agreements had included plans for reduced budgets in later years, following the Indian leaders' assumption that the number of placements would decrease. By the spring of 1993, the native agencies had placed more than 1,600 reserve children in care. The agencies found themselves with larger caseloads and, because of the smaller budgets, fewer case workers. The situation was ripe for tragedy.

Agency workers soon discovered that children were the real victims of the social disintegration on reserves. Workers were overwhelmed with neglected and sexually abused children. At the Child Protection Centre in Winnipeg, 35 per cent of the child sexual abuse cases between 1981 and 1987 involved registered Indians, yet this group represented only 6 per cent of the provincial population. The centre's reports concluded that the Manitoba experiment had failed. Placing children in the homes of relatives or friends on reserves often provided opportunities for other abusers who had not yet been detected. Within these small communities, children were pressured by relatives and abusers to recant their stories. One report examined a six-month period in 1983–84 and found eight reserve cases that involved thirty-three victims and twenty-three offenders.

Consultants' studies on four of the five new agencies during 1987 and 1988 produced similar findings. Indian case workers had little formal education. While directors and supervisors were likely to be graduates of a recognized school of social work, most case workers — the people in the field — had not finished high school. Workers could attend federal training programs, but universities would not recognize these courses for social work credit because they were not offered by an accredited institution. None of the available training was conducted in the communities where the workers lived, and the workers, with families of their own, were not willing to leave the reserve to take those courses. Thus, most case workers received only on-the-job training.

"It's easy to sit on the outside and blame them and say why was the system activated before people had the basic training to do the job properly," says Dr. Sally Longstaffe, a pediatrician at Children's Hospital in Winnipeg and one of Manitoba's experts on the treatment of abused children. "You can't blame the individual. They're doing their best. They haven't received the kind of training [they need] and they don't have the supervision and support they need."

Longstaffe says the workers wanted to help but did not know how. "We've got many, many people who are busting their rear ends but they don't know how to plan. They don't know anything about child development. They don't know how to recognize a child as being so damaged that they can't even learn. These are real, living, breathing victims who can only take a certain amount [of pain] and then they're damaged permanently."

The seriousness of the situation was made worse by the denial offered by most of the Manitoba Indian leaders. The reports and recommendations, for the most part, were ignored by native agencies and the bands that controlled them. Instead of acknowledging the problems with their model and trying to solve them, Indian leaders kept repeating the same mistakes.

Louis Stevenson, chief of the Peguis band in Manitoba, said in 1988 that the tragedies are an inevitable part of the growing pains of the Indian community as it regains control of its own destiny. "The child-caring agencies have their growing pains too, their share of problems, but I wouldn't write any of them off because it's not any worse than what our people were subjected to previously under the children's aid societies." Under the care and protection of Ottawa, Indian children were frequently physically and sexually abused and tormented — first in residential schools, and then when non-native child welfare agencies stepped in. "Let an Indian have one problem and it's all blown out of proportion and the whole system is labelled [bad]," Stevenson says. "But I know better now than to let people convince me that is the case. So what if we have a few problems, it's not going to be as great as many problems that we've been subjected to ever since someone else controlled our lives." Stevenson's words have come back to haunt him and the entire Indian community. His attitude, shared today by other leaders, allowed for no means of improving the lot of native children. Simply stated, Indians were now destroying their own people, and despite Stevenson's assertions, the new problems were at the least just "as great" as those that had preceded them.

The Giesbrecht Report

The suicide of a thirteen-year-old boy in Manitoba was the catalyst for a deeper debate about the direction of native-controlled child welfare agencies. Today, this debate, which continues to rage across the country, shows the extent of the disagreement between natives and non-natives. It also sheds light, for the first time, on the deep divisions between men and women in many native communities. Two events, an inquest into the boy's death and a public inquiry, which was called as a result of the inquest findings, have fuelled the arguments of the debate: in areas with widespread problems such as child welfare, what is the right solution — greater autonomy or greater intervention? The two reports, with their contradictory conclusions, should be mandatory reading for anyone involved in developing a functional native-controlled child welfare agency.

By all accounts, the death of Lester Desjarlais on March 6, 1988, was "unremarkable," states Associate Chief Judge Brian Giesbrecht in his report, *Inquest Respecting the Death of Lester Norman Desjarlais,* which was issued under the authority of the Fatality Inquiries Act (Manitoba). However, the details uncovered during the forty-day inquest, conducted more than three years after Lester's death, transfixed the entire province. Allegations of gross negligence by both native and non-native officials, missing files, and charges of political interference by band officials made daily front-page headlines. The inquest extended far beyond the circumstances surrounding Lester's death, examining in detail the day-to-day struggles of a nascent native child care agency in a way that no study had ever done before. No anonymous statistics or sociological jargon masked the severity of the tragedy, and the inquest itself was a real-life drama, with real people, unfolding daily in a court room and reported by the news media. Giesbrecht's report, released a year later, was 292 pages long. It contained 300 recommendations and bluntly stated its findings: the Indian agencies, the native community, and the provincial government have created an environment that literally destroys the lives of children.

"Although this is clearly not a general public inquiry, it has evolved into something more than a routine inquiry into the circumstances surrounding the death of a person," Giesbrecht wrote in the introduction to his report. "Lester Desjarlais hanged himself. A beautiful child is dead — a life wasted....The actual death itself was clearly a suicide, and though tragic in the extreme, was unremarkable....But the peculiar facts of this case and the way they developed have given Lester's short life an importance that it would not otherwise have had."

From witness testimony during the inquest, the story of Lester's life emerged; this account, while horrific, was typical of the community. He was an Indian child from a dysfunctional family surrounded by a dysfunctional community. He lived on one of the country's largest Indian reserves, Sandy Bay, which is located about 165 kilometres northwest of Winnipeg. The response of the Dakota-Ojibway Child and Family Services agency (DOCFS) was, as Giesbrecht concluded, typical of the Manitoba agencies. Testimony revealed that Lester was bounced from foster home to foster home, without a long-term plan. When it seemed that sensible plans were being formulated, a band councillor interfered or an agency worker refused to implement them. Lester had claimed that he had been sexually abused by a member of a prominent family on the reserve; these allegations were dismissed as Lester's fabrications or as the product of an overeactive non-native agency supervisor. Lester hanged himself in the home of a foster parent following an emotional meeting with his natural mother. In an earlier meeting with an agency worker, his mother had learned that, contrary to a plan worked out by a supervisor, she would soon be regaining custody of her child. Custody was the last thing she wanted. In meeting with her son, she fabricated an incident that led to his suicide.

The inquest revealed much more than just the events leading up to Lester's death. From the testimony of witnesses, Giesbrecht concluded that sexual abuse in the native community was rampant, that most child care workers were ill-equipped to cope with the situation, and that when they tried, elected officials or other members of prominent families in the community often interfered. Untrained agency workers routinely dismissed the directions of their superiors, sometimes on their own initiative or at the insistence of band politicians. Some politicians used their power and influence to protect family members from agency investigations; some of these protected individuals had been repeatedly convicted of child sexual abuse.

Giesbrecht found that Lester's case was not isolated. There were many others, including one involving Lester's younger sister. "She was used for sexual purposes by her own grandfather, raped by her uncles, beaten and intimidated by her own family, mistreated by her own community, allegedly sexually abused by the supervisor of the agency that stepped in to 'protect' her, and then bounced from one foster home to the next, willy-nilly, with no long-term plan, by the same agency."

Giesbrecht noted that despite the litany of horrors, there was no collective voice of outrage from the community. In fact, while the concept of community protection was a key component of the native child welfare system, Giesbrecht noted that the concept was not evident in Sandy Bay or in the DOCFS operation:

> The concept of the extended family was outlined in detail at the inquest, and it was explained how DOCFS incorporates this concept into the way DOCFS workers do their jobs....But with Lester, there are periods of time when no one was looking after him. He was truly on his own. His

mother was simply overwhelmed by her own problems, and was unable to protect Lester.

Other members of the family, or members of the community, offered a home to Lester for periods of time, but those placements always broke down. DOCFS was forced to intervene in crisis situations when it was clear that there was no other alternative....

When DOCFS did intervene, their efforts were half-hearted and ineffectual...DOCFS suggests that there are "native ways" understood only by Indian people that make what to a non-Indian might appear negligence, perfectly acceptable to the aboriginal community. The inaction of DOCFS...cannot be explained in this way. It was negligence and incompetence pure and simple.

Many of the initial allegations against DOCFS were made by Marion Glover, a non-native agency supervisor. Although it was revealed that she did not even possess university-level training, Giesbrecht believed most of her charges. His assessments of the agency and of the Indian leadership were corroborated by the testimony of a few native child care workers that came forward near the end of the inquest. "They told of an agency that was unable to function because of its internal confusion and disorganization," Giesbrecht wrote. "They described political interference that made it impossible for workers and supervisors to concentrate on child protection."

The problems at the DOCFS agency stemmed largely from the attitudes within the male-dominated native community; many Indians refused to admit that the problem of sexual abuse was rampant in their communities. As a result, few sought proper help for their children, who were paying a terrible price. Giesbrecht also found fault with the provincial and federal governments, which had maintained a hands-off policy despite the daily occurrence of similar tragedies. Their complicity, he said, proved deadly:

The chiefs and councillors insisted on injecting politics into the system at all levels, and meddling in the daily operation at the agency, out of the misguided notion that this would result in more community control.

In fact, exactly the opposite has happened. Workers have to worry about so many other things that they are not able to properly do their jobs. Lines of authority have been completely mangled. Anarchy and confusion prevail. The vision has been lost....

The situation that now exists, with the province wanting to play as small a role as possible in the reserve child welfare matters, and the Indian leadership recognizing minimal involvement only by the province, and the federal government funding only, is intolerable....

All three actors in this sad equation have shown themselves to be quite prepared to grind up a few generations of Indian children rather than resolve this [jurisdictional] dispute. This "triple whammy" of calculated neglect has helped to produce the parents of the neglected and abused children discussed at this inquest. Those tortured lives tear at the heart and shame us all.

Giesbrecht's initial assessment of Lester Desjarlais's death was correct: this suicide was, unfortunately, unremarkable, because similar horror stories continue to unfold across the province. However, Giesbrecht pointed out that this tragedy occurred despite repeated warnings by previous studies of the native child welfare situation in Manitoba. His recommendation was immediate government intervention: if the Indian communities are unable to police themselves, then the provincial government must intervene. Giesbrecht called for major reforms of the DOCFS agency, such as the elimination of political interference and the implementation of stricter standards for the credentials of the case workers. He added that if the agency refused to comply, the province must withdraw its mandate.

A tone of anger and frustration runs through Giesbrecht's report; there is a sense that, while Lester's death could have been prevented, similar tragedies will continue to occur, because the native leadership, the provincial government, and the federal government are guilty of turning a blind eye to this tragedy:

The evidence is abundantly clear that social problems on reserves are simply enormous. Women and children have no choice but to accept dangerous living environments that would not be tolerated by non-aboriginal people....

What all of this means for people living on reserves, the great majority of whom are decent, respectable people, is that they are forced to raise their families in a third world environment of dangerous and degrading social

problems, overseen by an Indian leadership that in too
many cases is more concerned with allegiance to family
and friends and the pursuit of political goals than with the
welfare of the community. And all of this meets with the
benign neglect from the government.

Children or Sovereignty

The public outcry in response to the inquest and Giesbrecht's report
led to the appointment of a task force made up of representatives
from the native community, Ottawa, and the province. While the
investigation covered much of the same ground that Giesbrecht had
examined, the task force report, *Children First — Our Responsibility,*
reached startling different conclusions. Instead of greater caution and
provincial intervention, the task force urged greater autonomy for the
native community. Ignoring the concerns raised by Giesbrecht about
the problems inherent in a dysfunctional native community, the task
force urged that the adoption of traditional methods should become
the ultimate goal.

Members of the task force visited fifteen reserves across Manitoba
and heard presentations from 170 different individuals; it released its
findings in November 1993. The report confirmed many of Giesbrecht's findings: the widespread sexual abuse of children in reserve
communities, frequent political interference, ill-trained staff, and
chaos caused by three levels of jurisdiction. However, the paper
softened the allegations of political interference on the part of chiefs
and councillors, portraying many of those charges as misunderstand-
ings by outsiders. In addition, it downplayed the importance of university-level training for case workers, citing a greater need for
individuals attuned to the native culture and lifestyle. Finally, the
report condemned the cold, bureaucratic nature of the native-run
child welfare agencies, adding that they were unresponsive to community needs.

In an unusual move for a judge, Giesbrecht himself appeared
before the task force to defend and explain his findings. Giesbrecht
informed the task force that he had chosen to issue a toughly worded
report because previous warnings had been ignored and child welfare
on reserves had become a political pawn. The judge warned of the
pitfalls of approaching the issue too gingerly; to do so, he said, would
produce a report that would be "incredibly sympathetic to the point
of being meaningless." The task force was not prepared to accept

such a message. After interrogating Giesbrecht for ninety minutes, chair Wally Fox-Decent concluded: "I suspect that had you been on the voyage of discovery we have been on, your report would have been much different."

The recommendations of the task force differed substantially from Giesbrecht's. The group called for reforms to eliminate political interference, but concluded that the ultimate solution to the crisis would be achieved through self-government, whereby Indian communities would develop their own standards of care and formulate a means to look after their own children, accountable to themselves and without interference from outside authorities. The task force had taken an amazing leap of faith. Without any evidence to support its conclusions, and ignoring vast amounts of its own research and Giesbrecht's work, the task force members believed that through the transformation towards self-government, severely dysfunctional communities would heal themselves. This group, without referring to it specifically, had opted for the Spallumcheen model. In the prelude to self-government, the task force called for the implementation of national Indian child welfare legislation and a directorate to oversee the workings of the native agencies. It wanted to decentralize the formal native agencies and revitalize individual community child welfare committees, by enhancing their responsibilities. When self-government becomes a reality, the task force believes that the new legislation will be obsolete, but that its standards will be upheld in each community. Individual bands themselves will decide if, like the Spallumcheen, they should run their own services or join other communities in running services on a regional basis:

> The Task Force firmly believes that a fundamental shift in authority must take place from those who exercise it to those who should exercise it — the First Nations people, and wherever possible, the First Nations communities. There is the inherent right of the First Nations people to self-government, and when this is achieved, child and family issues will become their responsibility and theirs alone.

The critical difference between the two reports was the ultimate solution each offered. The task force felt that the problems would only be solved when individual communities assumed complete control. Giesbrecht fully supported the concept of native responsibility, but he saw no magic solution in native control. When native communities proved incapable or unwilling to address their problems, Giesbrecht concluded that an outside authority must intervene. As of the writing of this edition, Ottawa, Manitoba and the Assembly of Manitoba Chiefs were still studying the ramifications of the task force recommendations. The provincial government stated that it supports the recommendations in principle, but that it could do nothing without the appropriate federal legislation. Giesbrecht's report has been denounced by the Assembly of Manitoba Chiefs and ignored by the province and Ottawa.

At a Crossroads

Native communities across the country want independence for their agencies from provincial jurisdictions, hoping to win the freedom the Spallumcheen band wrested from Ottawa and the British Columbia government. These bands have taken Ottawa's devolution policy for child welfare as far as it can go. Seeking to fulfil their self-government dreams, the Manitoba chiefs want the agencies to be accountable to their own people and hope to create a child welfare directorate, with its own culturally relevant policies and guidelines, to replace provincial participation. Ottawa has rejected this model, preferring the status quo. Despite the damning evidence gathered in Manitoba, Indian Affairs has insisted that those agencies are adequately funded and that they are to act as models for native child welfare service delivery across the country. It is not certain how the plan to dismantle the department of Indian Affairs in Manitoba will affect child welfare services. Ottawa's most recent report on the issue was released in October 1989. In *Indian Child and Family Services Management Regime, Discussion Paper,* Ottawa promises greater Indian autonomy, but actually attempts to place the agencies under tighter control, tying them permanently to provincial jurisdiction. Like the White Paper, released twenty years earlier, the proposals for self-government that Ottawa unveiled in the James Bay and Sechelt agreements, and Bill C–52 in 1984, this child welfare report rejects the Indian vision of self-government. The paper suggests the creation of more Indian agencies, but it adds that Ottawa does not have the funds to do so. It seeks autonomy for bands, yet it rejects the Spallumcheen model and demands that agencies remain under provincial jurisdiction. The report states that funding levels will match provincial levels, but it does not take into account the need for additional staffing and training, and their associated costs, to ensure that Indian agencies will avoid the problems documented in Manitoba.

The 1989 paper was not acceptable to the Indian community then, and it is not acceptable today. Native leaders in Manitoba are encouraging Indian case workers to stretch their authority from the reserves to Winnipeg and other urban centres where their people live, to license foster homes and approve adoptions. Case workers from non-native agencies now find themselves wrestling with native agencies over Indian clients. The provincial authorities resent this intrusion and threaten court action to force the Indian agencies back on the reserves. The Indian agencies see the reserve borders as artificial boundaries and argue that native people living off-reserve should still have access to agency services. This battle will undoubtedly be fought across the country as other bands try to break their ties with Ottawa and the provinces.

The Indian community has made quick strides over the past ten years in establishing control of its own child welfare programs. Yet, those gains were accomplished with numerous errors and far too many child victims. The consultants and the professionals investigating the situation initially concluded that Ottawa's unwillingness to fund serious preparation was the source of the problem. In Manitoba, the tragedies continued because the Indian leadership refused to acknowledge its own errors, and provincial and federal officials refused to meddle in what they perceived to be a native matter. Now, the native community finds itself in a dilemma: it cannot, and should not, revert to previous methods, but it cannot continue on its present course without making dramatic concessions and alterations. As the Spallumcheen band has already shown, the traditional approach can work, but only within the confines of a healthy community. Manitoba's experiment will only succeed if its participants admit that many native communities are in serious trouble and ensure that resources are put in place to heal entire communities while protecting their children at the same time. To do anything else, as Giesbrecht said, is to condemn another generation of Indian children.

9

Justice

Alvert Cherry slouches back in his chair and listens closely to the man sitting next to him. The nameless man, wearing a blue wind-breaker and a look of sheer concentration, is translating into English the lyrical Ojibway words Cherry has just uttered. The translation holds the attention of the 100 witnesses in the room almost as easily as Cherry's own hypnotic tones did only moments before. When the translator finishes, Cherry leans forward to make another point, his face in silhouette against the large, barred window behind him.

It is April 12, 1989, and Cherry, an inmate of Stony Mountain Federal Penitentiary in Manitoba, has been allotted fifteen minutes before the Manitoba Aboriginal Justice Inquiry. The two-man in-quest is investigating native experiences in the province's justice system. Cherry's testimony stretches far beyond his time limit, but neither of the inquiry's commissioners, associate chief judge Murray Sinclair, an Ojibway Indian sporting a long braid, and Justice Alvin Hamilton of the Manitoba Court of the Queen's Bench, a silver-haired non-native man, appear to be in any rush. As Cherry speaks, they both take copious notes.

Amid the day's stories of mistreatment and discrimination, and opinions on improving a justice system that incarcerates Canada's aboriginal people at phenomenal rates, one theme begins to emerge beyond all others. Cherry, speaking quietly and simply with the authority of a philosopher king, brings together the unconnected statements of the native inmates living behind the sandstone walls of this century-old institution and of the hundreds of others who have appeared before the commission in the months before. "The white man has been here for 500 years," Cherry says. "It is about time that the white man starts to learn about our different culture."

Throughout the day, the judges have heard about many instances of the prison system's lack of understanding and acceptance of native traditions and beliefs: the restriction of spiritual ceremonies to a weekly basis, following the Christian custom of worshipping only on Sunday; the removal of sweet grass and medicine bags in cell searches; the provision of only one elder to satisfy a diversity of native traditions (including the sweat lodge ceremony, which can be held only once a month because of its physically taxing nature).

With these examples and several of his own, Cherry illustrates just how foreign non-native society's concept of incarceration is for native inmates; the system not only removes them from society, but also meters out additional punishment by placing them in a world that fails to accommodate their beliefs. "We have our own values, our own way of life as aboriginal people," Cherry concludes in halting English. "We are in a very abnormal setting."

Weeks later, as the public hearings segment of the Manitoba inquiry winds up, Judge Sinclair reflects on the 800 presentations he has heard. "We have been told that we must look seriously at the ways that our justice system has come to grips with what has often been a matter of cultures in conflict," says Sinclair.

For more than two decades, studies of native involvement in Canada's complex legal system have been conducted; these investigations have explored native interaction with police, the courts, prisons, parole boards, and social service agencies. The most profound notion to have emerged from this body of work is the acceptance that forcing non-native rules of incarceration and methods of rehabilitation on native people might be discriminatory and unjust. A plethora of examinations into every conceivable native justice issue, viewed from every angle, have provided a mountain of often overlapping suggestions for improvement. However, as with most native issues explored in this book, actual change has been agonizingly slow, lending further weight to the often repeated lament of native people: "We have been studied to death with little to show for it."

In the late 1960s, in the glow of the civil rights movement in the United States, Canada began to examine its own civil rights record. Was racism behind the disproportionate number of incarcerations of native people? Or was poverty the cause? In search of answers and ways to dissipate the building tensions among native people, federal and provincial governments in Canada began conducting internal reviews on a wide range of issues, from hiring practices throughout the justice system to the treatment of native offenders at the hands of local police, the Royal Canadian Mounted Police, and all levels of the judiciary.

In 1975, the first attempt to explore the issue on a national scale took place during a three-day, federal-provincial conference in Edmonton, Alberta. The National Conference on Native Peoples and the Criminal Justice System attracted more than 200 delegates, including then solicitor general of Canada Warren Allmand, his provincial counterparts, and native leaders from across Canada. "Our expectations of this conference are high, and so they should be," Allmand stated during the event. "We share a determination to gain a better understanding of the problems we face and to move towards their solution."

The conference's six general guidelines and fifty-eight specific recommendations covered issues such as greater native representation in the criminal justice system and the education of non-native employees with respect to aboriginal customs and values. These suggestions reflected, in somewhat greater detail, many of the same concerns and viable solutions raised two years earlier in a more narrowly focussed investigation at the Conference on Northern Justice, which was held in Manitoba. In 1988, the solicitor general's office was nearing the end of a two-year study into the experience of native offenders from the day they entered federal prison to the day of their release. The interim report, based on interviews with inmates and staff at all levels, again issued the call for greater native involvement in programs and the education of non-native staff to encourage respect for aboriginal people. For the next two decades, this same message would echo through the multitude of examinations of the judicial system, conducted by all levels of government across the country. In fact, a 1993 report for the solicitor general of Canada on policing services for aboriginal peoples estimated that a total of fifty-two government-sponsored studies had been conducted since 1967, when the Canadian Corrections Association released its initial report, *Indians and the Law*. "The redundancy of [these] recommendations serves to highlight the continuing concern of the current system as well as the need for effective meaningful change," noted the 1993 document. Another distressing review, conducted in 1991, of the various aboriginal justice inquiries, task forces, and commissions, concluded: "The fact remains that apart from the modest reforms...most recommendations made by these inquiries have not been addressed."

Public Attention Focussed

In the late 1980s and early 1990s, Canadians were being bombarded almost daily by extensive publicity surrounding several independent, provincewide examinations of the treatment of native offenders by the judiciary.

In October 1993, a three-member inquiry into the shooting death of Cree trapper Leo LaChance of Saskatchewan by an admitted white supremacist released a report that raised serious questions about the diligence of police and prosecutors during the investigation. In January 1990, the Nova Scotia government released a two-year, $7-million study of the circumstances surrounding the wrongful conviction of Donald Marshall, Jr., a Micmac Indian who served eleven years in prison for a murder he did not commit. The scathing report touched on every level of Nova Scotia's judicial system. "The criminal justice system failed Donald Marshall, Jr. at virtually every turn," concluded the three judges in their seven-volume ruling. They added, in no uncertain terms, that racism had played a major role in Marshall's conviction and incarceration.

In Manitoba, the government launched the Aboriginal Justice Inquiry after the March 1988 shooting death of native leader John Joseph Harper by a Winnipeg constable. For months on end, Canadians watched as almost every level of the justice system, from the courts to police, was scrutinized as never before.

In April 1988, the Alberta government buckled after ten months of pressure and called for an inquiry into police relations with the province's aboriginal people. One of its mandates was to examine charges by the Blood Indians regarding improper police conduct during murder investigations involving band members. Less than three weeks before the inquiry was to begin, additional controversy was added to the already tense situation when a Lethbridge policeman shot and killed a Blood Indian named Heavy Runner, who had threatened police with a pair of knives. What was originally a six-month probe into five mysterious deaths ended eleven months later with more than 15,000 pages of transcripts and 160 exhibits on sixteen deaths. As with all other examinations into native issues in Canada, the $2-million inquiry, led by provincial court judge Carl Rolph, grew to explore the wide-ranging problems facing the Blood Indian band, from alcohol abuse to poverty.

The tension showed no signs of abating, as several Indian leaders across Canada called for similar inquiries within their own jurisdictions, and many began to talk about their expectations for the report of the beleaguered Royal Commission on Canada's Aboriginal Peoples, to be released in 1996.

While each of the later examinations has added new information based on particular circumstances, almost all reports have insisted that change will come only if the focus moves beyond the workings of the justice system and into the complex connections between poverty, discrimination, crime, and imprisonment. Neither startling revelations nor miracle cures for the high rate of native imprisonment are expected from the royal commission or any other sources. But, according to legal and other experts, what is expected to develop in the next few years is a growing acceptance among Canadians that it is time to give native people a chance to handle a problem with which non-natives have had little success. This acceptance is based on a striking admission — that native customs, methods, and values are credible and may offer tools of punishment and rehabilitation that are more effective than the traditional non-native approach.

The translation of this idea into action is often debated alongside discussions about the place of self-government in the wider Canadian context. Despite the numerous studies conducted and the apparent lack of progress, many experts in the late 1980s were hopeful that the accumulation of evidence would focus public attention on native justice issues and trigger the political will needed to make major changes. Legal experts, in particular, have predicted that the studies' conclusions and recommendations would result in marked changes for the entire country.

Professor Michael Jackson of the University of British Columbia is confident that the various reviews will do more than simply release tensions for a short period and then allow everything to settle back down, just to repeat the process all over again. "We are on the verge of a breakthrough," he argued in 1989. "There is just too much going on around the country. The 1975 conference was not much more than people coming together. There was no sustained effort." There is some evidence that he is right: things are changing.

Since 1987, numerous aboriginal police programs and training initiatives have been launched, providing some insight into how a native justice system might work. In April 1992, the federal government established the Aboriginal Justice Directorate to work in conjunction with the solicitor general of Canada and the secretary of state. The directorate oversees the Aboriginal Justice Fund, which finances the development of aboriginal programs and services, train-

ing and legal education projects, cross-cultural training, and consultations on native issues.

A 1992 inventory of aboriginal policing programs, conducted for
the solicitor general's office, profiled a number of native-run police
services. The Louis Bull Police Service in Hobbema, Alberta, was
one such case. In 1987, the province granted authority over policing
on the reserve to the Alberta band, which now offers twenty-four
hour police service. Band officers can enforce the Criminal Code and
other federal-provincial statutes, as well as band by-laws. The band
provides 99.5 per cent of the $670,000 annual budget; the province,
the rest. An evaluation of the "community-based" program after one
year indicated that "the crime rate has been reduced by about 50 per
cent." Dozens of similar initiatives have sprung up across the country, as have many more non-native initiatives aimed at improving
services to native communities.

More often than not, Indian leaders seeking some control over
native justice speak of programs that work within the basic laws of
the Dominion of Canada — the Criminal Code, as well as provincial
laws and regulations. For example, no significant native movement
exists to make Indian reserves separate political and legal entities
where armed robbery or rape would not be considered crimes. For
the most part, models being seriously considered by native leaders
and academics work within the Canadian legal system; similarly, in
the United States, independent tribal and reserve-based courts function as arms of the federal government. The maximum penalties that
American tribal courts can impose are one-year jail terms or $500
fines. The federal courts deal with serious crimes such as murder and
assault. Furthermore, native communities structure the courts to reflect specific traditions, using their own legal codes and frequently
relying on traditional customs to reach decisions. Some courts even
have their own jails.

In October 1994, the Saskatchewan-based newspaper, *Indigenous
Times,* carried details of the Federation of Saskatchewan Indians
Tribal Justice Plan for an independent native justice system. "The
First Nations Justice System envisioned…would exist as a parallel
[system] to the Canadian system," noted the article. "Provisions
would be made for cross jurisdiction between the two systems. Off-
reserve Natives charged with an offense could choose to be tried in
the native system. And non-Natives charged on reserve could opt for
trial in the Canadian courts." According to Ron Irwin, minister of

Indian Affairs, Saskatchewan has one of the most advanced proposals in the country.

Throughout Canada, native leaders have been able to influence both progress toward the establishment of their own justice systems and non-native treatment of native offenders. These changes have included a re-examination of punishments appropriate to the community and the offender. The common theme in the native-driven programs is healing; the focus is on finding ways to deal with offenders that will lead to a change in behaviour and an improvement in the quality of life for the entire community. A three-day round table discussion on native justice issues, held under the auspices of the Royal Commission on Aboriginal Peoples in November 1992, focussed largely on "reconciliation, restitution, rehabilitation, harmony and peace," according to the report.

The response of Canadians and government bodies to these initiatives has been, for the most part, positive. A 1993 report from the solicitor general of Canada recommended that "law enforcement agencies need to develop an awareness of the political values and beliefs that inform aboriginal culture, the education backgrounds of aboriginal peoples, and the sense of linguistic alienation experienced by many." Today, almost every major city in Canada provides some kind of sensitivity training for police officers and others in the judicial system who have frequent contact with native offenders. In Toronto, for example, an aboriginal peacekeeping unit staffed by three aboriginal officers was created in 1992, as one way of improving relations with the city's native population.

In September 1994, the *Indigenous Times* reported on the official signing ceremony at the opening of a wilderness camp for native offenders. The camp, at Lac La Biche in Alberta, is a joint venture between the Alberta Justice department, the province's environmental protection office, and the Métis Wilderness Camp Society. The twenty-five-bed adult institution allows elders to deliver counselling and personal development programs for minimum security prisoners. The camp was created in response to a 1991 provincial study on the need for better programs for aboriginal offenders.

In January 1994, the *Globe and Mail* reported that federal and provincial departments had approved funding for an alternative treatment program for sexual abuse that had been proposed by a British Columbia band at Canim Lake. The novel experiment offered amnesty from prosecution for anyone who confessed to a sexual assault during a two-week period. The program included a reconciliation process with the victims, to allow some abusers to gradually return to their families. The initiative was introduced in response to what was described as an epidemic of abuse in the community. One expert estimated that 80 per cent of the band's 483 members were potential candidates for the treatment.

The 1988 report, *Locking Up Natives in Canada*, by the staunchly conservative Canadian Bar Association, provided an indication that such ideas might be allowed to take root in Canada. After a two-year study, the association endorsed the concept that native people should be given the opportunity to run their own court systems. Similar endorsements, begrudging as they may have been, have resulted in slow but definite changes in the degree of Indian control over education, child welfare, and self-government. Only in the area of health care does the issue of native control lag further behind than in the legal arena.

Professor Michael Jackson, author of the Canadian Bar Association report, claims that the law is probably the most rigidly conservative institution in the Western world, and, like health care, it is one of the more intimidating areas for any group to consider taking over. "Sometimes these communities have the least ability to do something about it because they have so many other responsibilities, so many other issues to deal with that the idea of taking over the justice system is overwhelming. Justice takes a back seat, it seems intractable. It is fairly daunting to take on when you have no jobs, when your kids are dropping out of school, your people are on welfare."

As well, Jackson suggests that the idea of altering the justice system by offering culturally appropriate programs implies a shift in power, which is never relinquished easily. "It is the most cohesive part of a state's apparatus, the exercise of punitive power. It is always difficult to wrest power from the people who have it. The criminal justice system is awfully resistant to change."

According to Judge Murray Sinclair, co-chair of Manitoba's Aboriginal Justice Inquiry, moving into a position where the dominant society gives up some control has less to do with native people demonstrating the ability to handle the task (as many suggest) and more to do with a change in thinking on the part of the dominant society. "I think the real question is whether the people who had control of the football are prepared to hand it off. We have to understand that the process of self-government is one they [native people] are inherently familiar with. It has been part of their life for generations. What has not been part of the system is the respect for their history." This respect for native ways is what must evolve before real change can take place, Sinclair argues. "Not merely respect for it in the sense of it's all nice and thank you very much for telling me, but a trust in it and a faith in it and a willingness to divest and give up control where control now rests."

Still, even if the government is not ready to hand over complete responsibility, and native people, to accept it, work has begun. "What we tried to do in the Canadian Bar report was not to question native priorities, and not to suggest that if they all had tribal courts all the other problems would go away," Jackson says. "But I think that while these other initiatives play out, there are other things that can be done in justice to buttress those other initiatives."

The Pattern of Incarceration

The issue of native incarceration was not in the forefront of discussion when the 1969 White Paper was released. The document itself makes no mention of the issue, and the subject does not appear in the thousands of pages of White Paper briefs, memos, letters, and planned strategies, which circulated in Ottawa at the time. However, in its 196-page response to the government's proposals, *Wahbung, Our Tomorrow* (which was presented to the federal government more than a year later), the Manitoba Indian Brotherhood offered a few thoughts on the subject.

Referring to a study of native offences and the number of native inmates in the province, the document noted that, in 1969, Indians comprised about 4 per cent of Manitoba's population and just over 1 per cent in the Winnipeg area; however, they accounted for 23 per cent of the 5,472 offences in the city and 19 per cent of the 4,302 inmates at Headingley Jail (half of whom were being held for failing to pay fines). More than two decades later, the statistics were even worse. At Headingley in 1987, status Indians accounted for 25 per cent of the 2,703 prisoners. Including Métis in the count, the population of Headingley, which houses prisoners serving sentences of two years less a day, was more than 41 per cent aboriginal. Research continued to undercover large numbers of native people who had been jailed for failing to pay fines.

Between 1988 and 1990, Statistics Canada reported that native offenders, while making up less than 3 per cent of the national population, accounted for at least 19 per cent of provincial admissions and 11 per cent of federal admissions to penitentiaries across the country. Officials in the corrections department state that, for a variety of reasons, many inmates refuse to admit to their native heritage and that the actual rate is higher. When Alvert Cherry appeared before Manitoba's justice inquiry, a corrections official estimated that more than 45 per cent of Stony Mountain inmates were of aboriginal origin — status, non-status, Métis, and Inuit — based on information provided voluntarily by the inmates. Aboriginal people, including those who identify themselves as North American Indians, Métis, and Inuit, comprised 14 per cent, or 151,200 of Manitoba's population of 1.07 million, according to the 1991 Census. The registered Indian population stood at just over 10 per cent, or 62,635.

The pattern of incarceration reflects the distribution of native people across the country. According to Corrections Canada figures in 1990, for example, the number of native inmates in federal institutions in provinces east of Manitoba was between 1 and 5 per cent. The highest percentages were found in the rest of the country: 54 per cent in Saskatchewan, 40 per cent in Manitoba, 23 per cent in Alberta, 14 per cent in British Columbia, 44 per cent in the Yukon, and 75 per cent in the Northwest Territories.

The rate of incarceration in provincial jails, where inmates serve sentences of less than two years, is even more striking. In 1989–90, according to Statistics Canada, 18 per cent of the inmates in provincial jails were aboriginal people, a slight improvement over the 1987–88 rate of 22 per cent. Again, the numbers generally follow an east-west pattern: 4 per cent in Newfoundland and Nova Scotia, 3 per cent in Prince Edward Island, 5 per cent in New Brunswick, 2 per cent in Quebec, and 8 per cent in Ontario. The numbers jumped substantially in the Prairie provinces: the aboriginal inmate population in 1989–90 was 66 per cent in Saskatchewan jails, 47 per cent in Manitoba, 31 per cent in Alberta, 19 per cent in British Columbia, 65 per cent in the Yukon, and 88 per cent in the Northwest Territories.

"Aboriginal peoples are over-represented in proportion to their population in federal and provincial penitentiaries," states the 1993 report, *Policing Services for Aboriginal Peoples.* "In Manitoba, Saskatchewan and the North, aboriginal peoples represent more than 40 per cent of the prison population. The proportion of aboriginal youths who are considered delinquent is three times the national rate." The report estimates that 70 per cent of aboriginal offenders are jailed for crimes they have committed off-reserve and that the majority of aboriginal people in the justice system are women. "In recent years, aboriginal women have made up nearly one-third of inmates of the Federal Kingston Penitentiary for women, and a full 85 per cent of all provincial admissions in the justice system," notes a 1993 report for the solicitor general of Canada, which compares Canadian and Australian policing issues.

"The rate of growth of the aboriginal offender population has exceeded that of the general inmate population every year since 1982–83," notes the report on policing and native people.

Another fact particularly relevant to police work, according to the report, is the proportion of young people in the aboriginal population and their subsequent overrepresentation in the country's penal institutions. In the 1991 Census, 44 per cent of the aboriginal respondents were between the ages of fifteen and forty-nine. "The age group of fifteen to thirty-four will be the group most likely to come into conflict with the law," notes one report. Another states: "A male Treaty Indian turning 16 in 1976 had a 70 per cent chance of at least one incarceration in a provincial correction centre by the age of twenty-five." For non-aboriginal people, this rate was 8 per cent.

Such numbers are of particular interest to urban police forces. With the phenomenal growth in the urban aboriginal population in the last decade, police in cities have had their hands full. A 1992 federal review of aboriginal policing programs in the country noted two key concerns: "the 'over policing' of 'visible' aboriginal people in urban areas in terms of arrests, charges and treatment; and the 'under policing' of the less 'visible' violence against aboriginal people, especially violence against aboriginal women." The answer, suggested the document, would be the "continued development of community-based policing with much more grassroots aboriginal input" and sensitivity training, carried out by aboriginal people in their own communities, for police assigned to areas heavily populated by native people.

In June 1991, the federal government announced the First Nations Policing Policy, a plan to focus attention and resources on new ways of providing police services to Indians living on reserves. The policy noted the importance of ensuring that all aboriginal people were not assumed to be one homogeneous group and forced to accept the same solution for their problems. The reasoning behind the new policy was also interesting: "Increasing numbers, increasing militancy, such as the Mohawk–Canadian Armed Forces stand-off at Oka, coupled with pressures to deal with land claims and aboriginal sovereignty in the wake of the defeat of the 'assimilationist' white paper on *Canadian*

Aboriginal Policy...are combining to produce a major and largely irreversible demand for change in the treatment of aboriginal people in society." And more and more, the call has been for a separate native justice system.

At the 1992 round table on aboriginal justice issues, held by the royal commission, James MacPherson, dean of law at Osgoode Law School, York University, summarized the conclusions of the report, *Aboriginal Peoples and the Justice System.* "The current Canadian justice system, especially the criminal justice system, has failed the aboriginal people of Canada — Indian, Inuit, Métis, on reserve, off reserve, urban, rural, in all territorial and governmental jurisdictions. The principle reason for this crushing failure is the fundamentally different world view between European Canadians and aboriginal peoples with respect to such elemental issues as the substantive content of justice and the process of achieving justice." Ultimately, MacPherson wrote, "the linchpin of the current justice system (criminal and civil), namely the adversarial system, does not reflect the way aboriginal people think about or resolve problems."

The answer, according to at least some of the round table participants, was a separate native justice system. "It will not be a single system like the regimes in place at the federal, provincial and territorial levels at the present time," noted MacPherson. "Rather, it will be an individuated and plural system devised and implemented at the local community level...in recognition of the diversity of aboriginal people and because there are already, in Canada, a large number of separate aboriginal systems."

However, as MacPherson noted, the participants did not reach a consensus regarding future direction. Some legal experts continue to argue that the first step should be to reform the current justice system; if the effort failed, the next option would be a separate system.

According to Professor Jackson, some people argue that dealing with the disproportionate incarceration figures by granting a separate native justice system amounts to preferential treatment, in contravention of Section 15 (1) of the Charter of Rights and Freedoms. But those who make such arguments, he says, have missed the point. "The numbers alone tell us that quite distinctly what we have is a denial of equality." Critics of a separate justice system, Jackson argues, lack the understanding that native people have distinct rights and status as the first citizens of this country — rights that are recognized in another section of the Constitution and that are not shared by ethnic groups in Canada. "There is a constitutional basis for it, for native people, and there is not a constitutional basis for other groups." Jackson is referring to Section 35 of the Constitution and its recognition of existing aboriginal rights.

The same concept was described by Jeremy Webber, law professor with the Institute of Comparative Law at McGill University, in his submission to the royal commission's round table, *Individuality, Equality and Difference: Justification for a Parallel System of Aboriginal Justice.* "The mere fact that a parallel system of justice exists, one which reflects the culture of a particular people, does not mean that the interests of individuals have been sacrificed on the altar of 'collective rights'. We have to look more deeply to see whether the underlying value of individuality is protected."

The lack of understanding of this key point reaches the highest levels of both the judiciary and the government, and comprises one of the fundamental stumbling blocks to progress, Jackson argues. In January 1989, as Canada's newly appointed Conservative minister of Justice, Doug Lewis conveyed this lack of understanding in stating that creating a parallel justice system for natives could unleash a series of similar requests from other groups. While the new federal Indian Affairs minister, Ron Irwin, seems more receptive to the idea of a separate justice system, native leaders remain circumspect.

Professor Jackson also believes that the struggle of aboriginal people to control their own justice system is hampered by the large number of native offenders in the system. The people who will ultimately have to agree to relinquish power are those individuals involved in the judiciary. Based on their interactions with native offenders, these authorities have the distinct impression that Indian people cannot possibly handle an affair as complex as the administration of justice. "Those in criminal justice typically see native people at the worst part of their lives," Jackson says. "Police, sheriffs, judges, and prison staff don't see native communities and their leadership solving their own problems. They see the people who have failed. They rarely come into contact with the native leaders responding to problems in positive, effective ways. From that viewpoint, the response is predictable: 'How can native people do this when they can't stand up straight?' "

Other critics are concerned about the practical details of a native-run justice system. Traditional native justice systems were rooted in the aboriginal emphasis on co-operation, unlike non-native systems, which are adversarial. Co-operation was crucial to the survival of small Indian tribes that followed a nomadic lifestyle in the days before the Europeans arrived. While the traditional native justice system did administer punishment, the objective was to maintain the cohesiveness and survival of the group. Imprisonment was and often continues to be viewed as a destructive measure that harms not only the accused, but also the community. Historically, bands used various forms of ridicule before the larger group as a deterrent, everything from forcing a public apology to banishment from the group for a period of time. Today, customary punishments handed out in the American system include direct or indirect restitution to the victim of the crime or community work.

When Jackson released his 119-page report for the Canadian Bar Association, the media immediately latched onto one suggestion: the return to a separate, entirely native-run justice system. However, this model was only one among several presented in the document. Jackson never intended to suggest that Canada's aboriginal people must agree to a single system. Demanding that native people accept only one model disregards the vast diversity of aboriginal bands across the country. Canada's aboriginal people have many common roots, but their languages, customs, histories, and needs vary greatly.

"The government keeps asking why they can't agree about what they want," Jackson says. "There is this idea that somehow there should be this one model. Well, it is something they can't come up with."

Native-Based Justice

Yet another problem hinders progress in the creation of a native-based justice system. Some legal observers fear that, once control of justice is relinquished, the checks and balances that exist in the Canadian legal system to protect an individual's rights will be lost. In his paper, Jeremy Webber told the royal commission about members of a British Columbia native group who had kidnapped a delinquent member and forced him to undergo treatment against his will. This treatment consisted, Webber said, of a four-day spirit dance, which was supposed to resolve the man's personal problems. "The objection here is not so much to the fact of forcing a person to undergo treatment (or at least this is not the only objection), but rather to the way in which it was done." Webber argues that while Canadians will accept some limits on individual liberty, "they believe that these constraints should only be imposed through a carefully regulated public authority."

According to Jennifer Brown, a University of Winnipeg anthropologist specializing in native history, development of a new justice system based entirely on native traditions is improbable. For one thing, many native traditions have been lost, and, even if they could be recovered, approaches that worked in the past may not work in today's context. "I really think what you've got more of is a kind of innovation and adaptation," she says. "If people attempted to reconstruct tribal justice, it could be a form of justice that would incorporate quite a few traditional values and concerns and themes of native culture, but the actual form would have to mesh with what life is like now. One could go back to the traditionalist-oriented kind of system that would preserve certain themes, but I don't think it would be appropriate to call it traditional."

Brown sees evidence that indigenous leaders are well aware of these problems and are working towards systems that would both reflect an evolution of traditional ideas and function in co-operation with the Canadian justice system. "I think the native people are part of a world-wide phenomenon. They have suffered the impact of other groups coming in, sometimes in a very heavy-handed way, and ways have to be found to adapt to that, on both sides," she says. "History is not a reel of film you can run backwards."

Professor Jackson agrees. Old methods of punishment such as public ridicule worked in a world where offenders cared deeply about their peers' opinions. "How do you bring community pressure to bear when someone is not amenable to it? It requires new solutions." Jackson adds that native groups are not seeking answers that will isolate them from the rest of the country, but are looking for opportunities to develop justice systems in co-operation with the larger society.

The Canadian government does not have to look far to find examples of different models or evidence that various systems can thrive within a larger framework. As part of their research, Judge Sinclair and Justice Hamilton took their Manitoba inquiry south of the border to study the tribal court system run by the Navaho and Pueblo Indians.

Sinclair notes that American bands have been able to support their own justice systems despite the fact that the majority have a population of only 500 people. About half of Canada's bands have populations of more than 500, with several in the 1,000 to 5,000 range. "Many of them have their own tribal courts," Sinclair says of the American bands. "But they don't have full-time court administrators, they don't have full-time probation workers, they don't have full-time parole officers, they don't have a full-time jail, they don't have a full-time sheriff. What they do is rent. They rent a justice system. They generally rent a justice system from another tribe, an adjacent tribe with a similar culture."

Judge Sinclair and Justice Hamilton visited several Pueblo communities in Arizona and New Mexico. The largest band had a population of about 3,200 and its own full-time judge. "But the other Pueblos don't. They don't have the resources or the money or the crime to afford all of their own systems," Judge Sinclair notes. Instead, the smaller Pueblo communities rent time from the full-time judge, who uses the money to hire a part-time judge when necessary. The contract also includes the rental of a prosecutor and a legal aid officer.

The difference between the American system and Canada's circuit court system is that all the judicial players in the United States are Pueblos who spend up to a week in the communities, and they are paid by the bands. In Canada, only a few native people are among the provincially sponsored court parties, which fly into isolated reserves in the morning and leave at night. "The result is that these people don't feel like part of the community, don't feel answerable to the community. They don't feel any connection to the clients," says Sinclair, repeating one of the most common complaints about the circuit system.

Perhaps the most publicized fight against the fly-in justice system was the September 1994 episode in the Labrador community of Davis Inlet. Months after Canadians had been shocked by video images of gasoline-sniffing children who said they simply wanted to die, Davis Inlet was in the news again. This time, the residents had ordered a visiting judge and his fly-in court out of the community, after the judge had handed down what the community considered to be excessive sentences. The move forced a stand-off between police and Davis Inlet leaders who were demanding their own native justice system, with an emphasis on healing. From this incident, many Canadians learned about the justice system in remote aboriginal communities.

Professor Jackson's report noted that the United States has three Indian court systems — traditional courts, Courts of Indian Offences, and tribal courts. Each system offers insights into the potential problems of any Canadian proposal for a native justice system. There are eighteen traditional or customary courts operating among the Pueblo communities of the American Southwest. The tribal governor acts as a judge, enforcing laws based on long-standing traditions. The Pueblos have no written constitution or codes of offences, and customary law is handed down through oral tradition. The Pueblo council, a body composed of ex-governors, appoints a governor annually.

The United States government first established the Courts of Indian Offenses in 1883. These courts were part of an effort to destroy aboriginal culture by outlawing plural marriages, weakening the influence of medicine men, "civilizing" the Indians, and teaching respect for private property by breaking up communal or tribal land holdings. The aim was to have a court for every tribal government, a goal that was almost reached (seventeen still exist). Courts were staffed by Indian agents who applied the law according to a criminal and civil code drafted by the Indian commissioner. Customary Indian law was ignored or outlawed.

These Indian bands are now fighting to regain control. The United States Bureau of Indian Affairs appoints all judges to four-year terms, but the appointments are subject to the approval of the tribal council. All relevant federal laws, rulings of the Department of the Interior, and any tribal regulations or customs that do not conflict with federal laws are applied, as are provisions of the Code of Indian Tribal Offenses, which was established by the federal government.

The system has faced a number of criticisms. For instance, since there are few written decisions, case law has failed to develop any precedents. The issue of conflict of interest, which has been raised in the Canadian debate, has surfaced with charges that political or family considerations have interfered with the court's decisions; such a claim would be anathema to the non-native justice system.

In the 1930s, a change in thinking on the part of the United States government led to the Indian Reorganization Act of 1934, which returned some autonomy to Indians and resulted in the establishment of the tribal court system. The act allowed each tribe to enact laws governing internal matters, leading many bands to adopt their own tribal court systems. However, non-native political experts assumed that laws would be based on western — not aboriginal — customs and concepts. To this end, the Bureau of Indian Affairs drafted criminal code models to be followed. With limited resources to evaluate the codes or to create their own, tribes simply adopted what was given to them. In recent years, however, many tribes have redesigned their laws to complement contemporary self-determination goals.

Professor Jackson has explored court systems in Papua, New Guinea, Australia, and Canada — notably the Akwesasne (formerly St. Regis) and Kahnawake bands in Quebec. The Australian model basically adapted the national court structure by creating special courts for aborigines. These aboriginal courts, however, did not reflect existing models of aboriginal authority, but instead simply modified the regular court system to the special situation of aborigines. Jackson notes that the motivation behind the creation of the special courts was suspect. For example, the Australian Law Reform Commission suggested that creating the courts would be beneficial because judges in the regular court system were reluctant to convict the poverty-stricken aborigines, and believed more convictions would result in the special courts.

In Canada, two Quebec Mohawk bands have been running their own justice systems for several years, applying the Criminal Code and band by-law violations under Section 107 of the Indian Act, a section that was, ironically, designed to aid government assimilation plans. The band government collects fines and deals with prison terms through an arrangement with the Quebec government. Under Section 107, which was established in 1881, all Indian agents and their superiors within Indian Affairs were automatically appointed justices of the peace under the Indian Act, with powers to impose rules and regulations. Jackson argues that the motivation underlying the creation of the section was the same as that which sparked the establishment of the Courts of Indian Offenses in the United States; both actions provided a means of "civilizing the Indian population." Therefore, Jackson believes, Section 107 is unacceptable as a basis for launching a native-made model.

Jackson also argues against some bands' attempts to test their legal jurisdiction under Sections 81 and 83 of the Indian Act, which allow bands to set by-laws. Although bands have won a measure of success by using the by-laws to challenge federal fishing regulations and some provincial laws, Jackson notes that the by-laws affect only registered Indians on reserves and that, under the Indian Act, the minister of Indian Affairs retains the power to disallow any by-laws that the federal government considers questionable. Although his research presents some models that would work within these and other existing legislative frameworks, Jackson argues that, ultimately, the government must introduce new legislation specific to a native justice system. This new policy would, of course, require a degree of co-operation and understanding on the part of the federal and provincial governments that has yet to be seen in the native justice debate. Some observers believe that the defeat of the Charlottetown Accord, which would have recognized the inherent right to self-government, has delayed any implementation plans in the justice field. "A constitutionally recognized inherent right to self-government would have a significant impact on the structure and implementation of community justice initiatives, setting the stage for the development of a parallel justice system," concluded the report of a 1991 conference held by Correctional Services Canada and the Canadian Association of Elizabeth Fry Societies.

However, progress may yet be made, despite the lack of recognition in the Constitution of the inherent right to self-government. Liberal Indian Affairs minister Ron Irwin launched a self-government initiative in Manitoba in 1994, when he signed an agreement with the Assembly of Manitoba Chiefs which is to result in the complete devolution of authority from Indian Affairs to Manitoba's Indian bands. At that time, Irwin told the *Indigenous Times* that provincial authorities were the greatest obstacles to the introduction of native-run justice systems across the country. "Right now, those who have indicated a strong desire to move are Saskatchewan, Treaty 3 in Northern Ontario, the North Shore Tribal Council along Lake Huron, Walpole Island, and a few others scattered," Irwin said. "There's quite a few ready to move, if we can get the go ahead through justice and work it with the provincial bureaucrats." He added: "If we're ready to move, First Nations are ready to move, a provincial minister will want to do it, a provincial deputy will want to do it. It's middle management at the Attorney General's department in every province; it seems to get bogged down right there. I think that is where we have to put our effort, get through that group. The middle management at any AG's department in any province are reluctant to move...I think the first thing we have to do is recognize it, then attack it."

Meanwhile, the inquiries, the studies, and the recommendations pile up, while frustrations grow. The inquiry into the shooting death of J.J. Harper in Manitoba, the commission investigation into the murder of Leo LaChance in Saskatchewan, and the various reports being released by the royal commission have stripped away any notions that Marshall's experience of wrongful imprisonment was an isolated incident. The underlying problems of racism have been exposed for all to see. In 1993, a federal government report made the following admission in regards to urban police forces: "There continues to be significant evidence that police officers who are constantly in contact with the public develop strong feelings and beliefs as to attributes of individuals, based on factors such as appearance and ethnic background." The report used the word "bias" to describe the problem: "The working experience of many police officers exposes them to extremely selective cross sections of the urban population. Consequently, in the absence of balancing factors, attitudinal bias towards urban aboriginals may creep in."

In the months before his final report was released, Judge Sinclair sat in his Winnipeg office, speaking slowly, calmly, and with great patience about "how, as an aboriginal person, I feel this anger, and frustration and sense of wanting to strike out." Instead of lashing out, however, he finds himself guiding other native people to direct those feelings into productive change. "What we have said to [native] people in the course of our inquiry is that our report stays on the shelf as long as you're prepared to allow it to stay there. We expect that the inherent tendency of government will be to file it away and forget about it."

In large part, he is right. According to the royal commission's review of aboriginal justice inquiries, task forces and commissions, "the recommendations of the [Manitoba] Justice Inquiry have received no significant implementation." Among the recommendations in the inquiry's 1991 report were calls for community-based policing, employment equity programs to encourage greater representation of native people, retraining of any police officer found to have intolerant or culturally biased opinions of aboriginal people, and the establishment of a police advisory committee, which would establish programs, priorities, and recruitment efforts aimed at aboriginal people.

According to the royal commission review of the follow-up of some of the high-profile native justice inquiries, the Manitoba government responded with a proposal to create "a number of working groups, co-chaired by native groups, to discuss the possible implementation of those recommendations accepted by the government." However, aboriginal organizations were not happy with this weak response. "It has been emphasized that the government's invitation to aboriginal organizations to participate in and co-chair the working groups came only as a result of political action on the part of aboriginal organizations after the working group strategy was announced." In a striking revival of the centuries-old pattern, the Manitoba government had initially invited aboriginal people to participate in the process simply as "observers," a position that is no longer adequate.

Judge Sinclair believes that the Manitoba justice inquiry is one small contribution to the overall process of change. The inquiry's success, he said, lies in raising non-native Canadians' awareness about aboriginal people, and encouraging native people to talk among themselves about these issues. "I may go to my death bed never knowing if I accomplished those things. But I think I've contributed towards their accomplishment."

What about that sense of urgency and frustration after so many inquiries and the lack of action? "You have to understand the native culture. Urgency is not a concept....I don't know of any tribe that has a word for it. Patience is the virtue. The time in which things get done is less relevant than the doing. The point is that inherently there's a faith in our culture, in the outcome of life."

Perhaps more relevant, this time around, is a statement in Sinclair's closing remarks during the first part of the year-long inquiry: "We believe that, now, everybody is listening."

10

Native Organizations

Political organizations are the machines of action in a democratic society. They target issues, orchestrate lobby efforts, and force change in a complex world. In the past generation, native leaders and their organizations have emerged from near obscurity to become the increasingly effective voices of Canada's native people.

When the White Paper made its debut in Ottawa in 1969, there were fourteen fledgling native political organizations across the country. Two national organizations, the NIB and the Canadian Métis Society, made up the National Indian Council, which had been formed in 1954. In 1968, the two groups went their separate ways: the NIB moved on to foster the growth of the identity and culture of status Indians; the Canadian Métis Society began to lobby on behalf of all other aboriginal people. By the 1990s, both had once again shed their skins and emerged as new organizations with different names and mandates.

This pattern of tearing down and rebuilding organizations has been repeated since the time of the earliest recorded native political body, the Allied Indian Tribe of British Columbia, formed in 1915. Today, after more than a decade of constitutional war, most Canadians are familiar with the AFN. An association of 633 chiefs across Canada, the AFN was formed in 1981 to replace the NIB and, in 1995, is the largest predominantly political native body in existence. Its precursor was an association of bands that dealt with both the political needs of the country's native people and the responsibilities of a program funding body.

Before the 1960s, native organizations survived on the passion of their members and the small amount of money they could scrape together. Their leaders may have been household names in their own communities, but they were little known elsewhere in Canada. Political battles were more often than not one-on-one affairs with Ottawa bureaucrats — or with each other. By the 1990s, more than twenty native political bodies had sprung up. In 1995, Ovide Mercredi, the grand chief of the AFN, could be readily identified in native and non-native households alike.

Much has changed in the last twenty-five years. From their crises-oriented beginnings, native organizations have evolved into sophisticated, stable lobby groups, capable of launching and winning intricate court cases and political battles over everything from constitutional amendments to land claims and fishing rights. These groups have become masters at public relations and have managed to wrestle more and more control from their federal overlords. Some things, however, have not changed. The passion that fed the organizations throughout the 1960s is still apparent, and while their struggles for funding now involve much larger sums, the points of conflict are similar to those that hampered their efforts in the very beginning. As well, native organizations continue to be a target of government manipulation. Despite more than two decades of practice, native leaders still suffer with the frustration of working within a complex, cumbersome, non-native bureaucracy that remains in many ways unsympathetic to their goals. And, finally, despite their commonalities, native organizations continue to fall victim to internal bickering and dissension.

Examination of four major political events during the past twenty-five years — the 1969 White Paper, the 1982 repatriation of the Constitution, the 1990 Meech Lake Accord and the Charlottetown Accord, and Quebec's pending referendum vote — provides an opportunity to explore the evolution of native organizations.

The White Paper

Native organizations were one of the few specific targets of the White Paper. Government documents show that federal bureaucrats expected native groups, as young and inexperienced as some of them were, to become the main conduits for implementing the complex plan of the White Paper. Native organizations, particularly those with a specifically political mandate, had been offered little encouragement from Ottawa before the White Paper policy was announced, especially in terms of funding. But Ottawa now had a new policy to sell, and bureaucrats and politicians decided they needed strong provincial and national native groups to carry out the plan. "The Government proposes to invite the executives of the National Indian Brotherhood and the various provincial associations to discuss the role they might play in the implementation of the new policy, and the financial resources they may require," states the final page of the White Paper.

Invitations to speak with the federal players were not the only offering; money also began to flow. Ottawa offered the financially strapped Indian groups a grant package of $1 per capita for provincial organizations and 25 cents per capita for the NIB. The government provided a total of $300,000 to the associations in the first year of the multiyear program, with additional funding for special meetings held to discuss the White Paper proposals. Under Chrétien's plan, the struggling Indian bands would be given funds to support organizations, which in turn would lobby on their behalf at the government's bargaining table.

In 1969, that financing strategy translated into base funding of $61,000 for the NIB. In 1994, after an often bumpy financial ride that included some heavy debts, the AFN survived on an annual balanced budget of over $3.5 million, almost all of which comes from the federal government.

The funding of provincial native groups followed a similar pattern. In 1969, the newly created Union of British Columbia Indians received $46,046 from the government. By the late 1970s, the union had become something of a bureaucratic monster, with about eighty employees and a $1.2 million budget. A few years later, the union encountered serious financial problems, many of them linked to its lobbying efforts in the 1982 battle to repatriate the Constitution and to the recession of the early 1980s. By 1989, the monster had been tamed, according to its leader. Seven full-time and six contract employees were surviving on an annual budget of about $600,000.

Federal funding for Indian political organizations has always been a hotly debated issue. Native leaders have had to face the contradiction of accepting funding from the bureaucracy that their groups lobby against. As the Royal Commission on Aboriginal Peoples heard at its round table discussion in 1993, "The balance of power remains...in which aboriginal organizations are dependent upon government funding and resources to support change."

Native leaders in the late 1960s were aware of the potential trap they were entering when Ottawa first offered financial support. But with few resources and a membership heavily dependent on federal assistance programs, the leaders decided they had little choice but to accept the financial help in order to build their own political infrastructures.

The authors of the White Paper were evidently aware of the skepticism of native leaders and included in their plan a long-term goal in which native organizations would eventually be funded by their own bands and ultimately by the Canadian people. This community-based financial support would eliminate native organizations' dependency on the government, according to the theory.

In 1969, Indian Affairs minister Jean Chrétien believed that the White Paper plan would lift the majority of native people out of poverty within thirty years. Although the White Paper gave no specific time frame, supporting documents indicate Ottawa's presumption that Indians would be able to support their own lobby groups within this same thirty-year period. "In this way we ensure that all the Indian organizations are independent," Chrétien said of future funding plans. "We want money to come from the grassroots, and eventually it must, but many Indian people cannot yet afford to support the associations so we will feed the money in at the band level and let them decide who will speak for them, and what they want to have said." Few could argue against such a noble sentiment, even if it seemed naive to some. Ottawa failed to realize, however, that such a financial arrangement might actually cause problems for the poverty-stricken groups.

During the 1970s, a new hybrid of native political organization, the tribal council, emerged. Councils act as umbrella groups; they work on projects beneficial to a number of bands in a particular geographic area. The original intention was for tribal councils to eventually take over the work of Indian Affairs, once the federal bureaucracy had been dismantled — another White Paper proposal that failed.

As the Indian hierarchy became more complex, groups found themselves competing to stay alive. Saul Terry of the Union of British Columbia Indians states that, in 1983, he stopped approaching the tribal council for money. As proposed in the White Paper, the union was expected to tap into the council's money for part of its funding. But the competition for limited funds was detrimental to the native cause. "I told them this organization is not haggling over consultation funding. We don't want to fight with our own people over this."

Funding for staff salaries and for programs carried out by aboriginal political organizations and other native groups currently comes from a variety of sources, primarily the secretary of state for core funding and the Canadian Employment and Immigration Program.

The secretary of state began financing native organizations in 1971 through the Aboriginal Representative Organizations Program. In 1989, the budget for that program exceeded $11 million and was about to become the target of government budget restraints. Only funding from this source is provided to native political bodies specifically for their political work. Funds are granted instead for specific programs or research that falls under the mandate of various provincial or federal departments, such as Indian Affairs and Health and Welfare. Organizations compete for limited funds not only with other non-native groups, but also with each other. One Indian spokesperson says that using these various sources for money is "like reinventing the wheel." Securing adequate core funding from the secretary of state is difficult, and organizations frequently fall victim to government cuts and manipulation. In addition, the hiring and firing of staff becomes contingent on an organization's ability to formulate a program meeting departmental criteria, rather than providing any long-term stability for the group. Optimists viewed the 1969 financing arrangement, like most of the White Paper, as a gross display of naiveté on the part of the federal bureaucracy and its energetic new minister, Jean Chrétien. Skeptics, on the other hand, believed that the plan simply reflected the government's hidden agenda of forcing assimilation on Canada's native people: the native political machinery was being funded so that it could carry out the assimilation plan which, if successful, would make the organizations obsolete. Either way, the plan contained several miscalculations.

First, the federal government was certain that, with a little encouragement, native organizations would eventually support the changes proposed by the White Paper. To native leaders, this presumption was yet another example of the government's failure to hear what Indian people had been saying for decades about self-determination. Chrétien also assumed that, by 1969, the Indian political infrastructure had evolved to the point where it could function like a government bureaucracy. Finally, the government failed to consider the history of rancour within the native political movement.

In his book *Native People in Canada: Contemporary Conflicts*, James Frideres traces the roots of modern native political bodies to the nineteenth century and explores the efforts of native people to form regional and national organizations capable of representing their interests. According to Frideres, two basic reasons explain the eventual demise of the early groups — federal suppression and disharmony within the organizations themselves.

The disharmony, notes Frideres and other historians, can be linked to the natural divisions that exist within such a diverse group. The histories and experiences of native people across the country reflect their distinct regions. There are twelve different aboriginal languages, and religious beliefs, while often similar, are not the same. Native people come from numerous tribes and a variety of regions, both rural and urban, treaty and non-treaty. The federal government recognizes 605 different bands living on 2,597 separate reserves (some bands have more than one reserve). Adding to this diversity are the labels assigned by non-natives — Métis, Inuit, non-treaty, treaty, status, and non-status.

Over the centuries, attempts by native bands to unite have been thwarted by more than just the enormity of the task. Evidence of manipulation — both official and non-official — by Ottawa to prevent the emergence of a united political native force is well documented. One of the most blatant moves was the Indian Act of 1927, which prohibited native people from organizing politically beyond the local level. In the 1980s, forty years after the restriction was removed, there was still ample evidence that Ottawa used its powers to manipulate native political organizations to suit its own agenda. For example, funding for well-established groups was cut off with little notice, while new groups, friendlier to Ottawa's aspirations, suddenly found cash in their accounts. Federal bureaucrats have also been known to support or instigate smear campaigns against native leaders who have caused them grief. For example, in 1989, the Conservative government of Prime Minister Brian Mulroney launched what native leaders viewed as a campaign to undermine their goals and to cut funding. Alberta was the target this time, and the focus was the Lubicon Indian Band. The band has been involved in a protracted land dispute with the provincial government and Ottawa, and had conducted an effective, embarrassing campaign. Band members used every tactic, from blockades to keep oil companies off the land to demonstrations at the Calgary Winter Olympics. In an obvious attempt to undermine the Lubicon battle, the federal government agreed in July 1989 to sponsor a new Alberta band and create a new reserve. The new band consists of about twenty former Lubicon members who disagreed with the demands of Lubicon chief Bernard Ominayak. They wanted him to accept a government offer that he had already rejected. The federal move to support the splinter group overrode the long-standing policy against the recognition of any new Indian bands in Canada.

Such tension between native groups and the federal government was already well entrenched by the time Ottawa released the White Paper. The policy paper provided recommendations for bureaucratic support of the groups. Only after the White Paper's release, however, did many bureaucrats realize that some native people would not look favourably upon any of their organizations that accepted the new role. One month after the White Paper's release, one Indian Affairs supervisor wrote: "A surprising result of the Policy Statement has been the discrediting of the New Brunswick Association in the eyes of many Indians. It was reported that some Indians blame the association for the policy and have already resigned from it. The association is fairly new....If it falls by the wayside, we will be confronted with extra difficulties in embarking on the consultation and negotiation process in that province." In typical tunnel-vision style, this government official made no mention of the effect of the loss on the ability of New Brunswick natives to voice their concerns.

Harold Cardinal, the dynamic, determined leader of the Indian Association of Alberta in 1969, believes Canadians often forget that native people are new to the non-native political game. It was not until 1951 that the government removed from the Indian Act some of the restrictions preventing native political development: the right of Indians to organize outside of their reserves, the right to leave reserves without obtaining permission from their Indian agent, and the right of others to help Indians prepare claims against the government without legal penalty. "Those were part of a total range of instruments that the Canadian government was using as a policy to wipe out Indianness," Cardinal argued in an interview in 1989, referring to federal policies throughout the 1930s and 1940s. In the 1950s, Ottawa lifted some of the more restrictive elements of the Indian Act. "In 1951, it was clear that those kinds of laws could not be tolerated anymore. And, in a sense, that began the long, slow climb back."

Another significant event, according to Cardinal, occurred in 1960 when Indians obtained, for the first time, the right to vote in federal elections. Native people had already gained provincial and territorial voting rights in British Columbia, Nova Scotia, Newfoundland, and the Northwest Territories in 1949, and in Ontario in 1954. Those rights would come later in the Yukon, Manitoba, and Saskatchewan (1960), in New Brunswick and Prince Edward Island (1963), in Alberta (1965), and in Quebec (1969). Cardinal and other native leaders view the 1960 federal benchmark as the key that finally unlocked the door to true growth for native political organizations in the modern Canadian context: "With the granting of the franchise, that signalled the nation state's acceptance that we might be human after all," says Cardinal sardonically.

The native vote came amid early signs that times were changing for groups who had long been outside the mainstream political process across North America. The black rights movement in the United States, a revolution underscored by the introduction of the 1964 Civil Rights Act, was having an impact on the Indian rights movement in Canada. "I don't think our elders ever lost their sense of who they were individually, or collectively," says Cardinal, recalling his own political awakening during that era. "But the 1960s made it possible for them to very cautiously come out into the open from their catacombs recognizing that there may be a chance of living and practising the kinds of things they have been striving to protect through those years."

Cardinal is one of several native leaders who bristle both at the suggestion that the White Paper can be credited with turning native organizations into effective lobby groups, and at the idea that the Ottawa policy had anything to do with the evolution of Indian leadership. Cardinal points out that, before the White Paper was drawn up, the first national Indian body, the NIB, had been growing as an organization and was prepared to fight for Indian rights and the protection of Indian culture. All the policy did, he says, was force native leaders to regroup and focus their energies on fighting the latest government threat, instead of on their own goals.

Other organizations, however, such as the Union of British Columbia Indians, credit the 1969 government announcement and subsequent financing for their very existence. Indian organizations in British Columbia have had a troubled past; groups are frequently divided along religious or other lines or torn by fights over limited funding and attention. Still, the Union of British Columbia Indians celebrated its twenty-fifth anniversary in 1995. The union is one group that links its origins to the White Paper policy. Saul Terry, union president and chief of the Pine River band, described the birth of the union in 1969: "The idea was to pull all people together because of the fact the government was taking an action we did not think was conducive to our continued existence. I guess there was a common focus around which people were able to rally. It pulled people together for a time and broke down the traditional barriers."

Historians view the birth of modern native political organizations as the result of a number of factors, from the civil rights movement to the residential school system. "I don't think you can go to one cause," says Jennifer Brown, anthropologist and history professor at the University of Winnipeg. "There is an interesting generational factor," Brown explains, adding that, in a perverse sort of way, the much-maligned residential schools could be partly credited with helping native people from a variety of backgrounds reach some form of consensus about their goals, problems, and potential solutions. "A lot of young people were brought together from different reserves. They had common problems and they all underwent this sort of shared initiation. They began to share views."

The written response to the Chrétien document took native leaders almost a year to develop. During that year, they wrote hundreds of letters, lobbied the Queen of England, called on international bodies to hear their charges, and, on occasion, threatened federal bureaucrats with violence. For what many researchers and historians believe was the first time, Indians across the country put aside their differing interests and united as one voice.

In Manitoba, David Courchene, Sr., along with Harold Cardinal in Alberta and Walter Dieter in Saskatchewan, spearheaded the battle against the White Paper through provincial native bodies as well as the fledgling NIB. In the end, the co-operative effort was not in vain: Ottawa shelved Chrétien's White Paper and launched "A Search for Common Ground" one year after the paper's release, and soon after, native leaders submitted three reports, filled with statistics and specific recommendations for the government.

Before his death in 1992, Courchene recalled the early days of the national group the year before the White Paper policy was released. He relished the memories of those heady days of travelling from community to community, full of the desire to change the desperate conditions of Indian life. Although Ojibway, Chippeway, Cree, and Sioux were spoken in most of the Manitoba communities he visited, Courchene says the meetings he held across the province were largely conducted in halting English. "There was no money and no budget," says Courchene, who was the chief of the Fort Alexander band by the time the national organization was officially established in late 1967. "We used to have to pass the hat around in the community to get to the next community. But I was never short of a bed, or food, or smoke. It took me a year to get organized." According to Courchene, Indians across the country were being guided towards a national organization by Walter Dieter, the head of the twenty-year-old Saskatchewan Indian Association. Dieter, a Cree, would serve as the first president of the NIB. "We were into an exciting political, social, and philosophical state of development," says Harold Cardinal, the youngest of the dynamic trio. "We went out with a sense of adventure."

These three individuals were the first of a new breed of native leaders. Educated in the non-native school system and wise to the workings of the federal bureaucracy, they struck a common chord among their people and were able to communicate with the bureaucrats in Ottawa. Courchene recalls that native people were hungry to organize. "Getting together was new. But they had been in politics before." As a boy he had attended Métis conferences in Winnipeg with his father. "I think they had been ready a long time," he says of the people he met while forming the NIB. "It was just a matter of getting the internal work together." That — and money.

The early days were filled with creative financing. Courchene recalls obtaining his first funds from a government program aimed at helping farming communities: he claimed he was a communications arm for a community of farmers. Such funding escapades were not confined to national groups whose leaders had long been suspicious of Indian Affairs's largesse. Ottawa's 1969 announcement to fund political organizations was no exception. "When you get down to it," says Saul Terry, "it was still the department that had the say about how the funding would be appropriated. They still had accounting control."

And they still do. Cardinal views Ottawa's 1969 funding scheme even more cynically. According to Cardinal, in the year before the White Paper policy, native leaders had effectively tapped non–Indian Affairs sources for money and were gaining, at least in the western provinces, a sense of autonomy. "Of course, whenever a bureaucrat gets frightened he gets very conscious of democracy," says Cardinal. "He wants to know who is representing these upstart groups and can they prove they represent these interests."

As well, Cardinal believed that the 25 cent per capita maximum allotted in the White Paper to the NIB would effectively cut off other funding sources, thereby ensuring that the groups would have no voice. "We fought like hell to make sure that funding through [other sources] continued." According to Cardinal, the NIB lost the battle because Indian Affairs, faced with the political vacuum left when the White Paper was withdrawn, transferred responsibility for the groups over to the secretary of state and other federal bureaucracies. This change left Indians with the same funding restrictions that marked their relationship with Indian Affairs.

After the official withdrawal of the White Paper, Indian organizations with a purely political mandate began to multiply. Slowly, many leaders began to fight the advisory position given to them by Ottawa. By the 1980s, native groups had become fierce opponents, never far from centre stage.

Repatriation

By the late 1970s, the country's native organizations had moved away from their united stand against the White Paper and were again dealing primarily with regional concerns. Then, Prime Minister Pierre Trudeau's dream to end Canada's role as a British colony emerged, and the fight over the Constitution began. Once again, native leaders were called upon to unite. Their main goal, however, would be more ambitious than in 1969 — they would seek recognition as equal players within the federal framework.

This time around, native leaders used their treaties to back their demands. Those treaties, they insisted, were constitutional documents, and if the original signatory — the Queen — was about to hand over authority to a new party, then native people were entitled to be at the table, to ensure their rights were protected and incorporated into any new deal.

According to University of British Columbia law professor Douglas Sanders, whose detailed account of the native constitutional lobby effort has appeared in several publications, aboriginal groups began the debate with their three main organizations — the NIB, the Native Council of Canada (formerly the Canadian Métis Society and now the Congress of Aboriginal Peoples), and the Inuit Committee on National Issues. These groups united behind two general demands: aboriginal and treaty rights should be entrenched in the new Constitution, and Indians should be involved in the process of reform. This program would later be expanded to include recognition of aboriginal self-government, which would become a bone of contention between native groups and non-native power brokers. Considering that the Federation of Saskatchewan Indians had coined the term "Indian government" in 1977, native leaders faced a long uphill battle, with little time to explain to their own people and the rest of Canada what they envisioned their role should be.

Native people's initial efforts to be heard received only passing attention. Trudeau's response in the early rounds was an amendment stating that nothing, not even the equality provision of the Charter of Rights, would eliminate the special rights given to Indians in the Royal Proclamation of 1763. He then extended an invitation to the three key native organizations to attend the October 1978 FMC as observers. This gesture was viewed as an insult by many natives leaders, who had for decades argued that their rights went far beyond observer status.

Another invitation to observe was issued to native leaders for the February 1979 FMC. At the second meeting, with the 1980 Quebec sovereignty referendum on the horizon and the need for support growing for federalist forces, Trudeau offered to add a new item to the agenda that dealt with native issues in general terms. The three native groups rejected the overture as meagre and their leaders began to make other plans.

Twelve Key Points

In June 1980, one month after the Quebec referendum on sovereignty association was defeated, Trudeau's constitutional plan was accelerated. As *Globe and Mail* reporters Robert Sheppard and Michael Valpy describe in their account, *The National Deal*, two years of discussions and debate were reduced to twelve key points to be debated at a September meeting. All other issues were to be left for the "second round" of the debate, to be held after the Constitution was brought home. Aboriginal issues were not among the twelve points; native Canadians were being told, once again, to wait. Trudeau argued that the delay was the result of a failure of native leaders to offer clear definitions of their goals. Native leaders were furious and refused to bow out without a fight. They intensified their efforts. When the First Ministers met in September, the NIB held a concurrent conference that brought hundreds of native people to Ottawa and began making plans to send a team to lobby the Queen and anyone else who would listen, from parliamentarians to human rights groups.

In October 1980, the NIB opened an office in London, England. The Native Council of Canada also took the fight to the international stage, appearing in Amsterdam before the Bertrand Russell Peace Foundation in an international tribunal on human rights. The foundation declared the Canadian government guilty of "ethnocide," but the decision attracted little attention at home. In November, the Union of British Columbia Indians chartered a train called the *Constitutional Express*; more than 500 Indians made the trip to Ottawa. The pressure mounted.

In January 1981, Jean Chrétien, then justice minister in charge of constitutional matters, introduced an amendment: "The aboriginal and treaty rights of the aboriginal peoples of Canada are hereby recognized and affirmed. In this act, aboriginal people of Canada include the Indian, Inuit and Métis." There was also notice that the new Charter's equality provision would not negate the special status of native people. But two days later, under pressure from provincial premiers, Chrétien introduced another amendment that would allow any province and Ottawa to opt out of the aboriginal rights clause. Native leaders were outraged at Chrétien's motion which, in their minds, did nothing less than nullify the native clause. Faced with fierce opposition from native leaders, the federal New Democratic Party, and other sympathizers, Chrétien withdrew the offending clause almost immediately. But the die was cast.

While the provincial and federal leaders were suffering from last-minute jitters about the implications of the rights clause, many observers say it was ultimately the native groups who put the knife to the deal when their united front disintegrated. According to several accounts of the aboriginal role in the constitutional debate, native Canadians had arrived at the table to vie for an equal place with the provincial leaders with a largely unplanned strategy that would eventually prove too costly. Throughout their campaign, Indians leaders had failed to maintain a consensus within the national native community. Within days of Chrétien's last offer, the fragile native front dissolved as various native groups declared that the deal did not guarantee protection of their rights. Many status Indian leaders viewed the use of the words "aboriginal rights" instead of "Indian rights" as an attempt by the federal government to diminish their status and treaty rights to the same level as those of the Métis, and to discredit the growing recognition of Indians as an easily identifiable and unified force. (The Métis are wards of the provincial governments. Indian leaders claim that the provinces have done a poor job of providing for them and status Indians do not want to join their ranks.) The NIB was one of the groups that considered the word "aboriginal" to be a diluted version of "Indian" and a signal that the government was attempting to undermine both the growing strength and the national and international visibility of Indian groups. "The

tactic has always been that as long as you were dealing with identifiable, strongly visible Indian governments that say 'here are our
treaties,' then it was hard to deny the reality," says Cardinal. Using
the generic term "aboriginal" weakens the identifiable group, he
says. "It is as if all of a sudden you have put a smoke screen in front
of it. When you try and redefine it, then it becomes easier to mould
the kind of answers you have been working for all along."

By April, the NIB had withdrawn its support for the amendment.
By that point, lobbying efforts in England had also encountered
substantial roadblocks. British Columbia and Alberta natives had
launched lawsuits in the British court asking for support for their
position; they claimed that the British Crown was ultimately responsible for the treaties and that they had a legal right to participate in
the negotiation of repatriation of the Constitution. In January, the
British House of Commons Foreign Affairs Committee concluded
that treaty obligations had been transferred to Canadian jurisdiction
under the 1931 Statute of Westminster. Such a decision is binding in
the courts in England, and when the court decision came down, it
reflected the committee's findings. The Indian lobby moved back to
the British Parliament, but any hopes for progress on the international
front had died.

On November 5, 1981, the results of an all-night session attended
by Trudeau and nine provinces (Quebec was not included) were
released. Aboriginal issues had disappeared. Again, intense lobbying,
including a vow by the New Democratic Party to vote against the
resolution if changes were not made, forced the issue to be revived.
There was little celebrating, however. Only a watered-down constitutional amendment that recognized "existing aboriginal and treaty
rights" appeared in the final document. Ottawa also promised to hold
further discussions in a series of conferences.

Despite the near-defeat, the expensive five-year battle had not
been in vain. Native leaders across the country had once again been
given an opportunity to work toward a clearer definition of their
goals, both as a group and as separate individuals. As well, they had
succeeded in planting the term "self-government" in the national
conscience.

There were no doubts, however, that the lessons learned along the
way had been expensive and would remain a burden to many groups
for years to come. It is estimated that Canada's native organizations
spent $4.5 million fighting the constitutional battle. The Federation

of Saskatchewan Indians alone travelled to London six times in a two-year period.

The 1982 constitutional round was followed by the promised series of FMCs on aboriginal rights. The fourth and final conference ended in 1987 with the ministers' refusal to include "the undefined right of aboriginal self-government" in the Constitution.

Since this failure to win full recognition in the constitutional process, native people have continued to seek protection of their rights in the courts and on the political front. There has been much to keep them busy.

The Meech Lake Accord

In early 1990, as newspapers carried daily examples of victories for native people on a variety of fronts, Prime Minister Brian Mulroney's government delivered a series of blows to native organizations, particularly the higher profile tribal councils and the AFN. Three days after Finance minister Michael Wilson delivered a cost-cutting budget, which shifted much more financial responsibility onto the provinces, twenty-eight political and cultural native organizations across Canada were informed that, after nineteen years, their core funding from the secretary of state was being cut. Within three months, the twenty-eight groups would lose all of their base funding and be forced to survive on the program money they used to buttress their accounts. For many groups, more than 50 per cent of their budgets would be lost; other groups would see a reduction of 15 per cent. Total cost-cutting to organizations amounted to $3.4 million.

Lobby groups were not the only target. In the same move, the secretary of state eliminated a $3.5 million native communications program, creating a serious problem for native-language newspapers across the country and other native television and radio initiatives. Georges Erasmus, then national chief of the AFN, was stunned by the news. His organization was set to lose $562,000. "We're going to try and convince this government they've made a tragic mistake," he said. "It is extremely shortsighted and I think it's suicidal." Other native leaders charged that the move against their political bodies and communications networks was a direct attack against their growing power.

Ottawa denied the charge, saying simply that all Canadians had to tighten their belts and that only groups believed to have other sources of funding, mostly status Indian tribal councils, were hit.

Métis and non-status groups were informed that their budget would be cut by only 7.5 per cent because they had no alternative financial support. Status Indians were being told to beg for already scarce funds from Indian Affairs or their provincial governments.

Within hours of hearing the budget news, Erasmus was on the airwaves, telling Canadians that the government's move would be devastating. He had facts and figures, and a way of putting them together that allowed people to visualize the impact. "The situation among indigenous people in this country is absolutely deplorable. We are the Third and Fourth World Canada," he said. "The government is trying to keep us from explaining to Canadians the actual situation we live in." The Mulroney government had cut per-capita spending on native people by 11 per cent since 1985–86, Erasmus charged. To meet the 1985–86 level of $4,658 spent on each of the 440,000 Indians in Canada, the government would have had to increase native spending by $333 million.

Erasmus, a Dene from the Northwest Territories, is typical of native leaders of the 1980s and 1990s. A high school graduate, he honed his leadership skills in the late 1960s and 1970s at the grass roots level. He became heavily embroiled in the land claims negotiations of the Dene Nation (previously the Indian Brotherhood of the Northwest Territories) and fought the Mackenzie Valley Pipeline. He was elected vice-chief of the troubled AFN in 1983, and national chief, two years later. Like other native organizations that survived the recession of the early 1980s and the constitutional battle, the AFN carried a high debt load (more than $3.5 million) and was divided over its most recent election. But within three years, Erasmus had eliminated the debt and united the group to fight Ottawa.

Within this context, Prime Minister Brian Mulroney announced that the country would once again be called upon to deal with the Canadian Constitution. This time, the focus would be Quebec's role in the country.

During the three-year (1987–1990) debate over the Meech Lake Accord, the maturity of Canada's native organizations became evident. As in the repatriation debate of the 1980s, aboriginal people rejected the accord because it completely ignored them and their right to negotiate on their own behalf. One of the goals of the Meech Lake document was to entrench in the Constitution a vision of Canada that would recognize Quebec as a distinct society and the French and English as the two founding nations of the country. The role of Canada's first people was not mentioned.

While ignored at first, the native effort — spearheaded in large part by the AFN under Erasmus's leadership, and by the Assembly of Manitoba Chiefs, under the leadership of Phil Fontaine — slowly began to draw attention from the national media and federal politicians as the deadline for ratification neared and more groups added their names to the anti–Meech Lake forces.

To quell the growing protests, the federal government began to hand out concessions. When it came to the native handout, Ottawa borrowed a tactic from the 1982 campaign and offered aboriginal people conferences every three years to discuss their concerns. In addition, the government promised to strike a committee to study the idea of including aboriginal people and the multicultural mosaic as fundamental characteristics of Canada. It was not enough. On June 11, 1990, only twelve days before the ratification deadline, a lone member of the Manitoba legislature stood and stopped the progress of debate by challenging procedural issues. Elijah Harper, a Cree Indian from northern Manitoba and the first native member of the Legislative Assembly in Manitoba, became the unexpected hero of more than 440,000 native people across the country, as well as a growing number of Canadians who had come to despise the accord. Harper's actions, in large part co-ordinated by Phil Fontaine, Ovide Mercredi, and their organizations, indicated the degree to which native organizations had matured and thrived since 1982. While there is some evidence of internal bickering between the Manitoba chiefs and the Ottawa-based AFN, those disputes did not surface publicly during the Meech Lake battle. Instead, the sophisticated political and legal manoeuvres required to defeat the accord were executed with a deftness that earned native leaders and their people admiration and respect across the country.

Weeks later, however, those same leaders watched as violence erupted in Oka, Quebec, between Mohawk chiefs and the Quebec government. Some native leaders believe that the harsh response to the long-term land dispute was a direct response to the aboriginal role in the defeat of the Meech Lake Accord. The Canadian army was eventually called in, and the stand-off ended after 78 days. One Quebec police officer was killed, and dozens of heavily armed Mohawks were arrested and eventually convicted of crimes. For the first time in more than twenty-five years, violence as a political means of focussing attention on native issues had become a reality in Canada.

The Charlottetown Accord

By the time Mulroney was ready to re-enter the constitutional fray about a year later, much had changed on the aboriginal front. Ovide Mercredi had replaced retired national chief Georges Erasmus, and the country paid attention to the AFN leadership race as never before. Reporters crowned Mercredi the "eleventh premier" and federal politicians had little choice but to pay heed. This time, the AFN and other native leaders were treated virtually as partners in the process to create another constitutional document, the Charlottetown Accord. Among other things, the accord would, if passed, result in constitutional recognition of the right to native self-government "within Canada." Mercredi consulted with natives across the country and worded most sections of the accord pertaining to natives. He asked Canadians and aboriginal people to vote "yes" in the October 26, 1992, referendum. But it was not to be. For a host of reasons, including a palpable distrust of anything authored by Prime Minister Mulroney, Canadians voted against the document. Mercredi was livid and initially interpreted the results as a backlash against the native community. "Canada has said no to us," he said on national television. "And we are sick of it." He hinted broadly that civil disobedience would become the lobbying tool of future negotiating strategies with Canada.

However, days later, a much more subdued Mercredi reappeared on television, this time to apologize. On reserves across the country, 62 per cent of Indians had voted against the initiative. Mercredi may have done well to review events surrounding the White Paper and the repatriation debate; native people have often turned on leaders who are perceived as being too close to the non-native power élite. Behind the "no" vote were former allies Elijah Harper, now the MP for Rupertsland, and Phil Fontaine. Both argued that native Canadians had not had enough time to study the ramifications of the document. After hundreds of years, said Harper, what was the rush?

His leadership style and his propensity to focus on the federal government when seeking answers to the problems plaguing native communities, would haunt Mercredi in his second leadership bid in July 1994. Throughout the leadership convention in Saskatoon, it was not hard to find Mercredi detractors, including several members of the AFN's executive committee. Those who had worked closest with Mercredi during his first term in office charged him with being autocratic, among other things. They also blamed him for the AFN's

$2.3 million debt. Others made note of his failure to obtain consensus from the chiefs on several initiatives, including a fundamental change in the structure of the organization so as to allow a "one Indian, one vote" process for choosing leaders. In the end, Mercredi won. And while he warned Ottawa that the "chiefs are coming," it was obvious that much had already changed.

First, the Liberals, under the leadership of former Indian Affairs minister Jean Chrétien, were now in power, and native issues were high on the new government's priority list. Throughout the election campaign, the Liberals had promised that they would recognize the inherent right to self-government in the Constitution. (Details of this plan were not clear.) When the PQ came to power in 1994 and announced another sovereignty referendum for 1995, discussions about native recognition in the Constitution faded. But instead of dropping the idea of native self-government from the agenda, the Chrétien government, with the aid of Indian Affairs minister Ron Irwin, continued to move ahead with a regional strategy.

In March 1994, Irwin announced that the Assembly of Manitoba Chiefs, still under Fontaine, would spearhead the dismantling of that province's Indian Affairs department and oversee the experimental transfer of all responsibility to the sixty bands in Manitoba. The experiment is aimed at creating a self-government model that could be emulated across the country. In an interview with *Ottawa Citizen* reporter Jack Aubry in April 1994, Irwin presented his concept of self-government: "Almost every community will require its own mix of municipal, provincial and federal powers. Each deal will have to be negotiated. No community will be forced into any deal before the community is ready." In contrast to the 1969 White Paper, Irwin offered no estimates on a time frame for the dismantling of the department, in Manitoba or elsewhere; he expected the department to be around long after he had left his post.

The experiment, however, has left the AFN and its 633 chiefs without much influence on perhaps the most significant native initiative in this century. As a result, some antagonism has developed between the AFN and the Manitoba assembly, with Mercredi arguing that regional processes should not be advanced without constitutional recognition of the inherent right to self-government. Regional chiefs argue that, in the current political climate, they are wiser to take whatever control they can.

For the AFN and Mercredi, these events have forced a re-examination of the role of the national organization and its leader. Some observers suggest that if Mercredi fails to mend some fences and find a new role for the body, the AFN will simply become less relevant to the country's native people.

Quebec Referendum

It is possible that Mercredi and the AFN will find their renewed political voice through the debate surrounding the Quebec sovereignty referendum, expected in 1995. In May, Ron Irwin told Quebec chiefs that if Quebec chose to separate, the province's native people would have the option to stay in the country. And while Irwin was all but forced to retract his politically insensitive remarks later, polls show that Canadians, including Quebecers, agree. Some observers even envision a "Meech Lake II" scenario involving aboriginal people — perhaps with MP Elijah Harper saving Canada from the separation abyss.

It is also possible, however, that the AFN will be sidelined again, this time by the James Bay Cree of Northern Quebec. Well-schooled on the negotiating track in Canada (in 1994, they won a highly publicized, ten-year fight against the Great Whale hydroelectric project), the Crees are also experts on the international front. The Grand Council of the Crees has been involved with the UN Working Group on Indigenous Populations in Geneva since the group was formed in 1982. Today, the Crees are recognized as experts on international law and UN conventions as a means of advancing their rights. In 1995, a document called the *Draft Declaration of Indigenous Peoples Rights* will begin its final journey through the UN machinery. The document recognizes, among other things, that "Indigenous Peoples have the right to self-determination." The right is subject to international law, which includes the protection of the territorial integrity of states, i.e., the right cannot be used to support secessionist movements.

To date, however, Canada has led a campaign to all but eliminate this right from the draft, fearing that the clause could be interpreted to give native people the right to secede. The Crees say Canada's stance on the international front contradicts its position on the domestic front, especially if Irwin's retracted statement has any bearing on legal advice the government has obtained. The Crees argue that the UN declaration would support their claim that they have the right to choose Canada as their home, as they intend to, yet the Canadian government is opposed to giving them this leverage. The Crees may be interested in comments Chrétien made in 1969 on the question of native sovereignty. In a letter responding to complaints about the White Paper, Chrétien wrote: "I know that the Six Nations Iroquois Confederacy considers itself a 'sovereign nation'...But I must say that I consider the position of the Confederacy to be invalid. By definition, the sovereignty of Canada precludes the sovereignty of the Iroquois Confederacy. It is impossible to have a nation within a nation."

And to a twelve-year-old Indian boy, who had written in with his concerns, Chrétien wrote: "As I have said many times on many occasions, one can be a Canadian and yet be different. I am a Canadian who speaks French, and you are a Canadian Indian. But this 'differentness' must not be enshrined in legislation."

With Ottawa's acceptance of the Quebec referendum process, the Crees say that the Canadian government is giving Quebec tacit approval to separate if the vote is "yes." They hope, however, that their decade of work in the international arena will help them find allies who can pressure the Canadian government to clarify its responsibilities toward native people in a Canada with a separate Quebec.

Some native leaders argue that the battles they are being forced to fight today are the same as those fought more than twenty-five years ago, but on different battle fields; however, they have finally captured the attention of Canadians and the world, and their voice is one that will not be easily silenced. The new generation of articulate and sophisticated leaders includes a growing number of native lawyers, entrepreneurs, and civil service graduates who represent various bands and provinces. They all share the goal of self-determination, regardless of their stance on the intricate details.

Native people have long recognized that their small numbers frequently leave them at a disadvantage. But there is a growing sense of urgency, heightened by a demographic trend in the native population. According to the 1991 Census, the average age of the country's aboriginal population (Indian, Métis, and Inuit) is twenty; for the Canadian population as a whole, the average age is thirty. Almost 40 per cent of the country's urban Indian population is under the age of fifteen. The demands of this relatively young, frustrated, often angry group, with its keen awareness of native injustice, will become harder and harder to ignore. Throughout the debate on native issues, repeated warnings of potential violence have surfaced. To date, native people have, for the most part, turned this violence inward, destroying each other and themselves. In 1988, AFN leader Georges

Erasmus delivered another warning. "We say, Canada, deal with us today because our militant leaders are already born," he said in an Edmonton speech to the AFN.

Keith Penner, former Liberal MP and chair of a 1983 parliamentary committee on self-government, stated in 1989 that he still hears from Canadians who, seeing the poverty-stricken native person on the streets, ask how these people could possibly run their own affairs. He responds by telling them that they have simply never come face to face with some of the country's leading native spokespeople. When he hears the doubt in some people's voices, he draws them another picture: "When the White Paper failed dismally, the decision was made to turn the problem over to the native leaders which, in turn, began the politicization of Indian people. Since 1969, the number of Indian politicians has grown, and I would say that most of them are as good, if not better than MPs and premiers. In fact, I'm the one who feels inferior when I meet the top Indian leaders in this country."

Postscript

In October 1989, fifteen-year-old Nona Pariseau first posed the question that would eventually be included in the introduction to *The First Canadians*: "What is it that these Indian people want, anyway?" Her question led to several more, all filled with the frustration and impatience other Canadians have voiced about the apparent failure of aboriginal people to pull themselves together and lead productive lives, like the immigrants who have settled here. Pariseau's questions stemmed from her research for a high school history project on native issues, but her curiosity soon took her beyond the classroom.

After six months of talking to native people and debating the issues that have occupied the minds and hearts of Canada's aboriginal people for more than 200 years, the Halifax-born Pariseau was confident that she has found some of the answers. "Native people have been denied their basic human rights," Pariseau told a student audience called together to hear a debate on native self-government. "With the granting of self-government, natives will be getting back not only their human rights, but also a portion of what they had before white men began destroying them and their culture."

Pariseau had encountered many obstacles before reaching her conclusions. She was bombarded with the same questions she herself had posed only months before — questions asked by fellow students who suffered from the same ignorance about aboriginal history and who held the same negative attitudes about Canada's native people. "Kids asked me why Indians just couldn't go back to their own country, or why they wanted their own province. They said that after self-government, native people would just want to take over our country. They treat them like some communist state, like they are foreigners, and think that they are poaching off us."

Pariseau says that her experience has led her to conclude that racism was at the root of her initial evaluation of the native situation and of the comments classmates made during the public debates. "I was blown away," she explains, referring to the angry retorts that were tossed at her during the discussions. "I could not believe how prejudiced [the students] were. They still think that Indians are the bums on Main Street. But what they really need to see and do is to take a look at the reserves and to take a look at the fact that these people are human beings."

Looking back over her experience, she is straightforward and candid. "Yes, I was prejudiced, but I try not to be now. When I first came here, it was a lack of knowledge. But I think if everyone put aside their prejudice, they would come to the same conclusion…that native people need their freedom." And she has no doubts that the native leaders she met can run their own lives, and already do. "There will be mistakes, but so what? We've made mistakes many times, and no one talks about that."

Pariseau pauses a long time when asked if she thinks native people will win their battle for self-government. "I don't know," she says finally, with her new-found awareness of the struggle Canada's aboriginal people have faced over the centuries. "Look at how much we have taken away already. We have taken everything from them."

Pariseau believes that the strong native leaders and their communities will survive against all odds, but others may not. And she sees the possibility that Indian people might lose everything in their endless power struggles with the federal government, if Canadians remain apathetic and uninformed. Trying to get the native message across, she says, may be the toughest fight of all. "It's just so sad, because every generation has to learn it all, over and over again."

Bibliography

GENERAL

Canada, Department of Indian Affairs and Northern Development. *Basic Departmental Data*. 1993.

———. *First Nations Community Profiles, Manitoba Region*. 1994.

———. *Indian Act, Office Consolidations*. September 1989.

———. *Indian Conditions, A Survey*. 1989.

———. *Indian Register — Population by Sex and Residence, 1993*. March 1994.

———. *Main Estimates, 1967–1988*.

Canada, Department of Regional and Industrial Expansion. *Native Economic Development Program, Evaluation Study*. Prepared by Haskins-Sills, Deloitte (consultants).

———. *Review of Native Economic Development Program (NEDP), Element 1, Final Report*. 24 November 1988.

Canada, Report to Parliament. *Implementation of the 1985 Changes to the Indian Act*.

Canada, Statistics Canada. *1991 Aboriginal Data — Age and Sex*. March 1993.

———. *1991 Aboriginal Peoples Survey — Languages, Tradition, Health, Lifestyle and Social Issues*. June 1993.

———. *1991 Aboriginal Peoples Survey — Schooling, Work and Related Activities, Income, Expenses and Mobility*. September 1993.

———. *Canada's Aboriginal Population by Census Subdivisions, and Census Metropolitan Areas*. March 1994.

———. *1986 Census*.

Frideres, James. *Native People in Canada: Contemporary Conflicts*. Toronto: Prentice Hall, 1983.

MacGregor, Roy. *Chief, The Fearless Vision of Billy Diamond*. Toronto: Penguin Books, 1989.

York, Geoffrey. *The Dispossessed: Life and Death in Native Canada*. Toronto: Lester & Orpen Dennys, 1989.

THE WHITE PAPER

Asch, Michael. *Home and Native Land: Aboriginal Rights and the Canadian Constitution.* Toronto: Methuen, 1984.

Canada, Department of Indian Affairs and Northern Development. *Statement of the Government of Canada on Indian Policy (The White Paper).* 1969.

Canada. A Study Team Report to the Task Force (Nielsen Task Force) on Program Review. *Improved Program Delivery, Indians and Natives.* 1985.

Indian Tribes of Manitoba. *Wahbung, Our Tomorrow.* 1971 (obtained from the Department of Indian Affairs and Northern Development.)

Sheppard, Robert and Valpy, Michael. *The National Deal, The Fight for the Canadian Constitution.* Toronto: Macmillan, 1982.

RESERVES

Canada, Department of Indian Affairs and Northern Development. *The Incidence of Family Poverty on Canadian Indian Reserves.* 1993.

Canada, Department of Indian and Northern Affairs. *Survey of Bill C-31 Applicants.* Prepared by Coopers & Lybrand Consulting Group. 10 June 1988.

Canada. *DIAND's Costing Methodology and Questions on Bill C-31, a series of methodology papers prepared for the Assembly of First Nations Chiefs Committee on Bill C-31.* Prepared by the office of John Rayner, assistant deputy minister of Indian services. Spring 1988.

Canada, Indian and Northern Affairs Canada. *Highlights of Aboriginal Conditions 1981–2001, Part I, Demographic Trends.* Working Paper Series 89-3. Prepared by N. Janet Hagey, Gilles Larocque, and Catherine McBride, Quantitative Analysis and Socio-demographic Research. Finance and Professional Services. October 1989.

Canada Mortgage and Housing Corporation. Evaluation of CMHC On-Reserve Housing Programs and Summary Report. Program Evaluation Division, Operations Review Directorate. May 1987.

Lithwick, N.H., Schiff, Marvin and Vernon, Eric. *An Overview of Registered Indian Conditions in Canada.* Lithwick Rothman Schiff Associates Ltd., for Indian and Northern Affairs Canada. 1986.

URBAN INDIANS

Dosman, J. Edgar. *Indians, The Urban Dilemma.* Toronto: McClelland & Stewart, 1978.

Institute for Research on Public Policy. *Dynamics of Government Programs for Urban Indians in the Prairie Provinces.* 1984.

Krotz, Larry. *Urban Indians: The Strangers in Canada's Cities.*

Manitoba, Northern Affairs Department. *Workshop on the Development of an Indian and Métis Urban Strategy in Manitoba.* 1989.

Ryan, Joan. *Wall of Words: The Betrayal of the Urban Indian.* Calgary: University of Calgary, Department of Anthropology, 1978.

Urban Indian Association of Manitoba. *Economic Strategy for Urban Indians.* 1987.

SELF-GOVERNMENT

Angus Reid Poll. *Aboriginal Justice Issues.* 14 October 1989.

Canada, House of Commons Special Committee of Indian Self-Government. *Second Report.* 20 October 1983.

Cassidy, Frank and Bish, Robert L. *Indian Government: Its Meaning and Practice.* Oolichan Books and Institute for Research on Public Policy, 1989.

Brock, Kathy L. "Canadian and American Aboriginal Policy Compared: The Issues of Self-Government," in David Thomas, ed. *Political Issues in Canada and the United States.* Toronto: Broadview Press, 1993.

——. "On The Road To Self-Government," in Bob Kraus and Ron Wagenberg, eds. *Introductory Readings in Canadian Politics and Government.* Mississauga: Copp Clark Pitman, 1995.

——. "The Politics of Aboriginal Self-Government: A Canadian Paradox," *Canadian Public Administration,* 34. (Summer 1991), pp. 272-85.

Canada. *Consensus Report on the Constitution.* Charlottetown, Final Text. 28 August 1992.

Canada, Department of Indian Affairs and Northern Development, Assembly of Manitoba Chiefs. Framework Agreement — The Dismantling of the Department of Indian Affairs and Northern Development, The Restoration of Jurisdictions to First Nations People in Manitoba, and Recognition of First Nations Governments in Manitoba. 7 December 1994.

——. *Towards Manitoba First Nations Governments — Workplan, Drafts 4 & 12.* 22, 24 August 1994.

Chartrand, Paul L.A.H., "Aboriginal Self-Government: The Two Sides of Legitimacy," in Susan D. Phillips, ed. *How Ottawa Spends, 1993–1994: A More Democratic Canada...?* Ottawa: Carleton University Press, 1993.

Franks, C.E.S. *Public Administration Questions Relating to Aboriginal Self-Government, Background Paper Number 12*. Kingston: Queen's University, Institute of Intergovernmental Relations, 1987.

Liberal Party of Canada. *Creating Opportunity: The Liberal Plan For Canada*. 1993.

Prince, Michael J. "Federal Expenditures and First Nation Experiences," in Susan D. Phillips, ed. *How Ottawa Spends, 1994-95: Making Change*. Ottawa: Carleton University Press, 1994.

ECONOMIC DEVELOPMENT

Canada, Department of Indian Affairs and Northern Development. *DIAND's Evolution from Direct Service Delivery to a Funding Agency*. April 1993.

Canada, House of Commons Special Committee on Self-Government. *The Economic Foundation of Indian Self-Government*. Prepared by Thalassa Research Associates, Victoria, B.C. 31 May 1983.

Canada, Department of Industry Science and Technology and Manitoba Department of Northern Affairs. *Evaluation of the Canada/Manitoba Northern Development Agreement, Volume 1: Evaluations and Recommendations*. Prepared by the Advisory Committee to the Canada/Manitoba Northern Development Agreement. December 1988.

Canada, Department of Industry, Science and Technology. *Executive Summary: Mid-term Review of the Canada-Saskatchewan Northern Economic Development Subsidiary Agreement*. Prepared by Gail D. Surkan (consultant). n.d.

Canada, Department of Regional Economic Expansion. *An Evaluation of the Canada-Saskatchewan Interim Subsidiary Agreement on the Saskatchewan Northlands*. n.d.

Canada, Department of Regional Economic Expansion and Alberta Department of Tourism and Small Business, Northern Development Branch. *Canada-Alberta North Subsidiary Agreement Assessment*. Prepared by Co-West Associates, Edmonton, Alberta. 15 October 1980.

Canada, Department of Regional Economic Expansion. *Canada/Saskatchewan Northlands Agreement Evaluation: Future Directions for Cost-Shared Programs in Northern Saskatchewan*. Prepared by DPA Consulting Limited, Bell, Ahenakew & Associates, Damas & Smith. December 1982.

Hawthorn, H.B., ed. *A Survey of the Contemporary Indians of Canada: A Report on Economic, Political, Education Needs and Policies.* Two Volumes. Indian Affairs Branch. October 1966.

Canada. Department of Regional Economic Expansion. *Canada/Saskatchewan Northlands Agreement Evaluation: Main Report.* Prepared by DPA Consulting Limited, Bell, Ahenakew & Associates, Damas & Smith. December 1982.

HEALTH CARE

Canada, Health and Welfare Canada. *Annual Reports, Medical Services Branch, Manitoba Region and National, 1967–1987.*

———. *Suicide in Canada. Report from the Task Force on Suicide in Canada.* 1987.

———. *Vital Statistics.* Prepared by the Planning and Evaluation Unit, Manitoba Region, Medical Services Branch. 1986.

Lithwick, N.H., Schiff, Marvin and Vernon, Eric. *An Overview of Registered Indian Conditions in Canada.* Lithwick Rothman Schiff Associates Ltd., for Indian and Northern Affairs Canada. 1986.

EDUCATION

Assembly of First Nations. *Tradition and Education: Towards a Vision of Our Future, National Review of First Nations Education, Volumes 1 and 3.* Ottawa. April 1988.

Canada, Department of Indian Affairs and Northern Development. *Indian Education Paper, Phase 1.* 1 May 1982.

Canada, Indian and Northern Affairs Canada. *Basic Departmental Data.* Evaluation directorate. July 1988.

———. *Education of Indians in Federal and Provincial Schools in Manitoba, Evaluation Report.* 31 August 1978.

———. *Highlights of Aboriginal Conditions 1981-2001, Part III, Economic Conditions.* Working Paper Series 89-3. Prepared by N. Janet Hagey, Gilles Larocque, and Catherine McBride, Quantitative Analysis and Socio-demographic Research. Finance and Professional Services. October 1989.

———. *Post-secondary Education Assistance Evaluation Study, Final Report.* Prepared by DPA Group Inc. for the Evaluation Branch, Corporate Policy, INAC. January 1985.

Canada. *Main Estimates, 1967/68* through to *1988/90.*

Canada, Statistics Canada. *1986 Census — Characteristics of Ethnic Groups, Showing Single and Multiple Origins by Sex, for Canada.* 1988.

Chrétien, Jean. *A Venture in Indian Education* (speech). Address to Council of Ministers of Education. Regina, Saskatchewan. 23 June 1972. (Department of Indian Affairs and Northern Development).

Manitoba, Department of Community Services. *No Quiet Place. Review Committee on Indian and Métis Adoptions and Placements, Final Report.* Associate Chief Judge Edwin C. Kimelman, chair. 1985.

CHILD WELFARE

Canada, Department of Indian Affairs and Northern Development. *An Assessment of Services Delivered under the Canada-Manitoba-Indian Child Welfare Agreement.* Coopers & Lybrand Consulting Group. 27 August 1987.

———. *Indian Child and Family Services Management Regime, Discussion Paper.* October 1989.

Canada, Indian and Northern Affairs Canada and Family Services Task Force. *Indian Child and Family Services in Canada. Final Report.* 1987.

Canada, House of Commons Special Committee of Indian Self-Government. *Second Report.* Ottawa: Queen's Printer for Canada. 20 October 1983.

Johnston, Patrick. *Native Children and the Child Welfare System.* Toronto: Canadian Council on Social Development, 1983.

Manitoba, Department of Justice. *Report by Provincial Judge Brian Dale Giesbrecht on the Inquest Respecting the Death of Lester Norman Desjarlais.* 31 August 1992.

Manitoba. *Report of the First Nation's Child and Family Task Force: Children First — Our Responsibility.* November 1993.

JUSTICE

Canada, Solicitor General of Canada. *Correctional Issues Affecting Native People.* Correctional Law Review Working Paper. 1988.

———. *Native People and Justice Report on the National Conference and the Federal/Provincial Conference on Native Peoples and the Criminal Justice System.* February 1975.

———. *Native Policing in Canada: A Review of Current Issues.* 1986.

Canadian Bar Association. *Report of the Canadian Bar Association Committee on Aboriginal Rights in Canada: An Agenda for Action.* 1988.

Jackson, Michael. *Locking up Natives in Canada.* A report for the Canadian Bar Association Committee, Imprisonment and Release. 1988.

Morse, Bradford and Lock, Linda. *Native Inmates in Provincial and Federal Institutions.* For the Canadian Sentencing Commission's Native Inmate Project. 1985.

Simon Fraser University. *Conference on Northern Justice.* 1973.

Sinclair, Murray. *Closing Remarks for the Manitoba Aboriginal Justice Inquiry (Part One).* 28 April 1989.

Social Policy Research Associates. *National Evaluation Overview of Indian Policing.* July 1983.

Stevens, Samuel. *Access to Civil Justice for Aboriginal Peoples.* Conference on Access to Civil Justice, University of British Columbia. June 1988.

Index

AGMV
MARQUIS
Québec, Canada
1999